MAN OF EVEREST

The Autobiography of

TENZING

told to

JAMES RAMSEY ULLMAN

SEVERN

SEVERN HOUSE PUBLISHERS

First published in 1955 by
GEORGE G. HARRAP SONS & CO. LTD

This revised edition published 1975 by
SEVERN HOUSE PUBLISHERS LTD. LONDON

© 1975

ISBN 0 7278 0039 6

Printed in Great Britain by
Flarepath Printers Ltd, St. Albans, Herts
and bound by Wm Brendon & Son Ltd,
Tiptree, Essex

To
Chomolungma
in the name of all Sherpas
and all climbers in the world

Tenzing

AUTHORS' NOTE

We wish to make our grateful acknowledgment to all those who helped bring this book into being. And especially to Pandit Jawaharlal Nehru, Prime Minister of India; George V. Allen, former American Ambassador to India; Dr B. C. Roy, Chief Minister of West Bengal; John Hlavacek, of the United Press of America; Rabindranath Mitra, of Darjeeling; and the officials and staff of various departments of the Indian and Nepalese Governments.

T.N.S.
J.R.U.

CONTENTS

ILLUSTRATIONS

Between pages 96–97

MAPS AND SKETCHES
IN THE TEXT

The publishers are indebted to Mr J. A. Jackson for the colour plates reproduced in this book; to the Royal Geographical Society and Alpine Club of Great Britain for the half-tone illustrations facing pp. 48 (both pictures), 49 (top and bottom left), 64 (top left), 65, 81, 128, 129, 160, 193 (top), 208, 209, 224, 225, 256, 257, and 272; the Swiss Foundation for Alpine Research, Zürich, for those facing pp. 32 (bottom), 49 (top and bottom right), 112 (both pictures), 113 (bottom), 192, 193 (bottom), and 273 (top); Messrs Films de France for those facing pp. 145, 176, and 177; Mr Eric Shipton for those facing pp. 64 (bottom) and 161; Mr H. W. Tilman for those facing pp. 33 and 144; Mr Peter Jackson for those facing pp. 288 (top) and 305; the United Press Associations of America for those facing pp. 288 (bottom) and 304; Mrs Frank Smythe for that facing p. 64 (top right); and Mr Deane Dickason (Ewing Galloway, N.Y.) for that facing p. 80.

THE GENTLEMAN
FROM CHOMOLUNGMA

by

JAMES RAMSEY ULLMAN

LATE in the morning of May 29, 1953, two mountaineers, named Edmund Hillary and Tenzing
Norgay,[1] stood for fifteen minutes on the summit of
Mount Everest. They did what all climbers do when they
have reached their goal: shook hands, took pictures, looked
at the view, and started down again for the world below.
That world, however, was to be very different from the
one they had left. For Tenzing, in particular, it was a
world he never made and had never known. He went up
the mountain as a simple man, but he came down a *hero*.
And perhaps as much as any man in history he has reaped
the hero's reward—and ordeal.

It is hard for Westerners to realize the position that
Tenzing now holds in the eyes of the East. Probably the
most comparable phenomenon, in our own experience, is
Charles Lindbergh; but even Lindbergh, in his heyday of
hosannas and ticker-tape, did not receive adulation to the
point of actual worship. For millions in the world to-day
Tenzing is a manifestation of godhead—an avatar of the

---

[1] Tenzing has changed the spelling of his name several times, but promises
that the above form is final and official.

Lord Siva, a reincarnation of the Buddha. For still other millions, too sophisticated to confuse man with deity, he is a mortal figure of supreme significance. Symbolically as well as literally, Tenzing on Everest was a man against the sky, virtually the first humbly born Asian in all history to attain world stature and world renown. And for other Asians his feat was not the mere climbing of a mountain, but a bright portent for themselves and for the future of their world. Already his name resounds in song and story through the byways of the Orient. Already it is being woven into a fabric of legend and myth.

There he stands—Tenzing the Hero, Tenzing the Myth —a masked, faceless symbol raising his axe and flags upon the summit of the earth. This is one aspect of him; no doubt about it. Perhaps the aspect that will be best remembered. But there is another part of him too—beneath the mask and the padded clothing, beyond the victory and the tumult and the shouting—and that is the part he tells about in this, his book. "I am still the same old Tenzing," he declares, towards its end. And in this he is right, and we are fortunate. For "the old Tenzing," without benefit of myth or legend, is quite a person on his own.

The co-conqueror of Everest is often described as a small man, but this is hardly accurate. Alongside the towering Hillary he may appear so, but actually he is an average and well-proportioned five-foot-eight. Nor is there anything 'small' about his inner stature—anything of the narrowness, the constriction, the provinciality, that one is apt to associate with a peasant or mountain man. To a degree this is true of all the Sherpa people. Though of the simplest origins and for the most part unlettered (since there is no written Sherpa language), they have, through their specialized work and long contact with the outside world become a genuine élite among Himalayan hillmen. And Tenzing is the élite of the élite. He is fine of feature, fine of grain. His face is mobile, his eyes clear and quick. His tongue, his smile, and his mind are quick. His favourite drinks may be tea and his native *chang*, but he himself is champagne. There is bubble in him, pushing up at the cork. There is lightness and brightness. There is the indefinable essence called *quality*.

By now he has travelled a good deal. He has learned the ways, and a good many of the languages, of the world. He likes good food, good clothing, good living, good company. He has great curiosity and is avid for new experiences. But if certain of his habits are acquired ones, his instincts are his very own, and there is no faintest aura about him of the falseness or 'phoniness' that is so often the concomitant of sudden success. The "old" and the "new" Tenzing alike are possessed of taste and dignity, courtesy and grace. He was born to be not only a mountaineer, but a gentleman.

His new home in Darjeeling hums with life. Presiding over it is his wife, Ang Lahmu, a round and animated lady, with a shrewd eye and a girlish giggle. Completing the cast are two daughters, two nieces, an assortment of sisters, cousins, brothers-in-law, and cousins of brothers-in-law, plus a variety of semi-identified visitors (and cousins of visitors) who wander in and out at will. Dogs are everywhere. Scrapbooks, photographs, and souvenirs clutter the tables and walls. From upstairs, as likely as not, where a lama brother-in-law is in charge of the Buddhist prayer-room, comes the sound of chanting and a tinkling bell. And downstairs, whatever the time of day, it is a safe bet that tea is being served. In the centre of it all is Tenzing himself—busy, cordial, perhaps a little confused as to just what is going on; talking, it often seems, in several languages simultaneously. His dark eyes glow. His teeth are strong and white. You are very conscious of his teeth, because he smiles so much.

Not always, though. Sometimes the smile fades. The world presses in, massively, relentlessly; the crowds become too big, the pressures too great; the curious, the worshipful, the jealous, the predatory, close in upon him, until it appears that house and man alike will be crushed by their weight. There was a time when the ordeal became so bad that Tenzing collapsed, and for a while was seriously ill. Since then the pressure has eased a little, but there are still occasions when it is almost too much to bear. At such moments the Man of Everest undergoes a quick and unhappy change. Ease turns to tension. His lips tighten. His eyes take on a hunted look. In the next instant, you think, he will turn and run, disappearing up the nearest mountainside like an Abominable Snowman.

He is paying the price of fame, with no discount. As he himself puts it, he is an animal in a zoo, a fish in a bowl. And if the bowl exhibits him brightly it also holds him prisoner. The other Sherpas, his life-companions, go off on their immemorial expeditions, but he no longer goes with them. Now he is better off than they—but also worse—and amid the crowds and clamour he is lonely. He is paying not only for fame, but for being the man he is. If he were less intelligent and less sensitive he would be happier.

Tenzing, like most of his people, has had no formal education. But his knowledge of the world and of men, his sureness of perception and judgment, could put the blush to many a machine-tooled graduate. Nowhere is this more apparent than in his attitude towards politics and towards the many uses which men have tried to make of him since he came down from Everest. For he wants no part of special causes or propaganda, of racial jingo or loud-mouthed nationalism. Whatever label the world has sought to paste upon him, he has remained, in his own mind and heart, simply a human being.

Life is full of accidents. And among them are many accidental heroes—small and ordinary men who happened to be in the right place at the right time, and whom circumstance has spotlighted on the world's stage. But the Sherpa Tenzing Norgay is not one of these. Anyone who reads the pages that follow will know it was no accident that it was he, rather than some one else, who achieved what he did. It was William Blake, long ago, who wrote of his "Tiger! Tiger! burning bright"; but his imagined king of the forest burned no more brightly than does this latter-day, flesh-and-blood tiger of the snows. There is a flame in Tenzing, a marvellously strong and pure flame that no storm of man or nature can extinguish. It is compounded of dream and desire, will and struggle, pride and humility; and in the end, with the deed done, the victory gained, it is the man's humility that stands out above all his other qualities. In his moment of triumph what he felt in his heart was gratitude to Everest. His prayer for his future life is that it may be worthy of Everest.

If what I have thus far written gives the impression that I am somewhat enamoured of this man called Tenzing, that is precisely the impression I wish to give. Granted, I have a certain *a priori* weakness for mountains and those who climb them; but I think that, even without this weakness, even if I had never heard of Everest, I could still have recognized the rare and wonderful quality of the man. As he himself tells, towards the end of his story, there were complications about the birthing of this book. A formidable maze of trans-global red tape had to be threaded before the parties of the first and second part sat down together in that lively house in Darjeeling. But there, at last, we were. Here, at last, is the result. And, whatever the ultimate verdict on our collaboration, I for one, at least, am already content; for no work I have ever done has given me deeper satisfaction. I kept no count of the hours we spent together, but it was well up in the hundreds—first in India and later in the Swiss Alps, where Tenzing passed the summer of 1954. For the heavier going we had the help of his devoted friend-assistant-interpreter, Rabindranath Mitra. But Tenzing's own English is by now remarkably good, and he was able to tell much of his story without benefit of translation. Of its very nature, and his own, it is a simple story. There are, at least to my knowledge, no Freudian over- or undertones. But of one thing you may be certain all the way through: Tenzing says what he truly thinks and feels—whether he is speaking of his fellow-men, of mountains, or of God. The latter two, as will soon become apparent, have for him considerably more than a casual connexion, and throughout his life his identification with both has been so close that they seem sometimes almost indistinguishable. For him the high peaks are a place of pilgrimage. But they are also home. They are where he belongs. As his body moves closer to the mountain-tops his spirit moves closer to God.

"Why do men climb mountains?" goes the age-old poser. And generations of Westerners have wrestled with it in dubious battle. But there is no battle involved as far as Tenzing is concerned. No words are needed for the answer, because his very life is the answer.

So much for a ghost's introductory remarks. Now it is

time for him to fade into ectoplasm and for the flesh-and-blood man to tell his own story. It is the story of a hero. A certified, unaccidental, unmanufactured, authentic hero. But it is also, I think, something besides that—something more than that. It is the story of a fellow human being of whom we may all be proud.

I

IT WAS A LONG ROAD

MANY times I think of that morning at Camp Nine. We have spent the night there, Hillary and I, in our little tent at almost 28,000 feet, which is the highest that men have ever slept. It has been a cold night. Hillary's boots are frozen, and we are almost frozen too. But now in the grey light, when we creep from the tent, there is almost no wind. The sky is clear and still. And that is good.

We look up. For weeks, for months, that is all we have done. Look up. And there it is—the top of Everest. Only it is different now—so near, so close, only a little more than a thousand feet above us. It is no longer just a dream, a high dream in the sky, but a real and solid thing, a thing of rock and snow, that men can climb. We make ready. We will climb it. This time, with God's help, we will climb on to the end.

Then I look down. All the rest of the world is under us. To the west Nuptse; to the south Lhotse; to the east Makalu: all of them great mountain-tops, and beyond them hundreds of others, all under us. Straight down the ridge, two thousand feet down, is the South Col, where our nearest friends wait—Sahibs Lowe and Gregory and the young Sherpa Ang Nyima, who yesterday helped us up to Camp Nine. Below that is the white wall of Lhotse, four thousand feet more, and at its bottom the Western Cwm, where the rest of our friends wait at the advance base camp. Below the Cwm is the Icefall, below the Icefall the Khumbu Glacier. I see that Hillary is looking too, and I point. Below the glacier, 16,000 feet down, you can just see in the grey light the old monastery of Thyangboche.

To Hillary, perhaps, it does not mean much. To a man from the West it is only a far, strange place in a far, strange country. But for me it is home. Beyond Thyangboche are the valleys and villages of Solo Khumbu, and there I was born and grew up. On the tall hillsides above them I climbed as a boy, tending my father's yaks. Home is close now. I can almost stretch out my hand and touch it. But if it is close it is also far. Much farther than 16,000 feet. As we strap on our oxygen-tanks I think back to the boy, so close and so far, who had never heard of oxygen, but yet looked up at this mountain and dreamed.

Then we turn round, Hillary and I. We begin to climb.

It is many miles and many years that have brought me here.

I am a lucky man. I have had a dream, and it has come true, and that is not a thing that happens often to men. To climb Everest—which my people call Chomolungma—is what I have wanted most of all in my life. Seven times I have tried; I have come back and tried again; not with pride and force, not as a soldier to an enemy, but with love, as a child climbs on to the lap of its mother. Now at last I have been granted success, and I give thanks. "*Thuji chey*"—that is how we say it in Sherpa. "I am grateful." So I have dedicated my story to Chomolungma, for it has given me everything. To whom else should I make my dedication?

I have been granted much. But there is also much that I do not have, and the more I know the world the more I know this. I am an unlettered man. Dearly I would like to learn and teach myself many things, but when you are forty it is late for this and not easy. For my two daughters it will be better. They go to a good school, and will have a good education for the modern world. For myself I say, "Well, you cannot have everything. And at least you can sign your name." Since Everest I think perhaps I have signed my name more than most people write words in their whole lifetime.

It may seem strange, but one thing I have many of is books. As a boy I never saw one, except, perhaps, as some rare thing in a monastery; but since I have been a man and gone on expeditions I have heard and learned much about them. Many men I have climbed and travelled with have written books. They have sent them to me, and though I cannot read them myself, word by word, I understand what they say, and they mean much to me. Now it means much to have my own book. A book, I think, is what a man has been and done in his life; and this one is mine. Here is my story. Here is myself.

In the beginning there are some things I must explain. The Sherpa language, which is my native one, has no written form, and therefore no records. Also in our original home we kept time by the Tibetan calendar, and because of these things the facts and dates in my early life are sometimes uncertain. For my mountain career I could unfortunately keep no diaries, so for expeditions where a book was not written I am not always sure how to spell the names of the friends I have climbed with. For this I am sorry, and I hope they will excuse me if I have made some mistakes. To them and all my climbing companions I send my thanks and warm greetings.

Even with my own name there have been changes and often confusion. When I was born I was not even called Tenzing, but something else, and this I will tell about later. At different times the name has been spelled in Western languages with an *s* and a *z*, and sometimes without the *g* on the end. My second name has been given as Khumjung (for a village in my home country), Bhotia (which means "Tibetan")—and Norkay or Norkey, Norgya or Norgay (all of which mean "wealthy" or "fortunate," and many times in my life have made me smile). Even to myself this has been much of a mix-up. But it is not easy to keep such things straight without records or to spell in a language that has no spelling.

Actually my family, or clan, name is Ghang La, which in Sherpa means "snowy pass," but my people do not usually employ surnames, and the only use I have made of mine is for the name of my new house in Darjeeling. Various lamas, who are the scholars of our race, have recently told me that the best rendering of my name is *Tenzing Norgay*, and this is the way I now use and spell it. Often for official purposes I add the word *Sherpa* at the end, both to help in identification and to do honour to my people. But at home and with my friends I am just Tenzing, and I hope I can stay that way, and not wake up some morning and be told I am somebody else.

Many names—many tongues. That is typical of the part of the world I live in, and, as is well known, the question of finding a common language for her many peoples is one of the great problems of India. To-day one can hardly move from one small district to another without finding different speech, and I have travelled so much that, though unlettered, I have become quite a linguist. Sherpa, my mother tongue, derives from Tibetan, which I have also known from childhood, both in its northern and southern dialects. Next in familiarity is Nepali, which is natural, because Solo Khumbu is in Nepal, and Darjeeling, which has been my home for many years, is very close to it. Classical Hindi I have not learned, but I can get along in Hindustani, which is a mixture of Hindi and Urdu, and not very different from Nepali; and I have picked up a fair amount of several other languages, such as Garhwali, Punjabi, and Sikkimese, Yalmo (from Nepal), Pasthu (from Afghanistan), Chitrali (from the Northwest Frontier), and even a few words from the many languages of South India. All these, though, I have used only when travelling. At home with my own people my natural speech is still Sherpa, and for other purposes in Darjeeling I speak mostly Nepali.

Then, of course, there are the Western languages too. For many years I have gone to the mountains with British expeditions and known British people in India, and now my English is good enough for me to tell much of the story in this book without an interpreter. Also I have travelled with men of other nationalities and tongues, and do not always have to be a dummy. French?—"*Ça va bien, mes braves!*" German?—"*Es geht gut!*" Italian?—"*Molto bene!*" Perhaps it is just as well I have never been with a Polish or Japanese expedition, or by now I should be a little crazy.

I have had many journeys. Always to make journeys, to move, to go and see and learn, has been like a thing in my blood. When I was a small boy in Solo Khumbu I once ran away from home to Kathmandu, the capital of

Nepal. Later I left again, for Darjeeling. And from Darjeeling, for more than twenty years, I have gone out with expeditions to all parts of the Himalayan world. Many times to near-by Sikkim and back to Nepal; often to Garhwal, the Punjab, and Kashmir; sometimes even farther, to the borders of Afghanistan and Russia, and across the mountains into Tibet, and on to Lhasa and beyond. Then since the climbing of Everest I have been much farther. I have seen almost all of India, the south as well as the north. I have been to England and twice to Switzerland, and for a short visit to Rome. At the time that I tell my story I have not yet seen the rest of Europe or America, but I hope to do so soon. To travel, to experience and learn—that is to live. The world is wide, and you cannot see all of it even from the top of Everest.

I have said I am a lucky man. Especially I have been lucky with sickness and accidents, and that is not always so with my people, for many Sherpas have died in the mountains. Sometimes I have been ill, of course, but never too badly. I have never fallen on a mountain and never been frostbitten. Those who sweat a lot get frostbite easily, but I never sweat when I am climbing; and also I always keep busy, even in the camps when we are supposed to be resting, so that I can keep myself warm. It is when you sit and do nothing that you get frostbitten. Three times I have been caught in avalanches, but they were not bad ones. Once in the snowfields I lost my goggles and had much trouble with my eyes from the blinding sun, and since then I have always carried two pairs of dark glasses. Another time I broke four ribs and sprained my knees, but that was on a skiing trip, and not while climbing. The only time I have suffered an actual climbing injury was once when I broke a finger trying to catch and hold a companion who was falling.

Sometimes it has been suggested that I have "three lungs," because I have so little trouble at great heights. At this I laugh with my two mouths. But I think it is perhaps true that I am more adapted to heights than most men; that I was born not only in, but *for*, the mountains. I climb with rhythm, and it is a natural thing for me. My hands, even in warm weather, are usually cold, and doctors have told me that my heartbeat is quite slow. The high places are my home. They are where I belong. On a recent tour of India, with the heat and the crowds, I became more sick than I have ever been in my life on a mountain.

Yes, the mountains have been good to me. I have been lucky there. And I have been lucky, too, in the men with whom I have gone to the mountains, in the companions with whom I have struggled and achieved, failed and succeeded. There have been my fellow-Sherpas, of whom I am proud to be a brother. There have been Indians and Nepalese and men from many parts of Asia. There have been the men from the West—English, French, Swiss, German, Austrian, Italian, Canadian, American, New Zealanders. And it has been a great part of my life to meet and know them and to be their friend. It is not only people who are just alike who can be friends. Raymond Lambert, with whom I almost climbed Everest in 1952, is Swiss and speaks French. We could talk only with a few words of English and many gestures, but we are as close as if we came from the same village.

We are none of us perfect. We are none of us gods, but only men, and sometimes on expeditions there are difficulties. On the last British expedition of 1953 there were certain troubles, and I shall not deny it. But because it became so famous they were much exaggerated. They were twisted by outside people to their own purposes. Here in my book I shall not exaggerate or twist, but only tell things honestly as I saw them, with no complaints or resentment. Everest is too big for that; climbing Everest too great and precious. I shall tell only the truth, and the truth is that such differences as arose between British and Asian were as nothing to the bond that held us together. This was the bond of a common goal, a common love and devotion. The bond of all mountaineers in the world, that makes them brothers.

So much is made of politics, of nationality. Not on a mountain itself: there life is too real and death too close for such things, and a man is a man, a human being, and that is all. But later it begins—politics and more politics, argument and bad feeling—and no sooner was I down from Everest than it began for me. For the first thirty-eight years of my life no one cared what nationality I was. Indian, Nepali, or even Tibetan—what difference did it make? I was a Sherpa, a simple hillman; a man of the mountains, of the great Himalayas. But now everything was pushing and pulling. I was no longer a man, but some sort of doll to be hung from a string. It must be I who reached the top first—a yard, a foot, an inch, ahead of Hillary. For some I must be Indian, for others Nepali. The truth did not matter. Everest did not matter. Only politics mattered. And I was ashamed.

About reaching the top I shall tell later. About nationality and politics I can only say again what I said then.

Some people call me Nepali, some Indian. I was born in Nepal, but now I live in India with my wife and daughters and my mother. For me Indian and Nepali are the same. I am a Sherpa and a Nepali, but I think I am also Indian. We should all be the same—Hillary, myself, Indian, Nepali, everybody.

It has been a long road. Yes. From the bottom of Everest to the top. From the yak pastures of Solo Khumbu to the home of Pandit Nehru and a reception in Buckingham Palace. From a mountain coolie, a bearer of loads, to a wearer of a coat with rows of medals who is carried about in planes and worries about income-tax. Sometimes, like all roads, it has been hard and bitter; but mostly it has been good. For it has been a high road. A mountain road.

Always, wherever else it has taken me, it has led me back to the mountains. Because that is where I belong. And this I knew, this I felt in my blood on that blue May morning in 1953 when I climbed up with Hillary to the top of the world. Like the Buddhist Wheel of Life, my own life had made its great turning. I was back with Everest—with Chomolungma—where I started; with the dreams of a boy who looked up from the herds of yaks.

Only now the dream had come true.

2

NO BIRD CAN FLY OVER IT

IT is strange about the name *Sherpa*. The world hears it only in connexion with mountains and expeditions, and many people think it is a word meaning "porter" or "guide." But this is not so at all. The Sherpas are a people, a tribe. According to those who have studied such things, there are about a hundred thousand of us, dwellers in the high uplands of the Eastern Himalayas.

Sherpa means "man from the east." But all that is known to-day about our past is that we are of Mongolian stock, and that long ago our ancestors migrated from Tibet. In most things we are still more like Tibetans than any other larger group of people. Our language is similar (though we have no written form), and so are our clothing and food and many customs, especially among those who have not come into much contact with the outside world. One of the closest bonds is that of religion, for, like the Tibetans, we are Buddhists. Though there are no longer any Sherpa villages in Tibet, many of our people are attached to the great monastery of Rongbuk, on the far side of Everest, and there is much going back and forth between there and our own monastery of Thyangboche.

Also there are many caravans engaged in trade. And this, I think, is a remarkable thing for the present time; for

Tibet is now Communist, while Nepal is not, and here is one of the few places in the world where there is free trade and travel without passport; while everything else changes, life in the high Himalayan passes goes on the same as for thousands of years.

Over these passes our forefathers came south, many years ago, and settled in what is now our homeland of Solo Khumbu, in North-eastern Nepal. We usually say Solo Khumbu, as if it were one word and one place, but actually there is one district of Solo and another of Khumbu. The first is farther south and at a lower altitude, and its agriculture and ways of living are more like those of the Nepalese. The second is very high up, close under the great mountains and still very much like Tibet. Both I and most of the other high-climbing Sherpas come from this northern district of Khumbu.

Through Solo Khumbu flows the Dudh Kosi, which means "Milky River," pouring down in many tributaries from the high snows round Everest. Its deep valleys and gorges are the one main route to the south, and even to-day the only way to get to the rest of Nepal is along the steep trails that border it and its narrow, hanging bridges. In the cold winters and during the great rains of the summer monsoons it is a terribly difficult trip, and even in the good seasons of spring and autumn it takes almost two weeks to go to or from Kathmandu, in the centre of Nepal. Since Kathmandu itself is in turn partly shut off from the rest of the world, it can be seen that Solo Khumbu is very remote and primitive.

In the last few years Nepal has begun to open up to the outside world, and great efforts are being made to modernize it. At the present time there are only two extreme ways to get from India to Kathmandu: you walk or you fly. But now a road is being built across the foothill ranges that separate them, and soon for the first time it will be possible to go by car. Also there are plans for a big dam on the southern stretch of the Kosi river, which, though itself in India, will have much effect on Nepali agriculture. Like the rest of the world, Nepal has at last begun to change. But Solo Khumbu is still far away, and I think it will be many years before it is affected by such things, or people ride to it on rubber tyres.

Our home country is harsh and stony; the weather is bitter; but still we have both agriculture and pasturage. Wheat grows between eight and ten thousand feet (this is mostly in Solo), and barley and potatoes up to fourteen thousand. Potatoes are our biggest crop, and form the basis of much of our food, just as rice does for the Indians and Chinese. Some land is common ground and some privately owned, and many families have land in different sections, and travel from high ground to low in the different seasons for planting and harvest. Also the people travel while following their herds, which consist of sheep, goats, and yaks. Most important are the yaks. From them we get wool for clothing, leather for shoes, dung for fuel, milk, butter, and cheese for food, and also sometimes meat —though perhaps I should not say this last, because stricter Buddhists will frown on us. For the Sherpas, as for all high Himalayan people, the yak is the great staple of life. From it a man can get almost everything he needs to nourish him and keep him warm.

Solo Khumbu produces enough to eat, so that it does not need much from outside, but still there is trade along the forest trails to the south and the high mountain passes to the north. The greatest of these passes is the Nangpa La, which crosses the crest of the Himalayas at 19,000 feet, several miles to the west of Everest, and is one of the famous trade routes of history. Even to-day, as I have said, the caravans move up and down as they always have. Into Tibet go cloth and spices and small manufactured goods from India and Nepal, and out of it come salt and wool and sometimes herds of yaks. In Solo Khumbu the people buy such small things as they need from the merchants and traders who pass through. But they have no stores or business-places of their own.

Also there are no cities in Solo Khumbu, nor even a large town. In Khumbu the biggest village is Namche Bazar, which is now famous because of the recent Everest expeditions, and in the valleys around it are other villages, such as Khumjung, Pangboche, Damdang, Shaksum, Shimbung, and Thamey. Their houses are built of stone, with usually wood shingles for the roofs and wood for the doors and window-frames; and, of course, there is no glass for the windows. Most are of two storeys, with the lower one for animals and storage and the upper, reached by an inside ladder, for the family, including its living and sleeping quarters, kitchen, and latrine. It is that way now. And it was that way, too, when I was a boy, and when all my ancestors were boys before me.

It has often been said that I was born in the village of Thamey, but that is not quite right. My family lived in Thamey, and I grew up there, but I was born in a place called Tsa-chu, near the great mountain Makalu, and only a day's march from Everest. Tsa-chu, which means "Hot Springs," is a holy place of many stories and legends, and my mother had gone there on a pilgrimage to the monastery of Ghang La, that being also our clan or family name. Near it is a great rock, shaped like the head of the Lord Buddha, out of which water is said to flow if a pious person touches it and prays. But if an evil and godless person does so the rock remains only dry rock. In this region, too, there grow many herbs which are reputed to have great healing power. And round about are a number of lakes. The biggest of them is called Tsonya, which means "Lake of Fish," and there is another, smaller one that is the colour of tea. Along its banks, it is told, the Buddha himself used to walk in meditation, and, when he wished refreshment, paused and drank—and for him it was really tea that was in the lake.

There are many other stories about Tsa-chu and Ghang La. One of them is that in the old days there was a great battle here between two armies—those of Gyalbo (King) Wang and Gyalbo Khung. My ancestors, according to tradition, fought on the side of Gyalbo Khung, who was victorious, and served him so well that he gave them a gift of land at this place. Because it was called Ghang La they took the name as their own, and it has been so used by their descendants ever since. Anyhow, it was there that I was born; and my parents believed it lucky, and the lamas too. According to my parents, the holy men told them to take especially good care of me for at least three years, for if I was still alive then I would grow up to be a great man.

When I was born is not quite so easy as where. In Solo Khumbu time is kept by the Tibetan calendar, which has no numbers for years, but only names—like the Year of the Horse, the Tiger, the Ox, the Bird, the Serpent. There are twelve of them altogether, all named after animals, of which six are male and six female, and when they have passed the cycle begins over again. For most of my life I have not known my own age, but only that I had been born in the Year of the *Yoa*, or Hare; but recently, being

familiar with both the Tibetan and Western calendars, I
have been able to work back and find that this must also
have been the year 1914. With the twelve-year cycles it
could also, of course, by plain arithmetic, be either 1902
or 1926. But I hope I am not so old as the first and am
afraid I am not so young as the second. Thirty-nine sounds
to me just right for the age at which I climbed Everest.
And I am sure that it is.

The season of the year in which I was born was not so
hard to tell. It could be fixed by the weather and the crops,
and it was in the later part of May. This has always seemed
a good sign to me, for the end of May has been an important time throughout my life. The time of birth, to begin
with. The time of great expeditions and best mountain
weather. It was on the 28th of May that I almost climbed
to the top of Everest with Lambert, and on the 29th, a
year and a day later, that I reached it with Hillary. Since
we have no proper records, Sherpa people do not have
birthdays. But as an anniversary to celebrate this day will
do me for the rest of my life.

My mother's name is Kinzom. My father's name was
Ghang La Mingma. But, as I have said, the child does not
usually take the family name. My parents had thirteen
children—seven sons and six daughters—and I was the
eleventh; but life was hard and death always close in Solo
Khumbu, and of all of us only myself and three sisters are
now living. Two of them, with their husbands and
families, now live in Darjeeling, and the third, who is the
youngest, in Solo Khumbu. Neither my father nor mother
had ever visited the true outside world. The farthest
they ever went was to Kathmandu and to Rongbuk, in
Tibet, where my mother's brother was once head lama.
My father died in 1949. But my mother, who is now very

old, was until 1955 still in Thamey, and on the Everest
expeditions of 1952 and 1953 I was happy to see her again
after many years.

Now I must tell again about my name. When I was
born it was not Tenzing. My parents called me Namgyal
Wangdi. But one day I was brought to a great lama from
Rongbuk, who consulted his holy books, and he said that
I was the reincarnation of a very rich man who had died
recently in Solo Khumbu, and that because of this my
name must be changed. The name he suggested was
Tenzing Norgay—or Norkay, or Norkey, as it has so
often been spelled—and the reason was that, like the
lamas at Tsa-chu, he predicted great things for me. Norgay,
as I have said, means "wealthy" or "fortunate." Tenzing
means "supporter of religion," and it has been the name of
many lamas, and, indeed, of this lama himself. Anyhow,
"Wealthy-Fortunate-Follower-of-Religion" sounded like
a fine all-round name to go through life with, so my
parents made the change and hoped for the best.

Later, when I was a little older, it was decided that I
myself was to be a lama. I was sent to a monastery, my
head was shaved, and I put on the robe of a novice. But
after I had been there only a little time one of the lamas
(who are not necessarily saints) got angry with me and
hit me on the bare head with a wooden board, and I ran
home and said I would not go back. My parents, who
were always kind and loving to me, did not make me do
so, but now and then I wonder what would have happened
if they had. Perhaps to-day I should be a lama; I do not
know. Sometimes, when I tell this story, my friends say,
"Oh, so it was a whack on the head that made you so mad
about mountains!"

In Solo Khumbu the only people who could read and

write were some of the lamas—not in Sherpa, to be sure, for there is no such written language, but in classical Tibetan, which is the language of northern Buddhism. And when I ran away from the monastery I lost my one chance of an education. To-day there is a small lay school in Namche Bazar—not much of a one, but still a school— but when I was young there was none at all, so I played and did work like the other boys of my age. There are, of course, many things from that time that I have forgotten, but a few I remember well. One is riding round on the back of one of my older brothers, who is now long dead. Another is the animals in winter, when they were crowded into the lower storey of our house, and how they steamed and smelled as they came in out of the cold. Still another is the rest of us, the family, almost as crowded in the upper storey: all of us packed together in no space at all, with the noise and the stenches and the smoke from cooking, but happy and contented because we did not know there was any other way to live.

Some Sherpa fathers were stern and hard with their children. But not my father. I was very fond of him, and used to carry things and do errands for him even when I did not have to. Also I used to sit often beside my favourite older sister while she milked the yaks, and she would give me the hot, fresh milk to drink.

This sister's name was Lahmu Kipa, and she was like a second mother to me. Later she became an *ané la*, or nun, in the monastery at Thyangboche, where she stayed for seven years, and, remembering how good she had been to me when I was very small, I often brought her extra food. In the monastery she met a monk, Lama Nwang La, and finally they left together and got married. In our religion there is no disgrace if a monk or a nun gets married, but they can no longer stay in a monastery; and since then my brother-in-law has been only a sort of 'family lama.' He and Lahmu Kipa lived in Solo Khumbu for many years. Then after the 1953 Everest expedition they came back with me to Darjeeling, where they now live with their children. Their son, Gombu, went with me to Everest in that year, and climbed twice to the South Col; and although he is now only twenty, he is already one of the best of the younger Sherpa climbers.

But I am telling here of a time long before Gombu was born and before I had even heard the name of Everest. Many times as a child I saw it, of course, rising high in the sky to the north above the tops of the nearer mountains. But it was not Everest then. It was Chomolungma. Usually Chomolungma is said to mean "Goddess Mother of the World." Sometimes "Goddess Mother of the Wind." But it did not mean either of these when I was a boy in Solo Khumbu. Then it meant "The Mountain So High No Bird Can Fly Over It." That is what all Sherpa mothers used to tell their children—what my own mother told me—and it is the name I still like best for this mountain that I love.

For me, as for any child, the world was at first very small. There were my father and mother, my brothers and sisters, our house, our village, the fields and pastures and yaks. To the north were the great mountains, to the east and west other mountains, to the south the Dudh Khosi disappearing into the forests; and what lay beyond them I did not know. As I grew older, though, I of course began to hear a little of the outside world. The first was of Tibet and its holy city, Lhasa, which both my parents and the lamas would speak of many times. As good Buddhists my father and mother would have loved dearly to make a pilgrimage to Lhasa; but it was too long and expensive a trip, and they never got there.

As a grown man I have come to realize that in some ways I am a little different from most of my people. And I think the difference had already begun at this time. I remember I was very shy and stayed much by myself, and while the other boys chased one another and played games with mud and stones I would sit alone and dream of far places and great journeys. I would pretend I was writing a letter to an important man in Lhasa who would come and get me. Or that I was leading an army there. And sometimes I would make my father laugh by asking him for a horse, so that I could go. Always as a child, a boy, a man, I have wanted to travel, to move, to go and see, to go and find; and I think this a large part of the reason for what has happened in my life.

The dreams of Lhasa were when I was very young. Later I began to hear and think about other places. For many years Sherpas had gone from Solo Khumbu across the mountains and forests to Darjeeling, to work on the tea plantations or as porters and rickshaw coolies, and sometimes they would come back and tell about it. Then something even more interesting began to happen. An Englishman called Dr Kellas, who was a noted explorer and climber, hired Sherpas from Darjeeling to go out with him into the mountains; a little later General Bruce, of the Indian Army, also took some on his expeditions; and soon that was what most of the Darjeeling Sherpas were doing—working as porters and helpers on expeditions to the high Himalayas. Though, of course, I did not know it at the time, it was then that our people began to earn their reputation as the best of all mountain men, which we have kept with pride ever since.

In 1921, 1922, and 1924 there were the first three famous Everest expeditions, and many Sherpas went, both from Darjeeling and Solo Khumbu. They came back with all sorts of stories about the *chilina-nga*, which is the name we give to men from far places, and about climbing almost to the sky; and most of them wore big boots and strange clothes such as we had never seen before. I was so fascinated that one day I paid money to use a pair of the boots, but they were so big and heavy for me that I could not walk at all. Everest, Everest—they all talked about Everest—and that was the first I had heard of it. "What is Everest?" I asked. "It is the same as Chomolungma," they answered; "only we were on the other side of it, in Tibet. And the *chilina-nga* say it is the highest mountain in the world."

On the 1922 expedition seven Sherpas were killed in a great avalanche, and there was much sadness and mourning among our people. But in 1924 more than ever went back to the mountain. This was the year in which the climbers Mallory and Irvine disappeared close to the summit, and when the Solo Khumbu Sherpas came home afterwards I heard their names and never forgot them. Twenty-nine years later, when Hillary and I stood on the top, we looked around to see if there was any sign that they too had reached it before they died. But we could find nothing.

None of my own family went on these early expeditions. I would have given anything to go, but I was too young. Then for a while there were no more expeditions, and things were like they had always been in Solo Khumbu. I was big enough now to work with my father and older brothers, and there was always much to do. We grew potatoes, and also barley and little *tsampa*, which is a sort of maize, and we took care of the sheep and yaks, from which we got milk and butter and thick wool for our clothes. The only things we got from outside were salt and sometimes dried meat from Tibet. The slaughter of animals is not approved of in Nepal, which is mostly Hindu, and most Buddhists also have this prohibition, so we did not kill our own yaks. What we often did, though, was to draw blood from a yak's throat, without killing it, and then curdle the blood and mix it with other food. We found it very strengthening—as good as a transfusion of blood into the body, like they do now for sick people in a hospital. I remember we used to do this most of all in the autumn, and not only for our own good, because it was getting colder, but for the yaks as well. After they had eaten well all summer they would often get too active and begin to fight or run away, and the drawing of blood would quieten them down.

In the early days my family was very poor. But they say I was a lucky baby, because after I came things were better. The same year in which I was born a hundred young yaks were also born, and after that we had as many as three or four hundred at a time. As I have said, our house was small and crowded. We ate only the simplest food. But there was always enough of it—I do not remember ever being hungry—and from the yak wool and hides—we would take the hides if they died a natural death —we made clothing to keep us warm during the long, cold winters. Unlike other people of the East, most of whom live in warmer climates, we wore shoes in Solo Khumbu—mostly felt and hide boots of the sort they also wear in Tibet. In all my life I have hardly ever gone bare-foot. And although the Nepalese and Indians can do it easily, I should to-day have as much trouble as a Westerner in going without shoes in rough country.

What I liked best as a boy was to go out with the yaks and wander free and alone along the mountain-slopes. In winter you could not go very high, because it was bitterly cold and the snow was deep; but in the other seasons there was fine grass—just like I saw years later in Switzerland—and we would cut it to use in the winter for feed. Namche Bazar is at about 10,000 feet, Thamey at about 12,000, but I used to go up as far as 18,000, tending the yaks. This was as high as grass grew for them, close beside the glaciers and under the walls of the great mountains.

It is these regions that are the home of the *yeti*, which is known now throughout the world as the Abominable Snowman. I had heard about the *yeti* since I was no more than a baby, for Solo Khumbu was full of stories about it; and before I was born my father had met one face to face. I myself have never seen one, and it was not until I was more than thirty years old that I even saw one's tracks. But as a boy, up on the stone-slopes and glaciers, I would sometimes find the droppings of a strange animal that contained traces of rats and worms, and I was certain that this could only be the dung of the *yeti*.

I was a little frightened of the *yeti*, of course, but not as frightened as I was curious. And this was the way I felt, too, about the great silent mountains that rose around me. The lamas told many stories of the terror of the snows—of gods and demons and creatures far worse than *yetis*, who guarded the heights and would bring doom to any man who ventured there. But I knew that men, and among them my own people, had climbed high on the other side of Chomolungma, and, though some had been killed, more had returned alive. What I wanted was to see for myself; find out for myself. This was the dream I have had as long as I can remember. There they stood above me, the great mountains—Makalu, Lhotse, Nuptse, Ama Dablam, Gaurisankar, Cho Oyu, a hundred others. And above them all Chomolungma—Everest. "No bird can fly over it," said the story. But what could a man do? A man with a dream. . . .

The world was so big, Solo Khumbu so small. And as I grew older I knew that I must leave. But when I first left it was not for the mountains, or even for Darjeeling, but for Kathmandu, the capital of Nepal. I was only thirteen then, and I could not go openly; so I ran away, and I felt very guilty. My sister, Lahmu Kipa, has told me I was always the favourite child of my parents, and I was very fond of them and did not want to hurt them. But the desire was too much, too strong. I went to Kathmandu by a roundabout route, by way of Makalu, at first alone and then with some other travellers whom I met on the way; and it took a little more than two weeks to get there. It was the first city I had seen, and very strange and confusing—especially because I was from a Buddhist people, while those in Kathmandu are mostly Hindu. After a while, though, I found a Buddhist monastery that was hospitable to strangers, and this was where I stayed.

For about two weeks I went all round the city and saw the crowds and the bazaars and the big buildings and the temples, and all sorts of things I had never seen before. The Nepalese have a fine army, composed mostly of the famous Gurkhas, who come from Central and West Nepal, and I especially liked to watch them marching and hear the music they played. Also I was fascinated watching the people, who are not of Mongolian but Hindu stock, and whose faces and clothes and ways of doing things were different from anything I had seen before. But if I was curious I was also homesick, and when I met some other people from Solo Khumbu, who were about to go back home, I went with them. This time we took a more direct route, along the same way I was to go many years later with the Swiss and British to Everest. By the time I reached Thamey I had been gone six weeks, and my parents were so glad to see me again that they hugged me.

Then, when they had finished hugging, they spanked me.

For five more years after that I stayed at home. There were no Everest expeditions during that time, or the temptation to go would perhaps have been too great. But even so I knew that I could not stay in Solo Khumbu for ever—that I was not made to be a farmer or a herder—and late in 1932, when I was eighteen, I left again, this time not for Kathmandu but Darjeeling, and though once more I seemed to be turning my back on Chomolungma, I felt that really I was going towards it; for now the word had spread that there was to be another expedition in 1933, and I was determined to go with it if I possibly could.

Again I went without telling my parents. And this was a sadness, because they had been kind to me and I loved them. They were very simple and pious people, especially my mother, who through all her life has never worn good clothes or eaten good food, but has given them instead, whenever she has had them, to the lamas and nuns of the monasteries. Then and always she has been a true mother, my *ama la*. And I know that her devoutness, her faith, her blessings and prayers, have had much to do with the success I have been granted.

3

INTO A NEW WORLD

I HAVE had three lives. The first was as a child in Solo Khumbu. The second, lasting twenty years, was as a porter and mountain man, and was centred mostly on Darjeeling. The third began on the day I came down from the top of Everest, and where it will lead me to I do not know.

Now in late 1932, when I was eighteen years old, my second life was about to begin.

There were twelve of us who left home together—both boys and girls—and we had been planning it for a month, holding secret meetings and collecting food and supplies. All I had been able to get for myself, though, was one blanket, which I took from our house. I had no money, nor had any of the others. In fact, that was the reason why most of us were going—to earn money. And also to see the world.

One of my companions was Dawa Thondup, who has since become a famous Sherpa. He was older than I, and though he had never been to Darjeeling, he seemed to know a lot about it, talking about the new expedition that would soon be leaving for Everest, and how we would surely get jobs with it. He had me so excited that I would have liked to run all the way. But you do not run across the wild country of Eastern Nepal. You creep up and down, round and about, over steep ridges, through jungle valleys, across rushing rivers, on trails that you can hardly see. For most of the long journey we all stayed together; but then, when we got near the border of Nepal and India, there was some sort of mix-up, and the others went on without me, taking all the food. I was lucky, though. In a near-by town called Simana I met a well-to-do man named Ringa Lama, who took me into his house. At this time I knew only the Sherpa language and no Nepali, but here I was lucky too, because Ringa Lama knew some Sherpa. His family liked me and were very kind, feeding me and giving me new Nepali clothing; and in return I did work about the house and collected firewood for them in the jungle. But I was lonely and sorry for myself, away from my own people, and often, out in the jungle alone, I would sit down beneath a tree and weep. Already I was learning that dreams and reality are not quite the same thing.

After I had been in Simana awhile I told Ringa Lama how much I wanted to go to Darjeeling, and to my joy he said, "All right; I am going there myself on business, and I will take you." We made the trip in a car, which was the first time I had ever seen one. And when we got to Darjeeling there were all kinds of other things I had never seen before. It was not as big as Kathmandu, but much more civilized, and full of modern inventions and engines, including a railway. Also there were many *chilina-nga*—mostly Englishmen—and this was the first time I had ever seen Europeans.

At first I did not stay in Darjeeling, but in a near-by village called Alubari, which means "place where potatoes grow." It was Ringa Lama who took me there, and he arranged that I should live with a cousin of his who was named Pouri. Pouri had fifteen cows, and it was my job to take care of them and also to do general work about the place. Here I began to learn the Nepali language, which is much used in Darjeeling, and also Yalmo, another speech of the region. My best teacher was a man called Manbahadur Tamang, who worked with me cutting grass for the cows, and I was very grateful to him. To-day Tamang and I are old friends, and recently he has been working for me as a mason on my new house. Often we talk of those early days, remembering this and that— and especially how one day, when we were gathering firewood in a restricted area, a forest guard came along, tied us to a tree, and beat us.

Sometimes, when I was working for Pouri, I was sent into Darjeeling to sell milk. And these were the great days for me, because that was where I wanted to be. The town is built on the side of a steep hill, looking north, and about fifty miles away, across the deep valleys of Sikkim, is the main eastern range of the Himalayas, with Kangchenjunga in the centre. Often I used to look at it, standing great and white in the sky, and this would make me feel good, because I knew then that, even in this strange new world, I was not too far away from the mountains that I loved. Then, too, there was Darjeeling itself, and this was a marvellous place to a young boy from the country. At the bottom of the big hill was the old part of the town, with its bazaars and temples and narrow, crowded streets, which reminded me somewhat of Kathmandu. But higher up, in the strange part, everything was different and new. Here were the homes of the English and richer Indians; fine stores and tea-houses and a moving-picture theatre; Government House, a maharaja's palace, and a hotel like a castle. I am afraid I paid much less attention to my cans of milk than to all these wonders that lay around me.

Something even more exciting, though, was soon to happen, and this was the organization of the Everest expedition of 1933. Early in the year the climbers arrived from England, the whole town was upside down with the preparations, and Sahib Hugh Ruttledge, the expedition leader, sat up on the veranda of the Planters' Club while most of the Sherpas in Darjeeling went to see him about jobs. Now I did not think about milk at all. All I thought was: I must go too. They must take me too. At first I was afraid to go myself to the Planters' Club, so I went to my friend Dawa Thondup, who was already signed up, and asked him to speak for me. But now he said no, I was too young. "I am full-grown and as strong as any man," I told him. But he and the other Sherpas kept saying, "No, you are too young." They would do nothing for me, and I have never been more angry in my life.

Then I tried to get the job by myself, but everything went wrong. When I first came to Darjeeling I had had long braided hair, like all the men in Solo Khumbu, but people laughed at me and called me a girl, so I had cut it short. And also I was wearing the Nepali clothes that Ringa Lama had given me. This was all right for Darjeeling, but bad with the expedition, for they thought I was a Nepali, and they wanted only Sherpas; and I had no papers or certificate from a previous expedition to help me. I suppose it is the same with many young people looking for their first work. They ask you, "Have you done this before?" You say, "No." They say, "We only want people with experience." And you go away wondering if you will never get a job in your life, because you have not had one already.

Anyhow, they would not take me in 1933. When the expedition marched off from Darjeeling I stayed behind and was very miserable.

For many months I went on taking care of Pouri's cows and selling their milk. One of my customers was a young woman called Ang Lahmu, a Sherpani who had been born in Darjeeling and worked there as an ayah, or housemaid. I never spoke the Sherpa language to her, but only Nepali, and she did not even know I was a Sherpa; and we used to argue all the time when we did business. "If I buy from you you must give me an extra measure," she would say. "No, I cannot," I would tell her. "You are cheap and stingy," she would say. "And you are a hard bargainer," I would answer. This would not be an interesting story, and I would probably not even remember it—except that Ang Lahmu is now my second wife.

After I had been in Darjeeling about a year I heard from people coming from Solo Khumbu that my parents thought I was dead. I decided I must go back and see them; but Pouri did not want me to go, and said that if I left I must get a substitute to do my work. So I went into the town, found a man in the street, and brought him back. And then I left quickly, before Pouri could find any more objections.

When I reached home I found that the travellers had been right: my parents were performing rites for me as if I had died. At first sight of me they began to weep, but when they had finished weeping they were very happy— and this time there was no spanking. There had been an earthquake in Solo Khumbu while I was gone; part of our house had fallen down, and the first thing I did was help rebuild it. Afterwards I did the same sort of work I had done before, with the crops and the yaks, and when the next summer came I went for the first time to Tibet. This was to fetch salt, which is always scarce in my home country, and I went over the great pass of Nangpa La (*la* means "pass" in Tibetan), and round to a place called Thingri Gangar, near Rongbuk, on the far side of Everest. During the trip I had a chance to see the famous Rongbuk Monastery, which is far larger than that at Thyangboche, with more than five hundred nuns and monks. It was close to here that all the British Everest expeditions had made their base camps, but in this year—1934—there was no attempt. Otherwise that salt might have had to wait awhile before getting back to Solo Khumbu.

Later in the year, after I had been a few more months at home, my father asked me to go again to Tibet for the same purpose. But by now I knew for certain that I could never be happy in this life, and that I must return to the outside world; so instead of going I left once more, in the autumn, for Darjeeling. Although my father never came there, I saw him twice again in the next few years, when he himself came over the Nangpa La to visit the 1935 and 1938 Everest expeditions. But I did not see my mother again until I went with the first Swiss expedition to the south side in 1952.

Back in Darjeeling, I did not return to Alubari, with its cows and potatoes, but moved into the town itself. There were two districts where most of the Sherpas lived, called Toong Soong Busti and Bhutia Busti (*busti* means "village"), and I stayed in Toong Soong, which has been my home for much of the time ever since. By good luck I became a tenant in the house of Angtharkay, who was already an experienced mountaineer, and to-day ranks as one of the most celebrated of all Sherpas. And soon I was no longer the lonely outsider I had been before. Near by lived my old friend Dawa Thondup, now also a veteran, and all around were other men who had won fame on Everest and elsewhere.

In that autumn of 1934 all the talk was of the German expedition of the past summer to Nanga Parbat, in distant Kashmir. And it was not happy talk, because there had been a terrible disaster. Many Sherpas had been with the expedition—the first time most of them had been so far away from home—and six of them had lost their lives, along with four Germans, in a great storm high up on the mountain. As a result, there was mourning and grief in many homes in Toong Soong Busti, but there was also a certain deep pride in what our men had borne and accomplished. In particular, Dawa Thondup and Ang Tshering, who had been with the expedition and had survived, told me of the deeds of their friend Gyali, who was usually called Gaylay. In the worst of the storm Gaylay had been far up on the peak with the expedition leader, Willy Merkl. He himself had been all right. He could probably have got down to the lower camps in safety. But as they struggled to descend Merkl grew weaker and weaker, until finally he could go no farther, and, rather than leave him alone, Gaylay had stayed and died with him. Even though I had not yet been on a mountain, such a story made me, too, proud to be a Sherpa.

During this time of year there were, of course, no expeditions going out, so I had to be patient. As in Solo Khumbu, there had been a recent earthquake in Darjeeling, and for a while I was employed as a labourer on the rebuilding of the chapel of St Paul's School. For this work I was paid twelve annas a day[1]; and though this may seem very little,

[1] There are sixteen annas to a rupee. In the 1930's a rupee was worth about one and sixpence.—J.R.U.

it was considered good wages at the time, and more than most Sherpas could make during the off season. For, except for a handful of merchants and traders—most of whom had moved away—we were all very poor. In Toong Soong Busti we lived in wooden shacks with tin roofs, with usually a whole family in a single room. Our food was rice and potatoes. Our earnings, even when we were working, were very small, and the only blessing was that our wants were small too.

Early in 1935 I was married. My wife's name was Dawa Phuti, and Phuti means "lucky wife who brings children," which was soon to be true. She too had been born in Solo Khumbu, where I had seen her sometimes, though I did not know her well until we were both in Darjeeling. We found a little room of our own in Toong Soong Busti, and were very happy, but we were together then for only a short while.

For now at last, after so much hoping and waiting, my life in the mountains was about to begin.

4

TWICE TO EVEREST

THEY say you should start with little things and go on to big ones, but it was not that way for me. My first expedition, in 1935, was to Everest. This was the fifth of the big British parties to go out to the mountain.

Their first one, in 1921, had not been an attempt to climb, but only an exploration, and it was on this that a way was found through Tibet to the north side of the peak. To the Sherpas, who knew the route from Darjeeling to Solo Khumbu, it seemed strange to be going so far round to get to Chomolungma. But the reason was that the English had permission to enter Tibet, while at the time—and until only a few years ago—no Westerners at all could enter Nepal.

From near the Rongbuk Monastery, directly north of Everest, the 1921 explorers made many journeys along the glaciers and to the high passes, looking for a route to the upper mountain; and at last it was decided that the best one was along the East Rongbuk Glacier, and then up a steep wall of snow and ice to a pass, or saddle, more than 22,000 feet high, which they called the North Col. The famous climber George Leigh-Mallory, with some others, reached this col, and though they were not equipped to go farther, they felt sure they had found a good way up the mountain. Later they looked for still other ways, and climbed a pass near the Lho La, which looks over on to the south-west side of Everest and almost to Solo Khumbu. But Mallory did not think this side looked like good climbing; and, besides, it was in Nepal, where they were not allowed to go. So it was thirty years before anyone tried the mountain from that direction.

In 1922 the first real climbing expedition came. With many Englishmen and Sherpas, they set up camps on the glacier, another on the North Col, and still another on the steep ridge above. From there the strongest climbers went on to more than 27,000 feet, which is only two thousand feet from the top, and much higher than men had ever been before. But later there was the great avalanche on the steep slopes below the North Col, when a whole ocean of snow came pouring down on the roped porters. This was when seven Sherpas were killed, and it was the worst accident there has ever been on Everest.

Still, in 1924, both Englishmen and Sherpas came back, and this was the famous expedition on which Mallory and Andrew Irvine disappeared as they climbed together towards the top. This time there were two camps, not one, above the Col, and the higher, at 26,800 feet, was carried up by the three Sherpas Lhakpa Chedi, Norbu Yishay, and Semchumbi. From here, before Mallory and Irvine were lost, Colonel E. F. Norton and Dr T. H. Somervell made a fine attempt, in which Norton reached more than 28,000 feet. This remained the world altitude record until Raymond Lambert and I went a little higher on the other side of the mountain during the first Swiss expedition of 1952.

The fourth attempt on Everest was not until 1933,

which was the one on which I so much wanted to go, but was not taken. The result was much as in 1924, except that no lives were lost, and two teams of climbers—Wyn Harris and L. R. Wager together, and Frank Smythe, with Eric Shipton stopping a little below him—went to about the same place that Norton had reached. Again the highest tent, Camp Six, was set up by Sherpas, and this time the top men were Angtharkay, Pasang, Rinzing, Ollo, Dawa, Tshering, and Kipa. "Tigers," the Englishmen called them. It was not until 1938 that this title became official, and Tiger Medals were awarded to the porters who went highest. But already in the twenties and early thirties the name was used, and our men bore it proudly.

Then came 1935, and my first chance.

From the beginning of the year there had been much talk about another expedition; but there was trouble getting permission to enter Tibet again, and it was late before Eric Shipton, who was now leader, arrived in Darjeeling. Because of this it was decided that there would be no real summit attempt, but only a reconnaissance, as in 1921. For the monsoon, which blows up each June from the south, would surely come while we were still climbing, and after that it is almost certain death on a high mountain from storms and avalanches. A reconnaissance would not be a waste of time, though, because the British thought they might find a better route for the next year than the one always used before by way of the North Col.

As had happened in 1933, I was almost left behind again. The sirdar for the expedition—which means the one who is in charge of the porters—was Karma Paul, a businessman of Darjeeling, who did not know me; and also I still had no certificate for previous service. Mr Shipton and Mr W. J. Kydd, who was then Secretary of the Himalayan Club, interviewed the Sherpas, but picked only those who had climbed before or were recommended by Karma Paul; and I was very unhappy. Then, later, it was announced that they needed just two more men. There were more than twenty candidates, and I slipped into the line wearing a new khaki bush-jacket, and shorts, which I hoped made me look very professional. Mr Shipton and Mr Kydd checked one candidate after another, and when it was my turn they asked me again to produce a certificate. This was awful, and I wanted to argue and explain. But at that time, when I was only twenty, I did not yet know either English or Hindustani, and all I could do was make a gesture that I did not have one. The two sahibs talked together, then told me to step out of the line, and I thought that was the end of it for me. But when I started to leave they called me back, and the two men selected were myself and another young Sherpa, Ang Tshering, who was later killed on Nanga Parbat.[1]

Some of the older men were annoyed because I was a novice and had been taken in. But I was so happy that they could have beaten me and I would not have minded. The wages on the expedition were twelve annas a day, which would be raised to one rupee for every day above snow-line; so if I did well I should make more money than I ever

---

[1] There have been several other Ang Tsherings, including one who now holds a Tiger Medal. Indeed, many Sherpas have the same names, and in this book I shall do my best not to be confusing.

had before. It was not money, though, that was the important thing to me. It was that I was a mountain man at last—and going to Chomolungma! In 1953, when I saw Eric Shipton at a reception in London, I reminded him that it was he who, eighteen years before, had given me my first chance.

Like the earlier expeditions, we marched north from Darjeeling through Sikkim—first up and down, up and down, through the deep valleys and then high over the great passes into Tibet. In a straight line the distance from Darjeeling is only about a hundred miles, but we had to travel almost three hundred, going roundabout to the north and then off to the west. It was a long trip over wild, barren country, with much wind and dust. But one advantage of this old northern route was that you could carry things on mules almost to the base of the mountain, while on the new route through Nepal there are so many rivers and hanging bridges that everything must go on men's backs. On this 1935 expedition there were only twelve Sherpas, but many more non-climbing porters, mostly Tibetans, to take care of the mules and help with the unloading at base camp.

On the way through Tibet we went slowly and did much exploring. And when we reached Rongbuk we did not go right at Everest, but climbed many smaller peaks and passes around it. No better approach was found, though, than the old North Col route, and finally we moved on to the East Rongbuk Glacier, where the previous parties had made their lower camps. Here I had an unexpected and welcome visitor—my father—who had heard about the expedition and come across the Nangpa La from Solo Khumbu to visit us. He did not do any actual climbing, but stayed at the glacier camps for quite a while; and it was at this time that he had his second meeting with a *yeti*, which I shall tell about later.

Near Camp Three, below the North Col, we made an interesting and sad discovery. The year before an Englishman named Maurice Wilson, accompanied by only three Tibetans, had gone secretly to Everest, in the hope that he could climb it all alone; and he had not returned. Now we found his body. It was in an old wind-shredded tent—just a skeleton with a little dry, frozen skin, and bent over in a queer, stiff way, as if Wilson had died while trying to take off his boots. In fact, one boot was already off, and he was holding the lace of the other in his hand of bones. I think he had come back to his tent from trying to climb to the North Col, found no one there to take care of him, and then died from cold or exhaustion. We buried him under the rocks of a moraine beside the glacier.

Wilson had hired the three Tibetans in Darjeeling, and afterwards I met them there. Their names were Tewang Bhotia, Rinzing Bhotia, and Tshering Bhotia, and I asked them what had happened. They told me they had followed the usual expedition route, but had had to be very careful about patrols and officials, because Wilson did not have permission to enter Tibet. Reaching the Rongbuk Monastery, they had rested there fifteen days, and then gone on to make three camps on the Rongbuk and East Rongbuk Glaciers. At Camp Three the Tibetans had been unwilling to go on, and there had been a discussion. Finally Wilson said, "All right; I will climb up to the North Col alone. You wait for me here for three days." And so he went. The others waited the three days, so they told me, and then left; but, however long it was, they obviously did nothing to help him. I was angry and ashamed of

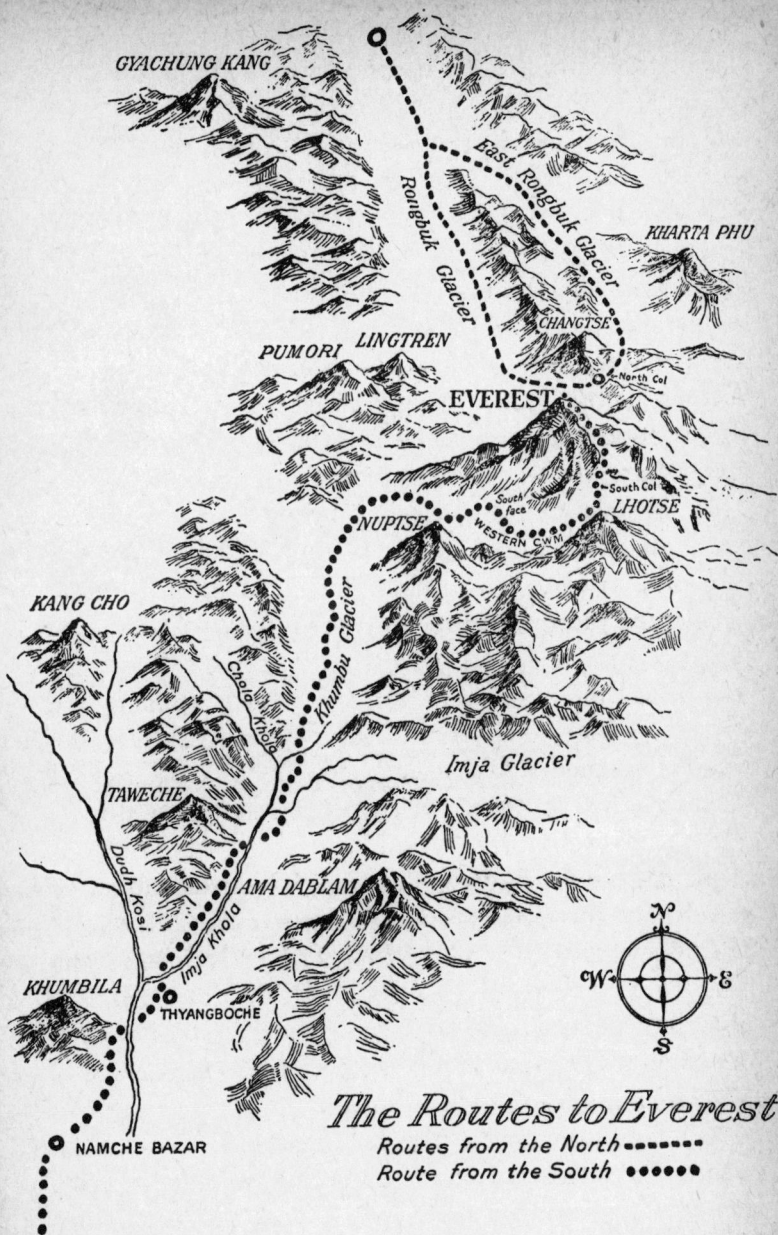

GYACHUNG KANG

East Rongbuk Glacier

Rongbuk Glacier

KHARTA PHU

PUMORI LINGTREN

CHANGTSE

North Col

EVEREST

South Col

South face

LHOTSE

NUPTSE

WESTERN CWM

KANG CHO

Chola Khola

Khumbu Glacier

Imja Glacier

TAWECHE

Dudh Kosi

AMA DABLAM

Imja Khola

Tim

KHUMBILA

THYANGBOCHE

N

W   E

S

The Routes to Everest

Routes from the North ------
Route from the South ••••••

NAMCHE BAZAR

them, because back in Darjeeling I saw that they had a lot of money, which must have been Wilson's. And, besides, they should have either gone out to look for him or at least waited longer for him to come back.

This time, in 1935, was my first on a big mountain, and it was very exciting for me. Especially this was so because it was not just any mountain we had come to, but Everest itself—the great Chomolungma. Here we were up on the glaciers, already higher than anything that lives, and straight in front of us, straight above us, is this tower of rock and ice, climbing still more than two miles, almost three, into the sky. It is strange for me to realize that my old home is only a few miles away; that this is the same mountain in whose shadow I grew up and tended my father's yaks. From this side it is, of course, all different. There is nothing that I recognize, and it is hard to believe that it is really the same. And yet I do believe it. Besides what others tell me I know it in my heart, because I know that no mountain but Chomolungma could be so tall and great.

The work was hard. Between the lower camps we carried sixty to ninety pounds on our backs, beyond them about fifty-five pounds; and it was not just once up, and that was all, but up and down, up and down, for days and weeks, until all the tents and food and equipment were brought up where they should be. I did not mind it at all, though, because, like all Sherpas, I was used to carrying heavy loads. And I thought, Now I am having my first chance to fulfil my dream.

Because this was my first expedition there were, of course, many things that were new to me. We were issued with special clothes and boots and goggles. We ate strange foods out of tin cans. We used pressure stoves and sleeping-bags and all sorts of other equipment I had never seen before. And in the actual climbing, too, there was much that I had to learn. Snow and glaciers themselves were nothing new to a boy who had grown up in Solo Khumbu, but now for the first time I had experience with the real techniques of mountaineering—using a rope, cutting steps with an axe, making and breaking camps, choosing routes that are not only quick but safe. As an apprentice porter, I was not given much responsibility. But I worked hard and was generally useful, and I think the sahibs liked me. Also the altitude did not bother me, even though I had never been so high before, and I was one of the Sherpas who carried loads to the North Col, at a height of more than 22,000 feet.

This was as far as the expedition went. As a reconnaissance, it did not have the equipment or number of men to go higher. And it was there on the Col, before we turned back, that I first realized that I was in some way different from the other Sherpas. For the rest of them were glad to go down. They did their work as a job, for the wages, and wanted to go no farther than they had to. But I was very disappointed. I wanted to go still higher on the mountain. Even then it was as it has been with me for all the rest of my life. When I am on Everest I can think of nothing else. I want only to go on, farther and farther. It is a dream, a need, a fever in the blood. But this time, of course, there was nothing I could do. We came down from the Col, and soon after left the mountain.

"Oh, well," I told myself, "you are only just twenty-one. There will be other expeditions. And soon, soon now, you will be a real Tiger. . . ."

Back in Darjeeling I spent a little time with my wife,

Dawa Phuti. A son was born to us, and we named him Nima Dorje. He was a very handsome boy, who later won first prize in a baby show, and it is one of the sorrows of my life that he died in 1939, when he was only four years old.

In the autumn of 1935 I went on my second expedition, but my part in it was very small. This was to the 24,000-foot mountain Kabru, which is in Northern Sikkim, near Kangchenjunga, and can be seen on a clear day from Darjeeling. The climbers were Mr Cooke, an engineer for the Indian Post and Telegraph Department, and a German friend of his; and the other Sherpas were Ang Tshering, Pasang Phutar, and Pasang Kikuli. Pasang Phutar is now one of my oldest friends, and has recently helped me in building my new home. Pasang Kikuli was at that time already one of the foremost Sherpas, and four years later he died as a hero on an American expedition to K2.

Since I was youngest in the Kabru party, I drew the heaviest load, which was eighty pounds of rice; but still I got to base camp first. That was as far as I went, though. I had been hired to go only to the base, and then I returned to Darjeeling. Mr Cooke and his companion were successful, and got to the top of Kabru in November, but unfortunately no Sherpa was with them.

During the winter, like most Sherpas, I rested and did odd jobs around Darjeeling. This gave me a chance to be with my wife and baby, whom I loved and was happy with. But I was young and restless, and knew now, after my first experiences, that my real life must be in the mountains. With the early spring of 1936 activity started again, and that year I was again on two expeditions.

The first was back to Everest; and this time I had no trouble in being included, because almost every one who had been out the year before was invited to join the expedition. Eric Shipton was again one of the party, as well as Frank Smythe and most of the other famous British climbers, but this time the leader was Hugh Ruttledge, who had also been in charge in 1933. Mr Ruttledge was too old to be a high climber, but he was a wonderful man, gentle and warm-hearted, and all the Sherpas were glad to be with him. This was a very big expedition, with more sahibs than there had ever been before, and a total of sixty Sherpas, which was five times as many as in 1935. With all the extra non-climbing porters to take care of the animals and help with the loads, we looked like a brigade going off to war.

This time we did not start our march from Darjeeling, but from Kalimpong, which is about thirty miles away on the direct trade route to Tibet, and all our equipment was hauled there by mechanical ropeway. From there on, though, the route to Everest was the same as before. We were so big a party that we travelled in two sections, a few days apart; and this was a good idea, because if we had all been together it would have taken half of each day to get the column started in the morning, and the other half to wind it up at night. During this trip I was assigned to the expedition doctor, and from him I learned many things about sickness, injuries, and first aid that were of much use to me in later years.

The English had great hopes for this expedition. It was not only the biggest there had ever been, but the best organized and equipped, and everybody was confident that we would get to the top of Everest. But we had no luck at all. From beginning to end the weather was terrible, and the whole time we were around the mountain it was as if we were in the middle of the monsoon. We made our Camps One, Two, and Three on the glaciers, with the snow falling steadily, and when we began to climb the steep slopes towards the North Col we found ourselves in drifts up to our chests. This was not only back-breaking work, but very dangerous, for the new snow hid many deep crevasses into which we might fall at any minute. And worst of all there was the threat of avalanches. It was impossible not to keep thinking of the awful accident that had happened here in 1922.

At last some of us reached the Col, and I was one of them. But the weather there was like nothing I had ever seen before. Half the time it snowed, so thickly that you could not see another man a few feet away, and the other half, when the snow stopped, the wind blew so hard that it almost threw us off the mountain. Indeed, we were lucky that we could crawl down again to the glacier. There we waited in the lower camps for good weather, but it did not come. It snowed, and then the wind blew, and then it snowed again. Some of the men, I think, would have tried to go up anyhow, but Ruttledge said, "No, we don't want any accident or loss of life. Everest will still be there another year." So at last, after many miserable weeks, we left. And we had got no higher than on the reconnaissance expedition the year before.

At least there had been no deaths on the mountain. But there was one on the way back at a place called Gadong Paga. Here was a big, swift river with a rope across it (which is what *paga* means), and the only way to cross was to tie each man up in a rope net, like a piece of baggage, and then haul him over by a sort of pulley. We all went across like this, except one Sherpa, and he said no, he did not need the net, but could get over on the rope by himself. So he tried, and when he was half-way he lost his hold and fell into the river. Some of the sahibs who could swim stripped off their clothes and jumped in after him, but the current was so strong they could not reach him. He wore his hair in a braid, in the old Sherpa style, and the last we saw of him was the bright ribbon at the end of it floating several hundred yards down the river.

When we got back to Kalimpong every one was disappointed about the expedition, and I was especially sorry for Ruttledge. He was a fine man and leader, but now he was getting on in age, and this would be his last expedition to Everest. I did not see him again until years later in London, after we had climbed the mountain, and then he grasped my hand and said, "Son, you have done a wonderful job. Now I am old. I tried and failed on Everest, but it makes no difference, because now you have succeeded. When you go back to India give my embrace to all my Sherpa sons."

He was right in calling us sons, for he had been a father to us all.

5

THE MAKING OF A TIGER

AFTER the 1936 Everest expedition I did not stay long in Darjeeling. Eric Shipton was going to Garhwal, in the Central Himalayas north of Delhi, and he took me with him. As when I came from Solo Khumbu almost four years earlier, this was a time of many 'firsts' for me—the first time I went down to the plains; the first time I rode in a train; the first time I saw big cities, like Calcutta and Delhi; the first time I felt real heat.

At Ranikhet, in Garhwal, Shipton introduced me to Major Osmaston, of the Royal Engineers, who was one of the head men with the Survey of India. He was going out to do work round the great peak of Nanda Devi, and it had been arranged that I should go with him. Over many years before and since then Major Osmaston has surveyed almost every part of the mountains of Garhwal, and this was the first of several times I went with him.

It was in this same year that Nanda Devi was climbed to the top. At 25,660 feet it was then the highest mountain that had ever been ascended, and it remained so until 1950, when the French climbed Annapurna, in Nepal. Its name means "The Blessed Goddess," and it is considered a sacred mountain by both Hindus and Buddhists. Also it had an especially interesting history, because until two years before no human being had even reached its base, and it was generally considered impossible to do so. Then in 1934 Shipton and his friend H. W. Tilman, another great English mountaineer, found a route. Following the Rishi river, they forced a way up past gorges and precipices, and came out at last into what they called the Sanctuary, a high, hidden, and very beautiful basin at the foot of the peak. They did not have enough men or supplies to go farther, but that was enough for one year. And in 1936, while Shipton was again at Everest, Tilman led out a full expedition to try to climb it.

Now, as Major Osmaston and our party moved in towards the mountain, we met these others coming out; and they told us they had been successful. Tilman and N. E. Odell (who had been on Everest in 1924, and climbed above 27,000 feet, all alone, searching for Mallory and Irvine) had reached the top together. And another climber, the young American Dr Charles Houston, had almost reached the summit, but had been taken ill at the highest camp from something he had eaten, and had had to go down. By this time he was fortunately all right again, and they were all very happy as they went down after their fine victory.

Soon after it was my turn to be ill, and it was the worst sickness I have ever had in the mountains. Perhaps it was from the heat of the plains on the trip from Darjeeling. Or perhaps because it rained all the time, or because I was still tired from the trip to Everest. Anyhow, I became very weak. I ran such a high temperature that sometimes Major Osmaston and the others had to carry me on their backs. No one has ever been kinder to me than Major Osmaston, and I promised myself that some day I would be of real service to him, as he now was to me. They told me that what I had was bilious fever, and some natives of the region said that if I ate a special sort of moss that grew on the stones it would help me. So I tried it. I boiled some moss in hot water and swallowed it, and then I vomited so much that I thought all my insides were coming out. But the fever went away. After that I was weak, but not sick any more, and able to go on.

Like the others before us, we went up to Nanda Devi through the great gorge of the Rishi, which is called the Rishi Ganga, and made our camp in the Sanctuary. As we had been told, it was a very beautiful place, with meadows of wild flowers all around and the great white mountain rising above them. We were not there to climb, though —only to survey and make maps—and that is what Major Osmaston and the others did for the next few weeks. Myself, I was still not strong enough to do much, and stayed mostly at the base camp, but at least I was getting better. Near the camp was the grave of a Sherpa who had become ill and died on the Tilman expedition, and I thought, Anyhow, I am luckier than he.

Finally we left the mountain and returned to Ranikhet, and from there I went back alone to Darjeeling. By now I was all right again, but not at all pleased with myself that I had been of so little use. Some day, I thought, I will go back to Nanda Devi and do better. And so I did.

One way a Sherpa could make a few rupees when he was not on an expedition was to take tourists to places of interest near Darjeeling. And I did this frequently during the next autumn and winter. Sometimes the trips were only to Tiger Hill, above the town, from which at sunrise you could often see the tip of Everest, a hundred miles away beyond the ridges of Nepal. Sometimes they were a little longer—along the trails to the north as far as Sandakphu and Phalut, from which on good days you could see much more of Everest. In a way it was satisfying to me. To know that it was still there, still waiting. But it was also unsatisfying, because I could only look and not go. There was to be no expedition that next year, and I would have to wait until 1938 for another chance.

Meanwhile, in 1937, I went back again to Garhwal. This was to climb with Mr J. T. M. Gibson and Mr J. A. K. Martyn, two teachers at the Doon School in Dehra Dun, which is the best-known English boys' school in India. It was a small expedition, for there were only the two sahibs, myself and another Darjeeling Sherpa named Rinzing, and ten Garhwali porters. The mountain we were trying to climb was Bandar Punch, which means "Monkey's Tail," and this was the first of three trips I have made there with Mr Gibson. It is 20,720 feet high, which is very little compared to Everest or even Nanda Devi. But it had never been tried before, and was not easy, and on this first attempt we were stopped by heavy snow at only 17,000 feet.

After this we tried no more ascents, but spent many weeks exploring the country and had many adventures. One day, while we were camped beside a big river, we split into two teams and went reconnoitring. Mr Gibson and Rinzing were on one side of the river, Mr Martyn and I on the other, and we were supposed to join forces again that night. But a great mist came down, and afterwards rain, so that we could not find each other, or even the camp. Mr Martyn and I had no tent or equipment and very little food. We wandered about, shouting, but in the mist we could not see where we were going, and then it rained so hard that we couldn't hear our own voices. We found a cave, and had to spend two days in it. And then at last the weather cleared, and we all found our way back to camp.

Later on we made a long march to a village on the border of Tibet. On the way back we got down from the high country into a deep jungle and were lost. After a while we ran low on food, but we were able to pick many berries, so we didn't starve. Still, we were very hungry. Then after a time we came upon some people from a near-by village who had stopped along the way to have their lunch. We saw they had plenty of food and asked to buy some, but they were unfriendly and would not sell. And suddenly I had an idea. I knew that among these people there is the belief that if a stranger touches their food it becomes unclean, and I told Mr Gibson to point at all the things to eat and touch them and ask, "What is this? What is that?" So he did this, and there was great excitement. But he touched everything very quickly before the villagers could stop him, saying, "What's this? What's that? What's this? What's that?"—and, as I had hoped, the people then wouldn't touch the food, but left it for us. The sahibs still wanted to pay, and offered them twenty rupees; but they would not accept it, and rushed away, saying they were going to report us to the chief of their village. Nothing happened, though, because soon we moved on and were able to avoid their village. And meanwhile we had nice full stomachs.

On this trip we were always having trouble about food. Once three weeks went by without our having anything fresh, and when we finally came to a village we bought a goat and killed it. We were so hungry that we stuffed ourselves, eating it all that same evening, and the next morning every one was sick. We felt so bad we stayed in that village for three days, and while we were there we bought some *araq*, which is a very strong liquor. Perhaps it was not the medicine a doctor would have ordered, but it seemed to cure us.

All this was after we tried Bandar Punch. On our travels we came to Gangotri and Gomukhi, which are famous places of pilgrimage, and then we passed close to the great mountains Badrinath and Kamet, and crossed Birnie Pass. This is 18,000 feet up, even higher than we had got on Bandar Punch, and was named after Captain E. Birnie, of the British Army, who had been on the expedition that climbed Kamet in 1932, and was the first to cross it. He had gone from south to north, however, and we were the first ever to cross it in the other direction. At this time we had very few local porters, and had to carry almost everything ourselves—which made it as hard as if we had been climbing a big mountain.

So I had two trips in two years to Garhwal, and they were very interesting. But they were not the same as Everest. And I kept thinking of Everest. Back in Darjeeling I waited impatiently, and in the spring of 1938 there was another expedition, and, of course, I joined it. This was the seventh expedition there had been to the mountain, and the third for me.

This time H. W. Tilman was the leader, and it was a much smaller party than the one in 1936. Besides Tilman, there were Eric Shipton and Frank Smythe, whom I had climbed with before; N. E. Odell, whom I had met the year before near Nanda Devi; and Peter Lloyd and Captain Oliver, who were going for the first time. Tilman was a very fine, quiet man, and all the Sherpas liked him. He had such shaggy looks and big eyebrows that we nicknamed him Balu—the Bear. It was he who started the custom by which high-climbing Sherpas do not carry heavy loads until they are actually on a mountain and the low-level porters have gone back. And he also started the official system of Tigers and Tiger Medals, which is now an established part of Himalayan expeditions.

The route to Everest was the same as before, and by early April we were in our base camp beyond the Rongbuk Monastery. Here I met my father once more, for he had again heard about the expedition and come over the Nangpa La to visit me. This, though, was the last time I was to see him, for he died in Solo Khumbu in 1949, which was before I returned there again. He had always been a good father to me, and I bless his memory.

From the glaciers we did not go right to the North Col, but, as in 1935, looked round to see if there was another, better way. Tilman, myself, and two other Sherpas (Ang Tshering and Jingmay), climbed to the high pass of the Lho La, near where Mallory had gone; and this was a great thing for me, because now at last I could look from one side of Everest to the other—right down to the south-west and almost to my old home in Thamey. Far below I could see yaks on the slopes near the Khumbu Glacier, and there was one man with them, and I wondered who he was. Tilman had hoped that we could go right across the pass to this other side and look round, but now we saw that the far slope was all ice and terribly steep. We could have got down it, perhaps, but almost surely not back up again. While we were on the Lho La there was much cloud and mist, and we could not see clearly into the great snow-basin above the Khumbu, which Mallory had given the Welsh name of Western Cwm. So we could not tell how the climbing would go there, and I could not have dreamed, of course, that fifteen years later this would be the route to the summit.

After we were again in base camp we set out for the North Col. And this time we reached it from two directions—the old way from the East Rongbuk Glacier and a new way from the main Rongbuk Glacier. But we found the new route very steep and even less safe than the old, which was dangerous enough itself. The snow-and-ice slopes below the Col, as I have said, are a place of great avalanche menace, and now for the first time I was caught in one. When it happened there were six of us climbing on two ropes—Captain Oliver, myself, and the Sherpa Wangdi Norbu on one, and Tilman with two Sherpas on the other. The snow is very steep, and also deep—as high as our waists—and we are moving slowly and with difficulty, when suddenly there is a sort of cracking sound all around us, and the snow begins to move too. The next minute we are all sliding down with it. I am off my feet, turning over and over. My head is under the snow, and it is dark. I remember, of course, what happened here in 1922, and I think, It is the same thing again. It is the end. But at the same time I am struggling, throwing my ice-axe back over my shoulder, trying to stop myself and dig out. And luckily the avalanche stops, and I am not too deep. My axe catches and holds on some solid snow, which allows me to pull myself up. I look around in the bright light, and I am still alive.

We were all lucky. The snow stopped sliding, and none of us was too deep. But only ten feet below us was a great crevasse, and if we had been carried into that we should not have come out. As it was, only one thing was missing. Captain Oliver had lost his woollen helmet.

We made our Camp Four on the North Col, and it was

my third time there. But now at last I was to go still
higher. For the upper mountain we divided into two
groups, and I was in the first one, which was led by Sahibs
Smythe and Shipton and had six Sherpas besides myself.
These were Rinzing, Lobsang, Wangdi Norbu, Lakpa
Tenzing, Da Tshering, and Ollo Bhotia. Following the
north-east ridge, which was the way the earlier expeditions
had gone, we carried up our loads and made Camp Five
at about 25,800 feet. Though this was the highest I had
ever been, the altitude did not bother me. But the weather
was not good, and the snow lay deep over the rocks, so
that we had almost to plough our way through it. Already
the sahibs were shaking their heads and saying there was
small chance of our reaching the top.

At Camp Five we waited and made ready to go on
farther and establish Camp Six, which would be the
highest. But two Sherpas behind us who were carrying
tents and fuel up from the Col could not get to Five, and
this made trouble, because we could not go on without
these things. There was a discussion about what to do.
The other Sherpas at Camp Five said that if they were sent
down they wanted to stay down, but I said I would go
down and get the things and come back again. So I went
alone. I found the tents and fuel about half-way down to
the Col, where the two Sherpas had left them before turning round, and, slinging them on my back, started up
again. And here I came the nearest to falling that I have
ever come on a mountain. In those days we did not wear
crampons—the steel shoe-spikes for steep snow and ice that
have been used on all recent expeditions. Suddenly I
slipped. It was a bad slip on an exposed place, and I was
just able to catch and hold myself with my axe. If I had
not I should have fallen all the way to the Rongbuk

Glacier, more than a mile below. Fortunately it was all right, though. I went on, and reached Camp Five just before dark, and Smythe and Shipton congratulated me. Later, when the expedition was over, I was given a special reward of twenty rupees.

The next day we climbed on and made Camp Six. This was at 27,200 feet, which was the highest I ever went until with the Swiss on the other side of Everest in 1952. Smythe and Shipton stayed there, but the Sherpas, including myself, descended the same afternoon to Camp Five. Here we met the second party of Tilman, Lloyd, and their Sherpas, who then continued up to Six, while we went down to the Col. There we waited. But we did not have to wait long, for soon the others began coming down too. From the highest camp both teams of sahibs had made a try for the top, but, as they had feared, there was no chance of success. It was not too cold, nor was there much wind; but everywhere the snow lay deep over what in 1924 and 1933 had been bare slabs of rock. It would not have been bad if the snow had been hard. But it was soft and feathery. At every step they had sunk in almost to their armpits, and more snow was falling all the time. The monsoon was beginning early, and it was the end of any hope for the summit.

One interesting thing about this expedition was that it was the first time I saw oxygen equipment. Tilman did not like oxygen—he thought Everest should, and could, be climbed without it—and most of the others did not use it either. But Lloyd carried a set the whole time above the North Col, and made many experiments with it. What sort of a mad thing is that? I wondered when I first saw it; and most of the other Sherpas laughed and called it "English air." It was a big, heavy apparatus, not at all like that we used on Everest many years later, and seemed much more trouble than it was worth. One of the big cylinders was later put to a very different use in the Rongbuk Monastery. When I returned there in 1947 it was hanging from a rope in the main courtyard, and every evening they would pound it as a gong when it was time for the monks and nuns to go to their separate quarters.

With the weather so bad, we were now ready to go down for good. But even that was not easy. The snow kept falling, and we were afraid of more avalanches, and also there was a sudden and unexpected misfortune. One morning, at Camp Four on the Col, I was bringing tea round to the tents for the sahibs and Sherpas when I found one of the Sherpas, Pasang Bhotia, in a dazed condition. I tried to stir him up, but with no result; and he also seemed half paralysed. Eric Shipton was at the time in charge of this camp, and he examined Pasang, but could do nothing either. At this time Tilman was still at one of the higher camps, and when he later descended he got Pasang down, with much difficulty, over the steep snow and ice to the glacier. No one ever discovered just what had gone wrong with Pasang, but he remained partially paralysed even after the expedition was over. And that was the only misfortune we had—other than not reaching the top.

As I have said, although the name was used loosely before, it was Tilman who made the title of Tiger official for the highest-climbing Sherpas. And this was the expedition on which it started. All of us who reached Camp Six in 1938 were later awarded a Tiger Medal, with the ranking entered in our record books; and since then the Himalayan Club, which is the chief mountaineering organization of India, has issued them to all Sherpas who have performed comparable feats on other expeditions. I was proud and happy, of course, to be among the very first Tigers, and back in Darjeeling I thought, Well, this time we got high. Perhaps next time, in 1939 or 1940, we will go all the way.

But I did not know then what it was like in the outside world, or what would soon be happening. Fourteen long years were to pass before I should have my next real chance at Chomolungma.

6

WAR YEARS

THE life of a Sherpa mountain man is, I suppose, something like that of a sailor. When things are good with him he is away from home much of the time and not often with his family. Perhaps it is a little better, though, for a Sherpa wife. For at least she knows that where her husband is going she does not have to worry too much about other women.

Later in 1938 I went to Garhwal. And again it was to go with Major Osmaston on a survey. This time we visited the Almora country, where the north of India touches both Tibet and Western Nepal, and it was a very wild region which had been visited by few outsiders. Sometimes we could look across the border of Tibet and see Mount Kailas, which, though only about 22,000 feet high, is the most holy of all the peaks in the Himalayas, both to Buddhists and Hindus. Near it are the great Manasarowar Lakes, which are also sacred, and a famous monastery; and through all history pilgrims have come to them from the far places of Asia. I wish that I too might have had a chance actually to go there. But Almora is the closest I have ever been.

Major Osmaston was a good mountaineer, but he did not go out to climb peaks—only to measure them and put them on the map. So on this trip, like the first, we did not try any big ascents. We were very busy, though, with fourteen assistants of the Survey Department in the expedition, plus many porters, and we were out in the mountains for more than two months.

Then I came back to Darjeeling and spent the winter there with Dawa Phuti. And the important thing that happened this year was that we had a second child, a daughter, whom we called Pem Pem. By this time our son, Nima Dorje, was more than three, and, as I have said, very handsome. Sometimes I would look at him and say to myself, "When you are too old to climb he will begin and take your place. And he will be the best of all Tigers."

Now it was 1939, and in the spring, as in all springs, I went out on a new expedition. A Canadian lady, Mrs Beryl Smeeton, came to Darjeeling to hire Sherpas through the Himalayan Club; but what she wanted them for was not a near-by mountain, but the great peak of Tirich Mir, far on the other side of India. In fact, it is not really in the Himalayas at all. It is beyond the Indus river in the Hindu Kush Range, on the border of Afghanistan, and at that time it seemed as remote to me as Europe or America. With a few other Sherpas, however, I decided to go. If I had not, I realized later, my life would have been very different during the next six years.

We went first a long distance to Lahore, in the Punjab, where we met Mrs Smeeton's husband, Captain Smeeton, and also a friend of theirs called Major Ogil.[1] Then we travelled almost as far again, until we came to the most north-western district of India—now in Pakistan—which is called Chitral. In the town of Chitral we made our last arrangements, and went on to Tirich Mir, which is a

[1] This is a name that is probably spelled wrongly, and I am sorry.

big and beautiful mountain, 25,260 feet high. We were a very small expedition, and it proved too much for us, since we did not have enough men or equipment, and with the wind and cold there was much danger of frostbite. Still, we got to 23,000 feet before we had to turn back. And Mrs Smeeton went the whole way with us, which was a wonderful climb for a lady. Tirich Mir was mostly snow and ice, with little rock, and not too difficult, and with more high-altitude equipment we could have got to the top. But we were climbing for pleasure, and not especially to reach a goal, so no one was too disappointed. I was interested to hear that it was first climbed in 1950 by an expedition from Norway.

On Tirich Mir I was in charge of both the Sherpas and the local coolies. But though there was much responsibility, this was unofficial. It was not until 1947 that I became a recognized sirdar, the official chief of all the porters on an expedition.

This climb had been in June and early July, and when it was over the other Sherpas went back to Darjeeling. But I stayed on in Chitral. On the way in to Tirich Mir I had met a Major White, who had been helpful to the Smeetons in organizing the expedition, and also very kind and friendly to me. He was from Scotland, and an officer in the Chitral Scouts, who are a famous regiment of the Indian Army, and now he suggested that I stay and work for him. So I did. At first I thought it would be for only a short time, and I should then go home to my wife and family. But I liked it so much that the months passed quickly, and soon it was almost the end of the year.

Then I had some very bad news from Darjeeling. My son, Nima Dorje, had got blood dysentery from drinking polluted water. He was only four years old. But now he was dead. "I must go home," I told Major White, and I did so early in 1940. Nima Dorje was gone, of course, but the family was no smaller; for now another child was born—our second daughter—and we called her Nima too. I stayed in Darjeeling only a short while. I had been very happy in Chitral, and, besides, there was now war in Europe, and there would certainly be no big expeditions for a long time. So I took my wife and two daughters with me, and went back to Chitral, and it was five years before I saw Darjeeling again.

Major White gave us a fine welcome. For a few months I again worked for him personally as orderly and assistant, and then, at his suggestion, I took a job in the officers' mess of the Chitral Scouts. There I had a chance to learn all sorts of new things about Western people and their habits and their food, and, if I say so myself, I became a first-class cook. Later I was made headman of the mess, in charge of all its operations. And since then I have sometimes thought, if there is ever any need for you to stop climbing mountains, you can always run a hotel.

We did not stay all the time in the same place. The regiment moved here and there round the North-west Frontier country, and I moved with them. Major White treated me like a son, giving me good clothes and many presents, and, best of all, he took me on many private trips when we could both get time off from our work. We did not do any climbing, but in the winter we went to Kashmir, and I learned to ski. I enjoyed skiing as much as anything I had ever done, and Major White suggested that some day I might find it useful in my mountaineering. Once I had a bad fall, in which I broke some ribs and sprained my knees, but that did not stop me, and I went at it again as soon as I could. The mountains you skiied on were not like the mountains you climbed. They were not really mountains at all—only hills. But I had never gone so fast before in my life—not even on a train—and that was what I liked about it. Climbing was so slow, and skiing so fast.

There were no other Sherpas in Chitral. In all the years we were there my family and I did not see another Sherpa or a Nepali. Sometimes, of course, this made me lonely, but there were good things about it too, because it taught me much of the world. I met Englishmen and Indians, Turkis and Afghans, Hindus and Moslems, Christians and Jews. I learned to speak Hindustani, Chitrali, and Pasthu, and improved my English, of which I already knew a little. I became used to dealing with men and problems of many different kinds. And as time went on I did not think so often of Darjeeling. I did not even think often of Chomolungma. It was so far away. One day Major White read a letter to me which officially notified me that I had been awarded the rank of Tiger for my work on Everest in 1938. But I did not receive the medal until I returned home in 1945.

During all this time the War went on and kept getting bigger. There had been a time when I thought there was only one country where *chilina-nga* lived, and that was England; but now I knew that there were a great many, both in Europe and all over the world. I would hear of them on the radio, and wonder about them and hope that some day I could go and see them. Sometimes when I heard news of the War I thought it might be the right thing for me to join the Army. But then I told myself I was already working for the Army, and if I was actually in it I should probably be doing the same work, only with less pay and more discipline. Besides the War, there also began to be much talk at this time about the struggle for the independence of India and a new country of Pakistan. Chitral was later to be part of Pakistan, and was mostly Moslem, but since I was not a Hindu I had no unpleasant experiences. In those days I knew little about politics or things of that sort, and all I wanted was to live my life peacefully and do my work to the best of my ability.

That was not hard then. But I wish more people would have let me do the same thing since the climbing of Everest.

I found out later that I could have made quite a lot of money in Chitral. There were many precious stones in that part of the country; you would see them all the time. Only I did not know they were precious, and neither did most of the local people, for they would often exchange them for a few bags of tea or a little something to eat. When I returned to Darjeeling I brought a few with me, and certain merchants there got very excited and told me they were valuable. Some of my friends then urged me to return to Chitral and get a whole supply, so that I could sell them and become rich. But I did not do it. Certainly I had no objections to making money, but I had an idea that somehow I should not be too successful as a merchant.

Besides Major White, I made another good friend in Chitral. This was Dr N. D. Jacob, the Civil Surgeon, who was in charge of all non-military medical services for the district. He was a very busy and important man, but with none of the stiffness of some of the English in India; and he was always kind and helpful to me and my family, treating us as well as if I had been a maharaja or a major-general. One of the greatest pleasures of my trip to London in 1953 was when I met him again after many years. And

I was deeply moved when I learned that he had travelled five hundred miles just to see me.

But there were sad things connected with Dr Jacob too. For much of the time in Chitral my wife, Dawa Phuti, was not well. The climate did not seem to agree with her, and though Dr Jacob did all he could, she grew steadily weaker. And in 1944 she died. This was a terrible thing for me, of course, and also for our daughters, Pem Pem and Nima, who were now five and four years old. With their mother gone, there was no one to look after them, and I was greatly worried and did not know what to do. For a while I engaged an ayah to take care of things, but it did not work out well. So early in 1945 I decided that we must go back to Darjeeling.

Over the years I had saved about fifteen hundred rupees, and that part was all right. But the War was still on, and transportation was very difficult. First I hired a horse and a pair of bags to sling across its back, and, putting the two girls one in each bag, I led the horse across the mountain-pass from Chitral to the town of Dir. At Dir there was a railway; but there were great crowds waiting to travel, and for days I could not get a train. Because of the girls I was desperate. I did not know what to do. And then at last I had a bright idea. Major White had given me one of his old uniforms, which still had officer's pips on the shoulders, and, putting it on, I looked really *pukka*. Going back to the station, I waited for a military train and walked right into a first-class compartment. No one objected, and soon we started off. And with the two girls I rode almost the whole way across India without the trip costing a single anna.

At Siliguri, near Darjeeling, I took off the uniform; for soon now we should be among people who knew me, and

I did not want to be arrested for my illegal masquerade.
Then we took a bus the rest of the way, and after six years
I was at last home again. To my old friends I was almost
a stranger. They stared at my strange clothes and laughed
at my way of speaking. And for a while they called me
"Pathan," which is the name for people from far North-
west India and Afghanistan.

Though I had been happy in Chitral, I was glad to be
back among my own kind. But there were still the girls
to be taken care of, and for a man alone that was very
hard. My friends said, "You must marry a good woman
who will look after them." And I answered, "Yes, that
is a good idea. But who?" Once more, though, I was
lucky. After a while I again met Ang Lahmu, the young
lady who had once bought milk from me and argued about
the price. And now it turned out that she was a cousin of
Dawa Phuti. We were married; she became the new
mother of my children; and for this, in the years to come,
I was to have much cause to be grateful.

7

THE MOUNTAINS ARE STILL THERE

TWO weeks after I married Ang Lahmu I went off on my next trip. I am afraid she was not too pleased about it, but that is the lot of a Sherpa wife.

This first trip was not a big one. It was not even mountain-climbing. At that time, with the War still on, there were many Americans in India, and often they would come to Darjeeling for their leaves. One of them, Lieutenant-Colonel H. Taylor, arrived with permission to enter Tibet, and engaged me to help make arrangements and go with him. So we took two horses for ourselves and some mules for the baggage and rode up through the valleys of Sikkim and across the high, windy passes. We did not go far—only to Gyantse, which is one of the nearest towns across the Tibetan border—but it was my first time in Tibet to any place but Rongbuk and Everest, and it was as interesting to me as to Colonel Taylor. He was very friendly, and kept telling me I should come to America, with the promise that if I did he would teach me to drive a jeep. Ever since then I have had jeeps on my mind, and if I can ever save enough money I will buy one, for they are just the right car for the steep roads round Darjeeling.

Besides being friendly, Colonel Taylor was also generous.

Later, when the War was over, he sent me a present of two hundred rupees before he left for home. But he still owes me those driving lessons, and perhaps when I come to America I will catch up with him.

This trip took only two months. Like Colonel Taylor, most of the Americans I had met liked better to ride than to walk, and now that I had had some experience with horses I thought of a new way of making a living. Back in Darjeeling I bought two horses with my savings from Chitral and hired them out. And for a while it went very well. While the other Sherpas worked hard all day, carrying loads and going up- and down-hill, I could just hire out the horses until noon, and then go back to my house for the rest of the day.

Actually, though, I did not do this often, because I was too active and would rather work than just sit. And in addition I took visitors about to see the sights, as I had used to do before the War. One day, I remember, I took seven American ladies up to Tiger Hill to see Mount Everest at sunrise. There were other guides and tourists there too, and the guides were doing what I am ashamed to say they did often—pointing out the wrong mountain to their people. From Tiger Hill, you see, Everest does not look very much.. It is a long way off, and stands behind Lhotse and Makalu, so that these other two look bigger, especially Makalu. For this reason the tourists usually think Makalu is Everest, and many of the guides just say, "Yes, that is Everest," because they don't care and are too lazy to explain. But I did not like that sort of thing. I told my seven ladies which was Everest and why it was the smallest one. And they were so pleased I was honest with them that later they hired horses from me, and also sent their friends to do so.

It is one of the good things about Darjeeling that so many different people are always coming there. One morning I was walking along the Chowrasta, which is the main street of the town, and there suddenly was Mrs Smeeton, whom I had not seen since Tirich Mir. There was a gentleman with her who seemed a stranger, and I waited for an introduction; but when he spoke I realized to my embarrassment that it was her husband. In the War, he explained later, he had been hit in the nose by a bullet, and it had changed his face amazingly. But both he and Mrs Smeeton were no different in their friendliness and kindness. They invited me to go with them for a week to Kalimpong, and we had a fine reunion.

As before, I used to take people on short tours to near-by places, like Phalut, Tonglu, and Sandakphu. And sometimes they were not the only ones who learned something from the trip. For instance, there was an English couple I had taken to Tiger Hill, and they wanted to see some more, so we hired horses and went off towards Tonglu. The sahib I do not remember well, but the memsahib was very pretty, and I noticed especially her good complexion and fine white teeth. At the end of the first day we stopped at a Dak bungalow,[1] where we spent the night, and in the morning, as usual, I brought them washing water and tea. As I appeared the memsahib sat up, and I thought, Oh, my God, I am in the wrong place!—because she was not young and pretty, but an old lady with yellow skin and no teeth. I put down the pot and pitcher and was about to run. Then I saw beside her some jars of creams and powders, and in a glass of water a fine white set of teeth; and I thought, Well, perhaps—— But I ran, any-

[1] This is the name given to rest-houses built by the Government for the use of travellers in wild country.

how. When she came out a little later she was as young
and pretty as the day before.

At last, in the spring of 1946, came the first real expedition in many long years. This was again to Bandar Punch
—the Monkey's Tail—in Garhwal, and again with my old
friends Mr Gibson and Mr Martyn, of the Doon School in
Dehra Dun. When their message came, asking if I could
join them, I was as excited as if I were not a grown man
but a boy. "You are going back to the mountains!"
That was all I could think, and it was like a great shout
inside of me. "You are going back to the mountains
where you belong!"

So I went to Garhwal and met them, and we started off.
Also in the party this time were Mr R. L. Holdsworth,
another master at the Doon School, who had been on the
1932 expedition to Kamet; Major Munro, of the Royal
Artillery; and Lieutenant N. D. Jayal, of the Indian Army,
with whom I was to have close association in later years.
Once again we did not have good luck on Bandar Punch.
The weather was bad, with heavy snow. But we got to
18,000 feet, which was a thousand feet higher than in 1937,
and it was wonderful to be up again in the sort of country
in which I am happiest.

"We will come back to it. Some day we will catch
that monkey by the tail," declared Mr Gibson, when we
said good-bye.

"Only it should not be called the Monkey's Tail any
more," I told him, laughing. "From now on it should be
the Doon School Mountain."

It is strange about Kangchenjunga. There it is, the
third highest mountain in the world, standing so near and
high above Darjeeling that I have spent half my life with

it in full sight. Yet I have never been on it. I have gone many times to Everest, to Garhwal, to far-away mountains in Kashmir and Chitral, but not to Kangchenjunga. No Sherpa of my generation has climbed on Kangchenjunga.

Years ago there were several attempts on it. In 1905 a small Swiss party tried to find a way up and were lost. In 1929 a young American named Farmer tried to climb it alone, like Wilson on Everest, and he too was lost. Then, in that same year and the next two, there were three big expeditions, two by Germans and one by Swiss, with also some English and Austrians in the party. This mixed expedition, in 1930, made their attempt from the Nepali side, but they had hardly started to climb when they encountered what was probably the biggest avalanche that men have ever seen. It seemed almost as if the whole wall of the mountain was coming down on them; and although it took only one life—a Sherpa's—it could so easily have killed them all that they decided to go off to another mountain. The two German parties, in 1929 and 1931, came from the other side, through Sikkim and up the Zemu Glacier. Each time they tried for weeks and months to cut their way up the great ridge of ice that is known as the North-east Spur, and at last, in the second year, reached the top of the spur at more than 26,000 feet, but could not find a way on to the summit. In this 1931 attempt a German climber and the Sherpa Cheden were killed in a fall of many thousand feet.

Since then no one has tried to reach the top of Kang-chenjunga. The chief reason for this is that, though it is so close to Darjeeling and easy to get to, it is also the closest of all the big mountains to the plains and the Indian Ocean, and the weather is very uncertain. The summer monsoon is here longest and heaviest, with the clouds so thick you often cannot see the peak from Darjeeling for months on end. And even at other seasons the warm air blows up and meets the cold of the snows, so that there are frequent storms and great avalanches. There are many lesser mountains round Kangchenjunga, such as Kabru, Jannu, Simvu, Jonsong, Kang, Koktang, and Pandim, and on most of these there have been expeditions —some successful. But because they are somewhat lower, conditions are not quite so difficult. Difficult or not, though, I do not think climbers can stay away for ever from the third highest peak in the world. In the last few years there have been several reconnaissance parties looking for new and better routes, and I shall not be surprised if soon there is another big expedition.

As for myself, as I say, I have never been on it. But I have, of course, been close to it many times. The first was in 1935, when I helped carry supplies to the base camp for Kabru. And now in 1946, after I came back from Garhwal. I went twice again within a few months.

Trip Number One was with Major Reed, of the Indian Army. It was not our purpose to climb a mountain, but only to explore the great glaciers, like the Zemu and the Yalung, and to go up to the high passes of the Nepal and Zemu Gaps. Also—and this is a sign of how dangerous it is in this region—there had been two expeditions there the year before, on both of which men had been lost; and we were on the look-out for any trace of them. One of these parties had been led by a Captain Langton Smith, who with three Sherpas had gone out to climb a mountain called Sugar Loaf, but had disappeared in a snowstorm and had not been seen again. From the other the missing man was an Indian, Mr K. C. Roy, who had been managing director of the Bengal Lamp Works, and before we left Darjeeling his wife, an American lady, had asked us to look for him and to bring back any relic we could find.

So we kept our eyes open, and, sure enough, after a while we found the body of one of Captain Smith's Sherpas. He was lying beside a big rock near a place called Green Lake, with the remains of a fire near by and a cooking-pan wedged under him. Not far away, among some stones, were several packets of photographic films that must have belonged to Smith, but there was no sign of him or of the other two Sherpas. There are many lakes in this district, and I think perhaps they had tried to cross one while it was half frozen and covered with snow, and had fallen in. A while later, when we were on our way back from the glaciers, we came upon the body of Mr Roy, from the other expedition—and this was also near Green Lake. Some one had tried to cremate it, but not very successfully, and we buried the remains. But first, remembering what Mrs Roy had asked, we took a small piece of charred bone and his wrist-watch, and these we brought back with us to Darjeeling.

This trip had not been especially to look for the missing men. We did that only by the way. But I had hardly reached home when I was sought out by Captain J. W. Thornley, of the Seventh Gurkha Rifles, who was going out on a special search for any traces of Captain Smith; and soon I was on my way back to the Zemu. Along with us came six other Sherpas, and when we reached the glacier we split into several teams and hunted carefully for many days. But this time we found nothing at all. Or, at least, no sign of Smith.

What we did find were the tracks of a *yeti*.

I will now tell what I know about the *yeti*, or Abominable Snowman. It is no more than most men know who have been long in the Himalayas, and perhaps less than some. This was the first time, on the Zemu Glacier in 1946, that I saw its tracks; and the only other time was in 1952, with the Swiss near the base of Everest. As I have said, I had often, when a boy in Solo Khumbu, seen animal droppings on the glaciers and high hillsides that I was sure could only be those of a *yeti*. And I had, of course, heard many stories about it, from my father and others.

Here are my father's stories.

The first time he encountered this strange creature was on the Barun Glacier, which is close to the mountain Makalu, and also to Tsa-chu, where I was born. He came upon it suddenly, and it was so close that, he said, he saw it very clearly. It looked like a big monkey or ape, except that its eyes were deeply sunken and its head was pointed at the top. The colour was greyish, and a noticeable thing was that the hair grew in two directions—from above the waist upward and from below the waist downward. It was about four feet high, and a female, with long, hanging breasts; and when it ran, which was on two legs only, it held the breasts up with its hands. My father was frightened, of course. But so was the *yeti*. Straight away it turned and began climbing a steep mountain-slope, making a high, shrill whistle, and soon it had disappeared. After that my father was much worried about what would happen to him, for there are many who claim that if a man sees a *yeti* he will surely die. He was lucky, though, and did not die. But he has told me that he was ill afterwards for almost a year.

There was another time also that he saw a *yeti*. This was in 1935, after he had come across the Nangpa La to Rongbuk, to visit me when I was with my first Everest expedition. One night he stayed alone at Camp One, on the glacier, while the rest of us were either at the base camp below or at the other camps higher up, and in the morning, when it was just starting to be light, he heard a whistling sound outside the tent. He raised the flap and looked out, and there was a creature a little way off, coming down the glacier from south to north. Again, of course, my father was frightened. He did not want to look at the *yeti*, but also he did not want just to hide in the tent, for fear it would then come closer, or even enter. So he stayed where he was until it had gone on down the glacier and was out of sight, and then he came as fast as he could up to Camp Two, where I was at the time. When he arrived he embraced me and said, "I come all this way to see my son. And instead what I see is a *yeti*." But this time he had not seen it so close, and he was not ill afterwards.

All over the Himalayas, among all the hill people, there are stories about the *yeti*. And it is hard to tell which are true and which come only from imagination and superstition. In Solo Khumbu there is the story that years ago many *yetis* came and lived close round the village of Targna. The Sherpas there would build their houses and cultivate their fields, but at night, or when the people were away, the *yetis* would come and make great mischief, so that the building or planting would have to start all over again. The strange thing was that the *yetis* did not just destroy. After they had done their damage they would try to rebuild the houses or replant the crops in their own way. But, of course, they did not do it right, and the villagers were desperate. Since they could never find the creatures when they went out to look for them, they decided they must use guile. So one day they went out to a place where they knew the *yetis* gathered, because there was much dung around, and there they left several bowls of *chang*, the strong Sherpa beer, and also many *kukris*, which are curved Nepali knives. When night came, as they had hoped, the *yetis* found the *chang* and drank it. And when they were drunk they picked up the *kukris* and began to fight. In the morning, according to the story, almost all of them were lying there dead, and the people of Targna could again go peacefully about their business.

Among the Sherpas it is believed that there are two types of *yeti*—the *metrey*, which is a man-eater, and the *chutrey*, which eats only animals. But of the two the *chutrey* is supposed to be the bigger—something like a big brown bear, except that, as with all *yetis*, its feet are said to point backward. Some Westerners and scientific men have thought that that is all the *yeti* is—a type of bear. The famous scientist Julian Huxley once came to Darjeeling, where I met him, and he gave that opinion. But there are others who think it is more like a big monkey or ape, which is how my father described it.

Only a few people claim actually to have seen a *yeti*. The native mountain people do not want to see it, because everywhere it is believed that then evil will befall you. For myself, as I have said, I have never seen one—either drunk or sober, walking forward or backward. I am not a superstitious man. I do not believe it is anything supernatural, nor do I believe many of the crazy stories I have heard. But I do not think my father was a liar and made his stories up out of his head. And certainly the tracks I have seen both on the Zemu Glacier in 1946 and near Everest in 1952 do not look like those of any familiar creature. Though I cannot prove it, I am convinced that some such thing exists. My belief is that it is an animal, not a man; that it moves about mostly at night and lives on the plants and small beasts of the highest mountain pastures; and that it probably is an ape of a type not yet known to us.

In 1954 there was an expedition to the Everest region, made up of British and Indians, that went especially to search for the *yeti*. And I would have liked to go with it, but was not able to. Like so many other parties, they found tracks and other signs—but no *yetis*—and though this was disappointing, it was also, perhaps, just as well. We now go to so many places, do so much, find out so much. I think it is all right if there are still a few things we do not know.[1]

---

[1] In 1955, on a trip to Solo Khumbu, I was lucky enough to come upon the skulls of two *yetis*; but this I will tell about later.

Family Man
Ang Lahmu is in the centre with Ghanghar. Pem Pem is on the right and Nima on the left.

My Mother with One of her Grandchildren
This picture was taken near her home in Thamey in 1952.

Namche Bazar—the Most Important Sherpa Village

Sherpa Boys

School in Namche

FOUR FAMOUS SHERPAS

Ang Nyima

Dawa Thondup

Angtharkay

Da Namgyal

H. W. Tilman

Frank S. Smythe

Eric Shipton

Summit of Everest from Camp Six in 1938
Camp Six was at 27,200 feet.

Darjeeling and Kangchenjunga

Winnowing Barley at Dingboche

The Job of Sirdar is not an Easy One
Here I am trying to get things organized for a day's march.

We carry Wangdi Norbu down after his Accident on Kedernath
I am the one on the right.

Preparing Parchment Scrolls for Use in Prayer Wheels

I baked the Cake on a Camp Stove, and admit I was very Proud of it

Village above Porche

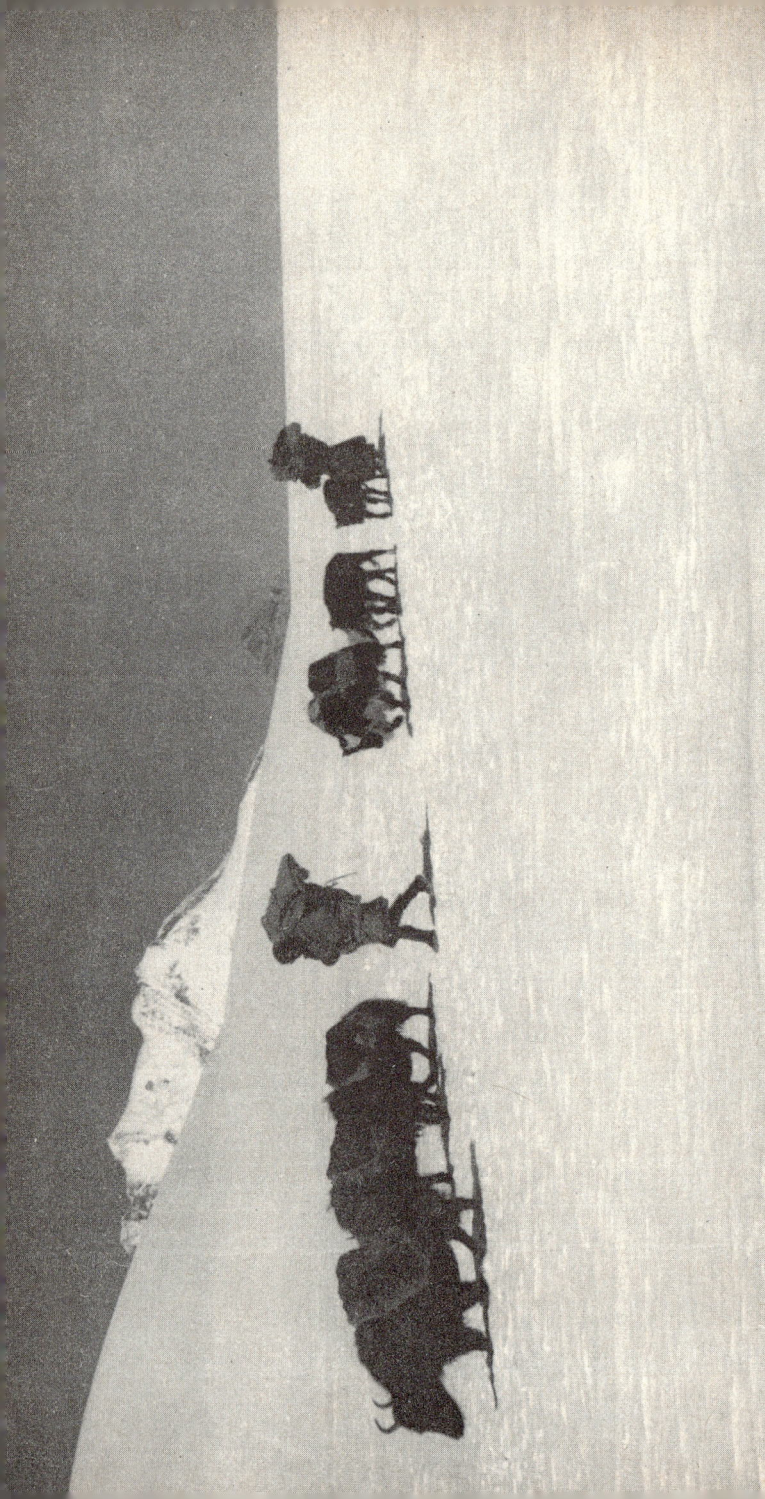

A Yak Caravan crossing the Nangpa La between Nepal and Tibet

Thyangboche Monastery

Back from the Eastern Summit of Nanda Devi

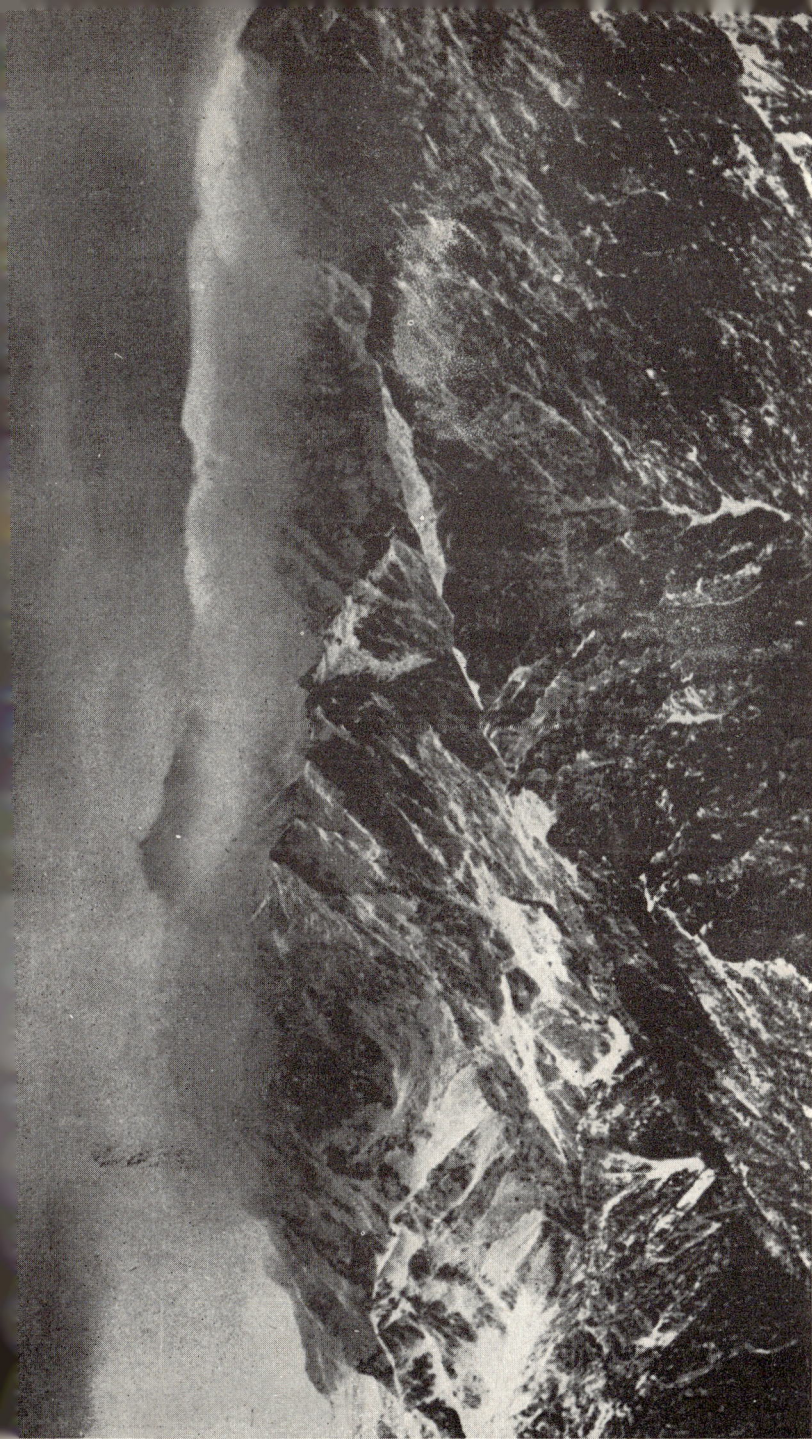

Nanga Parbat from the West

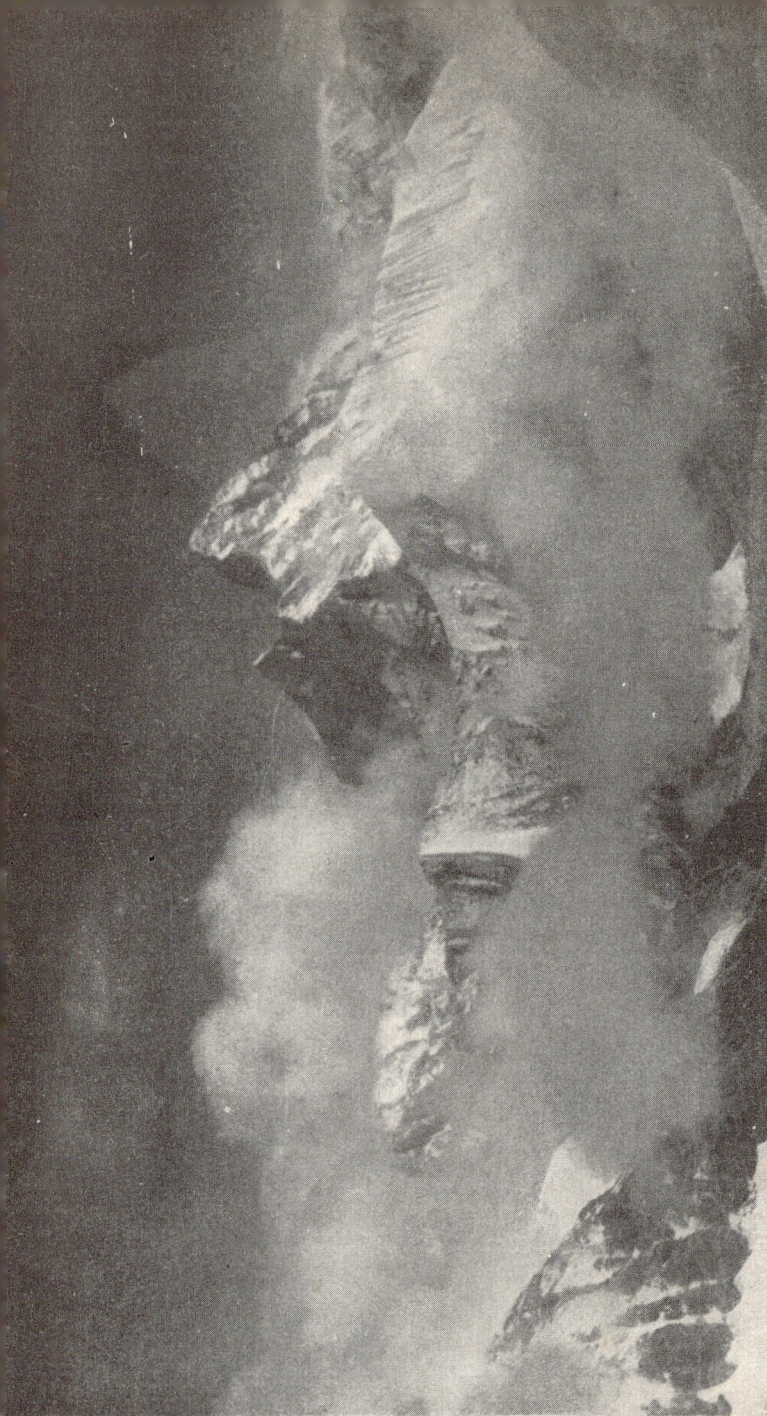

The Twin Peaks of Nanda Devi

8

DEFEATS AND VICTORIES

THE years immediately after the War were hard ones in Darjeeling. There were still no big expeditions going out, and very few of any kind. And now also, with the coming of independence for India, everything was uncertainty and confusion. The American military and Government people had already gone, with no tourists to take their place; and soon many of the English were following them. Several of the tea plantations shut down. Jobs were few, and there was much unemployment and poverty.

On top of this we had great personal trouble in the family, for my mother-in-law was ill and bedridden for two years, and, her husband being dead, it was up to us to look after her. For long periods I could find no work at all, my savings from Chitral were gone, and we were supported by my wife, Ang Lahmu. Part of the time she worked as an ayah, or maid, for various families; at other times as an assistant to the Smith Brothers, a firm of American dentists who had been in practice in Darjeeling for many years. I told her then, as I have told her often since, that I could never forget what she did for us all during those hard and bitter days.

As I have said, Ang Lahmu was born in Darjeeling.

Once as a child she was taken to Solo Khumbu for a short visit, but she had been so young she hardly remembered it, and had little knowledge of the primitive life of our homeland. Still, like almost all Sherpas, her family had been poor. She had worked hard since she was eight years old, carrying loads in the streets of the city, and later acting as servant for well-to-do families, which was what she was doing when I first met her and we had our arguments about milk. In 1938, though, a great change occurred in her life. A British family named Wallace, for whom she was then working, moved back to England and took her with them as an ayah to take care of their two children; and for several months she lived in the centre of London, at a hotel near Hyde Park, and saw the ways of the Western world. The trip was not too great a success, however, for Ang Lahmu, who had, of course, never been on a ship before, was sick much of the time at sea, and after she had been in London awhile she fell ill again and had to be taken to a hospital. By the time she came out Mrs Wallace had had to leave England once more, and, being out of employment and lonely, she made the long voyage back to India alone. This trip was at the time of much trouble between England and Germany before the War began, when no one knew what to expect. When we went to England together in 1953 Ang Lahmu said that what she remembered most vividly of her previous visit was being taught how to use a gas-mask while she lay in bed in the hospital.

Ang Lahmu is a woman who keeps her own counsel. Even now many people do not know that she was in England before 1953. Many do not know how well she understands English. And of the people who have employed her few know her real name, for she has always been called Nima when she works, instead of Ang Lahmu or Mrs Tenzing. Only recently, with the climbing of Everest, a funny thing happened because she was so quiet about herself. While I was on the expedition with the British she was working as ayah to the wife of an English officer who was staying at the New Elgin Hotel in Darjeeling. During that time my picture was often in the newspapers, and she would see it and be curious about what was happening; but since she could not read she would have to ask some one to tell her. One day she did this with an English lady who was a guest at the hotel, and the lady in turn was curious and asked why she was so interested. "Do you know this Tenzing, Nima?" she said. "Is he a friend of yours?" But my wife was still the same as always, and only answered, "Oh, he's one of the Sherpas from Toong Soong Busti, where I come from." That was all that happened then. But a few months later, after Everest was climbed, Ang Lahmu and I were given a reception in Calcutta, and among the guests was the same English lady. She came up in the line to meet us, but when she got close I saw that she wasn't looking at me at all, but only at Ang Lahmu, standing beside me. Then suddenly she stopped and stood still and looked as if she was going to faint. And all she could say was, "Good God, it's Nima!"

So it has gone with us through the years. Funny things and sad things; ups and downs—in our lives no less than on the mountains. It is a lucky man who has a wife to share and help in them, as I have had in Ang Lahmu.

But for a while then, after the War, there seemed to be no ups—only downs. My wife kept us going, and for myself there was only a day's work here, another day's there, all of them menial and dreary, and in between them nothing. Beyond the valleys to the north rose Kangchen-junga: high, white, beautiful—and now suddenly hateful, because it seemed to be mocking me. What had happened to me—or to the world—that I could no longer go to the mountains I loved and the life I was born for?

I did not go at all to Tiger Hill. There were no tourists to take there, and I did not want to go, anyhow. If Everest was still there it was at least better unseen. I did not want to see it or even think of it. . . . But I thought of it all the time.

Then in the spring of 1947 a mad thing happened. And it began when Mr Earl Denman came to Darjeeling.

Mr Denman had been born in Canada, grown up in England, and now lived in one of the British parts of Africa. There he had done a good deal of travelling and climbing in wild country, and he was obviously a man who could take good care of himself. But all the things he had done before or might do later meant little to him, because he had one great plan that had become the dream of his life. He wanted to climb Everest—and to climb it alone! . . . Well, no, perhaps 'alone' is not quite right. . . . He wanted to do it without a real expedition. Or, at least, he had no expedition. But he had to have *some one* to go with him, and that was how I met him. One day Karma Paul, the old sirdar, looked me up and said, "There is a sahib who has come to town, and he has an idea that might interest you." "About mountains?" I asked. "Yes, about mountains." And a while later, with another Sherpa, Ang Dawa, I found myself in Karma Paul's little office, meeting Mr Denman.

Right from the beginning it was like nothing I had experienced before. Denman was alone. He had very little money and poor equipment. He did not even have permission to enter Tibet. But he was as determined as any man I have ever met, and talked—mostly through Karma Paul as interpreter—with great earnestness and persuasion. He was especially insistent that he wanted me with him. Because I was a Tiger; because I had climbed to 27,000 feet on Everest; because I spoke Tibetan and also some English; because I had been recommended as the best of all Sherpas. And it was all very flattering—but still mad—and Ang Dawa and I said we must think it over.

What there was to think about I do not know, because nothing made sense about it. First, we would probably not even get into Tibet. Second, if we did get in we would probably be caught, and, as his guides, we, as well as Denman, would be in serious trouble. Third, I did not for a moment believe that, even if we reached the mountain, a party such as this would be able to climb it. Fourth, the attempt would be highly dangerous. Fifth, Denman had the money neither to pay us well nor to guarantee a decent sum to our dependents in case something happened to us. And so on and so on. Any man in his right mind would have said no. But I couldn't say no. For in my heart I needed to go, and the pull of Everest was stronger for me than any force on earth. Ang Dawa and I talked for a few minutes, and then we made our decision. "Well," I told Denman, "we will try."

As it turned out, he was not only without permission to enter Tibet, but had signed a paper promising not even to approach the border. So secrecy was of much importance, and instead of leaving Darjeeling together we met at a prearranged point outside the town and began our trip from there. Then we followed the usual expedition route through Sikkim. But that was our only resemblance to an expedition; for on such treks everything was carefully planned and organized, while we simply lived from day to day and hoped for the best, never knowing what the next would bring. Sometimes we travelled alone, sometimes with small caravans, from which we were able to hire pack animals to carry our loads. And gradually the valleys and forests of Sikkim fell away behind us, and we came up into the high Himalayan passes that mark the frontier of Tibet.

Here I recommended to Denman that we get off the usual expedition and trade route, that was sure to be patrolled; and, following a little-used pass, we were able to get across the border. Then we headed west over the great plateaux towards Rongbuk. Things went wrong, of course. Almost every day something went wrong. We seldom had enough food. Once the yaks that were carrying our loads plunged down a hillside, almost destroying both themselves and our baggage. Another time, as we had feared all along, a patrol caught up with us and ordered us to go back. But we were able to talk ourselves out of actual arrest, and after we had pretended to turn round were able to make a wide detour and continue on our way. From there on we avoided all towns and villages, and at last reached the Rongbuk Monastery, where we were received without questions or suspicion.

And now there, straight before us, was Everest—huge and white, with its streaming snow-plume, just as I remembered it after nine long years. The old excitement returned, as strong as ever. Here I was again where I was meant to be. But I had not taken leave of my senses, and, with the mountain looming above us, I was more conscious than ever of the hopelessness of what we were doing. I kept thinking of Maurice Wilson and his pathetic death in 1934, and I told myself, "No, we are not going to get into anything like that. No one is going to find our bodies dead and frozen in a tent."

Still we went on: up the glaciers, past the old lower camp-sites, towards the base of the walls below the North Col. With only the three of us, the work was back-breaking. The wind and cold were terrible. In fact, they seemed to me the worst I had ever known on the mountain, until I realized it was not so much they themselves as that we were so badly equipped. Our clothes were not wind-proof. Our food-supply was low, and we were already out of the most important item—tea. Our two tents gave us as much protection as a sheet of paper, and soon Denman, who at first occupied one of them alone, had to come in with Ang Dawa and me, so that our three bodies together could make a little warmth.

At least we moved fast. On a big expedition it takes days between the setting up of one camp and the next, while all the supplies are brought up in relays. But each day we set up a new camp, carrying everything we had in one trip, and soon we were at the foot of the snow slopes beneath the Col. I knew, though, that this was the end of it. Denman was less used to cold than Ang Dawa and myself and was suffering terribly. He could not sleep at night. Sometimes he seemed to have barely the strength to walk. From our highest camp—the fourth—we made a brief try at the steep snow and ice leading up to the Col; but the cold went through to our bones, and the wind almost knocked us flat. In a little while we were back in the tent, exhausted and beaten.

Even Denman knew we were beaten. He was a brave man—a determined, almost fanatic man with a fixed idea. But he was not mad. He was not ready to kill himself like Wilson, and he was willing to go back. For this I am as grateful as for anything that has happened in my life, for it would have been a terrible decision for Ang Dawa and myself if he had insisted on going on.

Our retreat was even faster than our advance. Now that he was defeated, Denman seemed only to want to get away from Everest as quickly as possible, as if it were a thing he no longer loved, but hated. We almost raced back to the Rongbuk Monastery, and then on across the wild, high plains of Tibet—almost as if the mountain were following us as an enemy. Now we were even shorter of food than before. Our clothes were in rags, and Denman's boots were in such bad shape that for a few days he had to walk barefoot. But we kept going. At least we were stopped by no patrols. And almost before I knew it we had crossed back from Tibet into Sikkim, and a few days later, towards the end of April, arrived in Darjeeling. The whole trip—to Everest, at Everest, and return—had taken only five weeks!

It was as quick as that. As strange and mad as that. In another few days Denman was on his way back to Africa, and it almost seemed to me that I had not been to Everest at all, but only dreamed about it. After a few months, though, I began receiving letters from Denman in which he said he was coming again the next year; and in the spring of 1948, sure enough, he was back in Darjeeling. This time he had better equipment than before, but what he still did not have was permission to enter Tibet. In the past year there had been much talk about our illegal trip; I had been criticized for acting as guide on it, and knew that if we tried to go back there would be serious trouble. So I had to tell him no, without permission I could not go again, and since he could find no one else he could trust to accompany him, he left once more and went back to Africa, giving me his equipment, which he could not afford to take with him. Since then I have not seen him, but we sometimes write to each other and remain good friends. Though a strange man, he was a brave one —a man with a dream—and I am sorry he did not get closer to realizing it. In 1953, when I reached the top of Everest, I was wearing a woollen balaclava helmet that he had left to me; so at least a little part of him has reached his goal.

But I am telling now about 1947. For months before Denman came, as I have said, there was no employment at all. Now, however, when we returned to Darjeeling, there was a sudden change, and on my first day home I got my next job.

This was with a real expedition, too. Not to Everest, to be sure, and not big as expeditions go, but well financed and well organized, so that it seemed almost miraculous after what I had experienced with Denman. The climbing was to be in Garhwal, but one of the party members, the famous Swiss mountaineer André Roch, had come in advance to Darjeeling to hire Sherpas, and almost before I knew what was happening I had signed up. Then with Roch and several other Sherpas I made the trip to the Garhwal jumping-off place, and met the other members of the expedition. These were Alfred Sutter, a wealthy business-man, who was also an experienced climber and hunter; René Dittert, with whom I later climbed on Everest; Mrs Annelies Lohner, a young lady mountaineer; and Alex Graven, one of the leading guides in the Alps. They were all Swiss, and this was my first experience with the people with whom I was later to have so close a bond of friendship.

We were not out to climb a single great mountain, but,

rather, several of the second rank—though they surely would not be called that anywhere except in the Himalayas. For all were 20,000 feet or more in height, and none had been climbed before. The first one we went for was a big snow-peak called Kedernath, and after a long trip across-country we reached its base and began setting up our camps. Higher and higher we went, looking for the best route upward, until finally we were sure we had found it and were ready for the try for the top. As it turned out, though, I was not one of the summit party; for the job I had been given was that of personal assistant to Mrs Lohner, and, though she was a fine climber for a lady, she was not taking part in the highest ascents. So I stayed with her, as was my duty, in the highest camp, and while I was, of course, disappointed at being left behind, at least I could not have been left in more charming company. On the morning of the summit attempt we waved good-bye to the others, and then waited through the day for them to return.

Well, they returned all right—but not at all as we had hoped and expected. Even as I saw them coming down the snow-slope above us I knew that something was wrong, and when they reached us they announced that there had been a bad accident. High on the mountain and approaching the summit, they had been roped in pairs, and while mounting a steep, narrow ridge of snow, one of the pairs had slipped. This had been Mr Sutter and Wangdi Norbu, the head Sherpa of the expedition, and before they could stop themselves they had fallen from the ridge, rolling and tumbling a full thousand feet down the slopes below. The others had been horrified. Looking down so great a distance, they could not tell if the men were alive or dead. And, of course, they could not go straight down after them, but had had to descend the ridge and circle far round, which meant that several hours passed before they reached them. To their surprise and relief, Sutter was not badly hurt. In fact, he was with them now, shaken and bruised, but still able to walk. With Wangdi Norbu, though, it had been a different matter. One of his legs was broken, and the other had been badly cut by Sutter's steel crampons during their tangled-up fall. After their tremendous climbing, both up and down, the others were too exhausted to carry him on down to camp. The best they had been able to do was set up an emergency tent, make him as comfortable as they could, and stumble on down themselves.

It was already evening when they arrived. Nothing could be done in the darkness. But at first light the next morning the rescue-party set off, and this time I, of course, went with them. Indeed, it was I, I felt, of whom most should now be expected, because the others had worn themselves out the day before, while I was fresh and rested. Besides, Wangdi Norbu was an old friend and climbing companion, a fellow-Tiger from Everest back in 1938, and at all costs he must be rescued and brought down alive.

Luckily the weather held good, and in a few hours we reached his tent—the tiniest brown speck on the white miles of the mountainside. We opened the flap, and what we expected to find I am not sure; but certainly it was not what we did find. Wangdi Norbu was there all right. And he was alive. But now, besides his two injured legs, he had a great bloody gash across his throat. What had happened, he told us later, was this. The previous day, when the others had left him, he had been so dazed from his fall that he had not understood when they told him they would be back in the morning. All he knew was that he had been left alone. To freeze. To die. And in his pain and misery he had taken out his knife and cut his own throat. Two things had saved him. First, that he was too weak to cut hard and end it all at once; second, that as he lay bleeding he thought of his family and decided that for their sake he must try to live. So for the rest of the night he had lain still. The blood had clotted and stopped flowing. And the next day, though weak and in great pain, he was still alive.

On our backs and with a makeshift stretcher we got him down to camp, and then gradually to the lower camps and down off the mountain. From there we sent him on with local porters to Mussourie, which was the Garhwal hill-station from which we had begun the trip, and after some time there in the hospital his injuries healed and he was able to go home. He was never the same again, though. When I saw him later in Darjeeling it was obvious that what he had suffered had had a lasting effect, not only on his body, but on his mind. Old Tiger Wangdi never climbed again, and he died in his home a few years later.

Even though we could not guess its final result, we were, of course, badly upset by his accident. But calling off the expedition would have done him no good, and we went back to our mountain. As I have said, Wangdi had been the headman, or sirdar, of us Sherpas; but now that he was gone a new one was needed, and I was appointed. It was a great honour. To be a sirdar is the ambition of every Sherpa, a turning-point in his life. And I was deeply pleased and flattered. But I was also sorry that I first reached this rank because of the misfortune of an old friend.

Again we moved up to the high camps. Again we made ready to try for the top. As usually happens after an accident, most of the Sherpas were for the time being nervous and refused to climb high. But now I was to have my first chance, and was anxious for it, so the summit party consisted of the four Swiss sahibs—Roch, Dittert, Sutter, Graven—plus myself. Leaving the highest camp, we pushed up the long snow slopes, up the ridge where the accident had happened, and arrived at last, safely, on the flat white platform that is Kedernath's pinnacle. It is only some 22,000 feet high—no more than the North Col of Everest, which is only a sort of base for *that* mountain. But we were all happy and proud in our victory, and to me it was an especially great moment. For, in spite of all the years I had climbed and the heights to which I had gone, this was the first time I had ever actually reached the top of a big mountain. "Mission accomplished," as I had heard some fliers say. And it was a wonderful feeling.

Kedernath was only the beginning of our climbs on this expedition. From there we moved on to its slightly higher neighbour, Satopanth, and here, too, we were successful; but I am sorry to say that I myself did not get to the top, because of stomach trouble I suffered at the highest camp. Then from Satopanth we moved over towards the Tibetan border, where all of us, including Mrs Lohner, climbed a somewhat lower mountain called Balbala. And finally we went up one called Kalindi, which is not at all like most of the Himalayas, but an almost snow-free rock-peak of the sort I was to see later in Switzerland. Four virgin peaks—four first ascents. It was a record that I think, perhaps, has not been matched by any other expedition.

Between climbs we of course saw much of the country of Northern Garhwal, including the holy cities of Badrinath and Gangotri, and many smaller places where I had not been before. Another pleasant thing was that through-out the trip we ate very well, for Mr Sutter, besides being a climber, was an expert hunter, and we were seldom without fresh meat. It was a fine change from my trip to Garhwal the year before, when "The Doon School Expedition" did most of its travelling on empty stomachs.

Indeed, after the accident to Wangdi Norbu we had no trouble at all until the very end of the expedition—and this was trouble of a different kind. The summer of 1947 was the time when the British were giving up the government of the country; India and Pakistan were splitting into two separate nations, and everywhere there were bloody riots between Hindus and Moslems. When we came out of the mountains and reached Mussourie the town was under military law, with troops everywhere, most of the shops and business-places closed, and a curfew which allowed no one in the streets at night. Also transportation had practically stopped, and for a while it looked as if we would never get out. Finally the local authorities arranged for the Swiss to go on to Delhi in an Army van, but we Sherpas, ten of us altogether, were stranded for another two weeks. It reminded me of the trouble I had had getting out of Chitral during the War; but this was even worse, because we soon used up our expedition earnings and had nothing in reserve.

Well, almost nothing. I still had fifteen rupees, and with this I went to the police station and asked to see the chief. Of course they told me I couldn't see him, and then the fifteen rupees came out, and one of the orderlies decided that perhaps it could be arranged. When I saw the chief the first thing I said was that we were members of an expedition, and he almost put me in gaol then and there, because he thought I meant something political. When I explained, though, he calmed down, and finally he arranged for a lorry that took us to Dehra Dun. Here we had more trouble. Not political trouble, but monsoon trouble. The roads were washed out by the rains, and we were stranded again; but this time it was not so bad, because Dehra Dun is where the Doon School is located, and we were taken care of by my old friend Mr Gibson. When the roads were again clear he helped us to get out, too, and at last we got home to Darjeeling. But not until we had had all kinds of trouble with other police and railway officials. Everybody, I suppose, has his favourite sort of people and his opposite-of-favourite, and police and railwaymen have always been my opposite.

So another expedition was over. The accident to Wangdi Norbu had been bad. The trip home had been bad. But all the rest had been good—the best it had ever been on a mountain trip—not only in the success of our climbs, but in the enjoyment we had from them. I had liked the Swiss tremendously. Even though there was much language difficulty, I had felt truly close to them, and thought of them not as sahibs or employers, but as friends. And that is how it has been ever since.

Besides the friendships, there had also been the beginnings of a romance on the expedition, and it was to cost me a minute's embarrassment six years later. When I arrived in Switzerland in 1953, after the climbing of Everest, my old friends met me at the airport, and there were warm greetings. "*Comment ça va? Wie gehts?*" I asked in my finest French-German. "How are you, Mr Roch—Mr Dittert—Mr Graven—Mr Sutter—Mrs Lohn . . ." Then I stopped. Perhaps I blushed. "I mean Mrs Sutter," I said.

For now they were married.

9

TO THE HOLY LAND

THE year 1948 was like no other I have ever had. There
was no climbing in it. No mountains. Instead, for
nine months, I was on a journey to Tibet—all the
way to Lhasa and beyond. To Westerners Tibet is known
as the Forbidden Land, but for Buddhists it is the Holy
Land, the Land of Pilgrimages. Along with the fight for
Everest, my visit there is one of the great memories of
my life.

Back home after the Garhwal expedition with the
Swiss, things were no better than they had been before. I
had spent all my earnings getting back to Darjeeling. Jobs
were scarce. There were no more expeditions going out,
and the autumn and winter dragged by. Ang Lahmu still
worked as an ayah, but the girls, Pem Pem and Nima,
were getting bigger and needed more food and clothing,
and there was seldom enough of either. "What do we do
now?" I thought bitterly. "Eat my Tiger medal?" Meanwhile my mother-in-law, who had been bedridden for
two years, became worse and worse, and at last she died,
at the age of seventy-six. Just before the end she put out
her hand from her bed and blessed me, saying that I had
been good to her and that God would reward me and
make things better. And what she said came true. Soon

after her death our fortunes began to improve, and they have never been so bad again.

In the spring of that next year I heard that an interesting man had come to Darjeeling—Professor Giuseppe Tucci, an Italian, who was a famous scholar of Oriental art and literature, and had already been seven times in Tibet. Now he had come back for still another trip, and was making arrangements for helpers and porters with the sirdar, Karma Paul. I hurried to apply for a position, but by the time I got there the needed men had already been hired and left for Gangtok, in Sikkim. It was a great disappointment, and I was very depressed. But a few days later a lucky thing happened. Professor Tucci sent back word that he was not satisfied with the men; that he especially needed some one who was a linguist and could speak at least a little Tibetan, Hindustani, Nepali, and English. And these were exactly the languages, apart from Sherpa, that I knew best. One morning Karma Paul called me into his office, and the same day I was on my way to Gangtok.

Professor Tucci was a strange man; indeed, one of the most remarkable I have ever met. He was very serious and absolutely devoted to his work. But, unlike the mountaineers I had known, who were mostly quiet men, he was terrifically excitable and temperamental, and everything had to be just so, or there was a great explosion. No sooner did I reach Gangtok than I found it wasn't just he who was dissatisfied with the Sherpas he had hired. They were afraid of him, said he was too hard a task-master, and wanted to go home. When he interviewed me I could see all right what they meant, for he fired questions at me in different languages—*bang-bang-bang*, like a machine-gun. And then suddenly he said, "All right; you're hired." The other Sherpas thought I was mad to take the job, and for a while I thought so too. But in time I grew to like Professor Tucci as well as any man I have ever known.

When the arrangements had been finished we headed north from Gangtok. Besides the professor and myself, there were three Italian assistants, one other Sherpa, who served as cook, and a Mongolian lama, on his way from Darjeeling to Lhasa—plus the usual local porters, who stayed with us a few days at a time and then were replaced by others. More than most expeditions, we made use of animals, with about a hundred mules, loaned by the Sikkim Government, for our baggage and horses for ourselves. The loads, besides the usual food and equipment, consisted of many boxes and crates in which Tucci planned to carry the things he collected, and also guns and other manufactured goods to be distributed as gifts in Tibet. From the very beginning I was put in charge of all these things. "I don't want to be bothered," he said. And he even gave me the keys to his personal baggage and a lot of money to use for our expenses on the way. He may have been a hard man to work for, but I was pleased and flattered at this trust he showed in me.

Up and down we went through the Sikkim foothills. For the first time I rode all the way, and, not being used to it, my backside was sorer than my legs had ever been on a mountain. Some days we made long journeys, some days short ones. You never could tell when Tucci would start or stop or go right off the route to some town or monastery where he thought there might be interesting things. As I have said, he was a great scholar, knowing much more about the country than the people who lived there. And I have never been able to count how many languages he knew. Often his conversations to me would begin in one, change suddenly to another, and end up in a third. In fact, about the only languages we couldn't use were our two native ones—Italian and Sherpa.

From him I learned all sorts of things I had not known before. It was like travelling and going to school at the same time. A monastery was no longer just a house built of stones with some monks living in it, but a place full of manuscripts and old works of art. Everything we saw had a history and a meaning. As we came up to the real mountains we passed Kangchenjunga on our left, and even about this mountain, which I knew so well, I learned all sorts of new things. About its name, for instance, which I had always just taken for granted, as one does with familiar things. Now I discovered that it is made up of four Tibetan words—*kang*, meaning "snow"; *chen*, meaning "great"; *dzod*, meaning "store" or "treasure"; and *nga*, meaning "five." So if it were transcribed exactly it would be spelled Kang-chen-dzod-nga, and its meaning is "The Great Snow with the Five Treasures" (which refers to its five separate peaks). These treasures are specifically named too, and according to tradition are: *tsa* ("salt"), *ser dhang yee* ("gold and turquoise"), *dham-choy dhang nor* ("the holy books and wealth"), *mtson* ("weapons"), and *lo-thog dhang men* ("crops and medicine"). Since then I have never forgotten that our mountains are not merely things of ice and snow, but are full of history and legend as well.

With Kangchenjunga behind us, we crossed the high border into Tibet, and there at the first town, called Yatung, we had some trouble. Tucci's three Italian companions, it seemed, did not have the proper permission to enter the country, and since they were not prepared to dodge and hide like Earl Denman, they had to go back.

To the rest of us, though, the Tibetans were hospitable. As the Sikkimese had done, they loaned us animals for our transport. And soon we were heading on. To Professor Tucci it was all familiar, for he had been on the route often before. But though I had been to Tibet six times, it had always been only to the region of Everest and Rongbuk, and from this point northward everything was new to me. My heart beat faster. I was as excited as if I were approaching the base of Chomolungma. For I was going to Lhasa at last!

Om mane padme om. . . . *Om mane padme om.* . . .

Englishmen have told me that it sounds to them like "money-penny-hum," repeated over and over, again and again. It is the sacred, mystical chant of Buddhism. What it literally means is "the jewel is in the lotus," but it also has many hidden and symbolic meanings which only the most learned lamas can understand. Everywhere where there is Buddhism you hear it, and especially in Tibet. Beside the turning prayer-wheels; beneath the streaming prayer-flags:

Om mane padme om. . . . *Om mane padme om.* . . .

Tibet is the holy land, and Lhasa the holy of holies. Every Buddhist would like to go there in his lifetime, as a Christian to Jerusalem or a Moslem to Mecca. My parents had always longed to go there, but were never able to, and now I felt I was going not only for myself, but for them. I was going for all my family, all who were dear to me. I bought yak butter to light lamps for them in the temples and monasteries. I spun the prayer-wheels with their parchment scrolls inside. I thought that perhaps it was the blessing of my dead mother-in-law that had made this trip of mine possible, and for her I said special prayers. It is said among my people that unless a man visits Lhasa his life on earth is useless. Now I was living many lives within my own.

I am a religious man. I believe in God and in the Way of Buddha, and in my home I have always had a prayer-corner or prayer-room, which is the Buddhist custom. But I am not an orthodox man. I do not believe greatly in ritual, and not at all in superstition. In my life I have been on too many mountains to think that they are the home of demons. Nor do I put much stock in ghosts; and, indeed, a few years ago, used to go out searching—unsuccessfully —for a much-talked-of lady ghost who was supposed to be haunting Toong Soong Busti. Also, and more seriously, I have known too many men of other faiths to believe that they are all wrong and Buddhists alone are all right. I am not an educated man—not a lama or scholar who can speak of matters of theology. But I feel that there is room on earth for many faiths, as for many races and nations. It is with God Himself as it is with a great mountain. The important thing is to come to Him not with fear, but with love.

True religion is one thing. Its outward forms and practices, unfortunately, can be another; and in Buddhism —as in all Churches, I suppose—things happen that do not seem to have much to do with the worship of God. Some of our lamas are truly holy men. Some are great scholars and mystics. But there are others about whom you wonder if they could take care of a herd of yaks, let alone human souls, and you are pretty sure they are monks only because it gives them the best living with the least work.

There is a story told among the Sherpas that I have always liked, and I think perhaps it is not altogether made up. It is about two lamas who were travelling from village to village, and in one place they came to a house where a woman was cooking sausages. For a while they watched her, chanting and turning their prayer wheels; then the woman left the stove and went to another room, and one of them jumped forward and grabbed the sausages from the pan. Before they could eat them, though, the woman came back, and the lama who was holding them, not knowing what else to do, put them quickly under his pointed hat. Then they were ready to run away. But the woman, who had not yet noticed that the sausages were missing, asked them to say a prayer for her, and they had to begin chanting again. For a few minutes it went all right, but then the second lama saw that the sausages, which were on a string, were hanging down from under his friend's hat. Wanting to warn him, without their being found out, he made a quick change in his praying, which the woman could not understand, anyhow. "*Om mane padme om*," he chanted, "the sausages are showing. *Om mane*—the sausages are showing—*padme om*." But, instead of the other's doing anything about it, he suddenly began to chant louder than ever and to jump up and down with strange jerky movements. His friend grew desperate. "*Om mane padme om*," he kept repeating. "The sausages! The sausages!" But by now the other was hopping about as if there were a hundred devils inside him. "I don't care if the whole pig is showing," he yelled suddenly. "My head is on fire!"

I am not anxious to contribute sausages for lamas to

hide under their hats. A short while ago, after the climbing of Everest, I was asked to give money to a certain monastery near Darjeeling, but after thinking it over I decided against it. I preferred to donate it towards the building of a hostel or guest house which could be used by all poor people visiting the town, rather than to a group of monks who would use it only for themselves.

But I have said, and I say again, I am a religious man. And I like to think that perhaps I am the more so because I care only for the truths of my faith, and not for appearances and sham. On the top of Everest I bowed my head and thought of God. And on that journey through Tibet I thought of Him too; I thought of my parents and my mother-in-law, whose faith had been so great; and I knew that I was making the journey not only for myself, but for them.

Om mane padme om. . . . *Om mane padme om.* . . .

We passed the *mani* walls, always on the left. We passed long rows of *chortens*, that guard the spirits of the dead. We passed streaming prayer-flags and turning prayer-wheels and old monasteries set on lonely crags above the great plateau.

I was going to Lhasa at last.

The trip in from Gangtok took about twenty days. When we moved we moved very fast—at least, for that part of the world—for Professor Tucci was tireless and impatient. But often we would stop at the monasteries to look for interesting things. What he was after chiefly was old books, manuscripts, and works of art. But he was not like a tourist in a bazaar; he knew exactly what he wanted and did not want; and usually the lamas were astonished that he had more knowledge about their possessions than they had. At night in his tent he would sit up late, studying and making notes, and be very angry if anyone disturbed him. Then suddenly, at midnight or later, he might jump out of the tent and announce, "All right; I have finished. Now we go on." And we would all have to get up and start moving.

Then the great day came. Ahead of us one morning were no longer the dusty plains and the yaks and the lonely monasteries, but a great city in a broad basin between the hills. There were streets and squares, bazaars and temples, crowds of people and animals, and high above them, on the city's edge, the great palace of the Potala, which is the home of the Dalai Lama. We stopped and looked, and I remembered my prayers. And then we rode on into Lhasa.

Professor Tucci was well known from his previous visits, and we were given a fine welcome and a large bungalow to live in. Also many receptions were given by the Government and private people—some of them on horseback on a field outside the city, which was a sight I had never seen before. At first people could not decide what I was. My face is much like a Tibetan's, but my clothes and manners were different, and they were surprised when they found I could speak their language. When they learned I was a Sherpa they asked me many questions about mountains and mountain-climbing, and at one reception I talked to high officials and showed them photographs of my expedition with the Swiss to Garhwal. It was Everest, however, that interested them. The other mountains they had never heard of, but every one knew Chomolungma. "Do you think it will ever be climbed?" they asked me. And I answered, "Nothing is impossible for a man. If he tries he may one day succeed." Then they said, "But aren't you afraid to climb it? It is the home of gods and demons." And to this I answered, "I am not afraid to die. Walking in the street you can meet easily with an accident. So why should I be afraid on a mountain?"

The most important thing that happened in Lhasa was that we met the Dalai Lama. Not only once, but twice. Going to the Potala, we were taken up through many rooms and long corridors, and presented to him in his private quarters; and, though he was then only a boy of fifteen, he bore himself with great charm and dignity. Usually one may not look up at him, but must sit with bowed head in his presence. As an old friend, however, Professor Tucci was privileged not only to pay his respects, but to have long talks with him, and while they spoke I was lucky enough to be allowed to stand by, watching and listening. Then at the end of each meeting the Dalai Lama blessed us. And I left the Potala thinking of my parents and Ang Lahmu's mother—and with my heart very full.

Now that I have used the name Dalai Lama, perhaps I should explain something about it that I think few Westerners know. No Tibetan ever calls the head of his religion by this title, but uses instead the name Gyalwa Rimpoche. Gyalwa means "one who has conquered or mastered"; in other words, the godhead or Buddha. Rimpoche means "the precious or holy one." Sometimes this last name is used also for other lamas of great rank and incarnation, but Gyalwa is reserved only for the highest of all—the incarnate godhead. A Tibetan unfamiliar with the outside world does not even know what Dalai Lama means. To him his leader has only one title, and that is Gyalwa Rimpoche—the precious or holy Buddha.

In Lhasa we also met two interesting outsiders—Heinrich Harrer and Peter Aufschnaiter. They had been members of a German climbing expedition to Nanga Parbat away back in 1939, but had been caught in India by the beginning of the War and interned by the British. After several tries they escaped successfully, made a tremendous trip across the Himalayas, and were allowed to settle in Lhasa—all of which Harrer has since told about in his well-known book *Seven Years in Tibet*. By the time I met them they had already been there most of that time, and, though they loved Tibet and wanted to stay, they were, of course, anxious to hear of the world beyond. Harrer particularly wanted to know what had been happening in mountaineering, and I told him. Then he said, "You are a lucky man, Tenzing. You can go where you want—to the mountains, on fine expeditions. But I was a prisoner-of-war; now I am a sort of prisoner too; I will probably never get to the mountains again." Suddenly he smiled. "Perhaps you and I should go off on a climb," he suggested. "Straight away. What do you say?" For a while we discussed it, almost seriously, but there were, of course, too many problems and objections. And soon after I left Lhasa. A few years later, however, I met Harrer again in Darjeeling, after the Communists had taken over Tibet. He had left the capital with the Dalai Lama, who was then planning to escape to India; but at the frontier town of Yatung the young ruler had changed his mind, and Harrer came on alone. In those seven years he had come greatly to love Tibet, and it saddened him to think that he might never return.

With Professor Tucci I remained in Lhasa for one month. Then we set out on our travels again, and for the next seven months journeyed all over Tibet. He had hoped to go the whole way to the Chinese border, in the east, and then follow it round; but this did not prove possible, because already the Communists were preparing to invade the country, and even Tucci, who was afraid of nothing, did not want that sort of trouble. So instead we doubled back and forth across the other parts of Tibet, visiting more towns and monasteries and places of pilgrimage than I had thought there were in all Central Asia. It was a wonderful trip for me, on which I could see so much of the Buddhist holy land, and especially so because I was no simple tourist, but had some one to explain everything that we saw. I do not think there are many, even with much schooling, who have had a famous professor all to themselves to teach them for so many months.

Tucci was bored and impatient with money matters, and more and more he had me handle them. Also, when he was occupied elsewhere, he would often send me off alone to a monastery, with a letter in Tibetan saying what he wanted; and if the things were there I would make a deal for them and bring them back. Because of this the lamas began calling me his *nyeba la*, which means "agent" or "manager," and, for my part, I learned so much that I could have written a guide-book to Tibetan monasteries. Gradually our many chests and crates were filling up with the professor's collections. And with mine, too, on a smaller scale. For I have always loved rare and interesting things, and this was the chance of a lifetime. To-day my house in Darjeeling is filled with souvenirs—masks and swords, scarves and head-dresses, bowls and prayer-wheels —that I brought back from this trip.

But the greatest prizes, for both Tucci and me, did not come until near the end of our journey. On this eighth visit of his to Tibet there was one thing he was searching for above all others—a famous religious manuscript some two thousand years old, written in Sanskrit on the bark of a tree, which scholars believed still existed, but none had been able to find. According to Tucci, it had originally been written in Turkestan, where Buddhism had spread at that time, but it was his theory, based on long study, that it had years ago been transferred to Tibet, and specifically to an old monastery called Ghangar. So to Ghangar we went and began our search. And it was not an easy one, for the lamas there seemed to know nothing about it, and there were thousands of ancient scrolls and manuscripts to be sorted and pored through. Days went by, and then more days, while we worked in the dust and the cobwebs, and I became very discouraged. It was either not there, I decided, or, if it was, we would never find it. But Tucci was not a man to give up, and still we kept searching. When his mind was on his work he could not think of anything else, and was very absent-minded, and one morning I noticed that he was wearing his shirt inside out. "That is a lucky sign," I told him. "Perhaps to-day we will find it at last." . . . And we did. As it happened, it was I who came upon it—a dusty, tattered old thing almost buried under piles of other manuscripts. But Tucci had described it so well that I knew at once that it was what we were looking for, and when I brought it to him he was as excited as another man would have been if he had found a gold- or diamond-mine.

Meanwhile, as a sideline, I was finding another prize of my own; and this was neither gold nor jewels nor precious manuscripts—but dogs. All my life I have been fond of animals, and here among the lamas I found two long-haired Lhasa terriers which I liked so much that I wanted to take them with me. The lamas were kind and generous.

They gave them to me as a present. And I named one Ghangar, after the monastery, and the other one Tasang, and took them back with me all the way to Darjeeling. Tasang I later gave to my old friend Angtharkay, but Ghangar still lives with me and, along with Ang Lahmu, runs the household. We have mated him to another Lhasa terrier, and our place is now full of pups. But this does not satisfy Ghangar, for he is no stay-at-home, and I think that now half the mongrels in Toong Soong Busti are his children or grandchildren.

The lamas would also not take money from Professor Tucci for their Sanskrit manuscript. The way they put it was that knowledge should not be for sale, but given freely to those who wanted it, and they asked only that he make a copy after he reached Italy and send the original back to them. When we left, however, he insisted that they accept a gift of five hundred rupees for the monastery.

By this time we had been in Tibet many months, and with the precious relic in his strongest travelling-chest Tucci felt that his trip had been successful. So at last we headed south and crossed the high passes that lead down to Sikkim and India. Though I, of course, did not know it then, this was to be the last time I should visit Tibet—at least, until the present—for soon after the Communists came, and now the Forbidden Land is more tightly closed than ever. As a Sherpa, I suppose that I might be able to go back to Solo Khumbu and cross from there over the Nangpa La with one of the caravans that still use it. But the strange thing is that I should probably have to go in disguise, as the Westerners used to do; for now that my name is known I think that if I went as myself I should be called a suspicious character and probably turned back.

At least I am grateful that I could make the journey

while there was still time. I have Ghangar to remind me of it. I have lovely and precious things in my home. And I have many memories—of Lhasa and the great Potala; of the Dalai Lama and his blessing; of the shrines and temples on the lonely hillsides; of the pilgrimage I made for my loved ones to the Holy Land of my faith. When the prayer-flags flutter I can still see it. When the prayer-wheels tinkle I can still hear it.

Om mane padme om. . . .   Om mane padme om. . . .

10

MY HOME AND MY PEOPLE

M Y HOME, I say. But what do I mean by home? In a way Tibet is the home of my spirit, but as a living man I am a stranger there. Mountains are my home, but one does not build his house and bring up his family there. Solo Khumbu was once my home, but I am now only an occasional visitor. To-day my home is Darjeeling. And it is the new and true home of many of my people.

Not of all my people, of course. Most of them are still back in Solo Khumbu. Some are in Rongbuk, some are in Kalimpong, and a few are scattered over Nepal and India. But Darjeeling is the centre for what might be called the "new" Sherpas—those who have left the old homeland and old ways of living, who go out on the great expeditions, who have become part of the modern world. From Lhasa, from Everest, from Garhwal or Chitral or Delhi or London, it is to Darjeeling that I return "home."

As I have said, the migration from Solo Khumbu began many years ago. Those who came first did so for many different reasons and did various kinds of work. But about fifty years ago some of the British explorers of the Hima-layas, like Dr Kellas and General Bruce, began using Sherpas for work in the mountains, and almost at once it was apparent that here was a case of the right men in the job. During the big Everest expeditions of the twenties and thirties more and more of my people made the journey from Nepal to India, and it was not long before Sherpa porters were considered as important a part of these expeditions as tents or food or ropes, or even the climbers themselves. Not all our men, of course, took up this work. But enough did, and they did so well that to-day, in most people's minds, the name Sherpa is the same as mountaineer.

We came originally from the mountains. Now we go back to the mountains. But it is in a very different way that we go to them, and between expeditions our lives are different too. In Solo Khumbu we were all country people, but in Darjeeling we are town people, and few of us have any longer anything to do with raising crops or cattle. I have mentioned the tea plantations, and sometimes, during the busy seasons, both our men and women work on them. I myself did this once for a few months before the War. But mostly the able-bodied men are on expeditions for about half the year, and during the other half work as labourers, animal-drivers, or tourist guides. For myself, of course, there has been much change in all this since the climbing of Everest, and I will tell about it later. But for many years my life in Darjeeling was the same as that of most other Sherpas, and it is of that which I am telling now.

We are a people in the midst of change, and what will happen in the future is hard to say. But so far, though we have left our homeland, we have stayed pretty much together, and there has not been much intermarriage with outsiders. Most of the Sherpa homes are in Toong Soong Busti, which is on a steep hillside on the outskirts of the town, and the rest in near-by Bhutia Busti, where there are also Sikkimese and Tibetans. We live a communal sort of life and share many things, including our houses, which are usually long wooden buildings with several rooms—one or two to a family—with such things as kitchens and latrines being used in common. In recent years a power-line has been extended to Toong Soong, and some of the families have an electric light or two. But most of the facilities are very primitive.

Like most people, we are poor and worry about money. But we are simple folk, not used to a great deal, and so far we have not worried too much. Back in Solo Khumbu, what little money we used was Nepali, but in Darjeeling, of course, there is the Indian rupee, and that is what we are paid in for all expeditions. This is worth more than the Nepali rupee, and when we have some savings we try to send some to our relatives who are still in the home country. But more often than savings we have debts. Then it is fortunate that we all live much like one big family; for we are always helping one another, loan money without interest, and try to even things up when we receive our pay at the end of an expedition. The deepest I myself was ever in debt was just before the Everest expedition of 1953, when I owed a thousand rupees to my friends. And if things had not turned out as they did, with all the rewards that came afterwards, it might have taken me years to pay them back.

Some of our old customs have already disappeared, and others are changing quickly. We do not, like people with older cultures, cling to ancient traditions, but adapt ourselves easily to new thoughts and habits. In certain things, however, we still follow the ways of our ancestors, and one of these, having to do with money, is that a younger son inherits more than an elder (the same holds true for daughters), as well as the family title, such as, in my case, Ghang La. A new-born child is supposed to be given its name on the third day, but this can be changed later—as, again, in my case—if there seems good reason for doing so.

Among outsiders there has always been some confusion about Sherpa names. Some say this is because they repeat themselves so often, but I do not feel this is especially true, for certainly there are no names more common among us than, say, Smith with the British or Singh with the Sikhs. Rather, I think, the difficulty is for two other reasons: first, that we have no last names that are used regularly for all members of a family; and, second, that, since Sherpa itself has no written form, they are spelled in all sorts of different ways by people who write them down. What you do not know you do not miss. In Solo Khumbu a name was a sound you made with your voice, and that was all there was to it. But in the modern world things are more complicated, and sometimes you have to supply different names for different occasions. Strangely, it is simplest at the bank in Darjeeling, where I now have an account. When I make out a cheque to my wife (which seems very often) I simply put down Ang Lahmu and sign it Tenzing. But to foreigners who meet her Ang Lahmu seems too intimate, and they usually call her Mrs Tenzing, which would not possibly be used in our language. Then with my daughters, who are now in a Western-run school, it is still different. When they were registered there Pem Pem and Nima, which are their only Sherpa names, were not enough for the records; so my second name, which has nothing to do with family, was brought into use, and they are now, to their confusion, known as the Misses Norgay.

As in most languages, Sherpa names have meanings. My own—"the wealthy fortunate follower of God"—I have already told about. The very common first name, *Ang*, used for both men and women, means "darling" or "beloved." *Lahmu* means "goddess"—and if my own name were not so easy to make jokes about I would, perhaps, have some husbandly comment to make. Among other much-used names, *Phu* (more properly *Bhu*) means "son," *Nyima* means "sun," *Norbu* means "gem," *Namgyal* means "conqueror"; and there are also several familiar ones taken from days of the week, such as *Dawa* (for "Monday"), *Pasang* ("Friday"), and *Pemba* ("Saturday"). Of the family or clan names, most—such as my own, Ghang La—derive from places or events in the family's history, and among the best known are Murmi, Sheray, Rhukpa, Mendava, and Thaktukpa. To those who ask why they are not generally used my best answer is that, to Sherpa ears, it would sound as strange as it would to an Englishman if some one called himself William Piccadilly or Trafalgar Jones.

In every country, I suppose, there are jokes about the people of another country looking all alike. Westerners on expeditions have sometimes said that they cannot tell the Sherpas apart, and we have our troubles too, especially when the Westerners, as they usually are in the mountains, are half hidden behind big beards. We ourselves, like most Mongolian people, have very light beards, and the average man shaves only about once a month; but it is possible for us to grow moustaches if we work hard at it, as I, for one, have demonstrated during the past few years. Back in Solo Khumbu most of the men, like the women, wear their hair in long braids, Tibetan style, and attach rings or gems to their ears. Almost all who have come to

Darjeeling, however, have long ago given up these customs. As I have said, I first cut my hair short as soon as I
arrived, and·have never worn it long since; and I have not
used earrings since I was a boy, though the holes for them
are still there in my lobes.

Black hair, dark eyes, and smooth yellow-brown skin
are typical of my people. Our features are, of course, pre-
dominantly Mongolian, but not nearly as distinctively so
as those of the Chinese, or even the Tibetans, and our noses
and eyes come in all sorts of shapes and sizes. In height
we are on the smallish side, and in build generally solid and
sturdy, though often not as much so as one might expect,
considering the work we do and the great loads we are
able to carry. I myself am five feet eight inches, and in my
best condition weigh about eleven stone six, which makes
me somewhat taller and thinner than the average.

In Darjeeling most of our womenfolk still wear the
traditional Sherpa dress, which consists principally of a sort
of wrapped-round dark robe and a woven woollen apron
with bright-coloured horizontal stripes. The men, however, have largely taken to Western clothes, especially
sports shirts, knickerbockers, sweaters, and similar items
which they have acquired on expeditions. Unlike the
Indians and Nepalese, almost all of us wear shoes; of
Western style if we can afford them, otherwise the Tibetan-
type felt boot. For formal occasions since the climbing of
Everest I have worn mostly the Indian ceremonial dress
of tight white trousers and knee-length black coat with a
high collar. At other times I wear almost entirely British
or Swiss sports clothes, and have reached the point where
I feel almost as if I am in costume when I put on the traditional dress of my ancestors.

The reason we Sherpas have been so successful on climbing expeditions lies not only in our strong backs and legs, or in our love of mountains, but also in our eating habits. Most peoples of the East—Hindus, Moslems, orthodox Buddhists, and almost all the smaller groups—have strict religious rules about diet, and it is very hard to keep them properly fed out in the wilderness. But a Sherpa will eat anything—fresh, dehydrated, or out of a tin—and sharing the fare of his sahibs imposes no need to bring special rations along. At home in Darjeeling, as back in Solo Khumbu, our main food is apt to be some sort of stew, usually with potatoes as a basis and with meat or vegetables mixed in. Also, since coming to India, we eat a great deal of rice, often with a curry sauce for flavouring; and a great favourite is the traditional Sherpa dish called *mo-mo*, consisting of soup full of flour-and-meat balls, which, according to Professor Tucci, are very much like Italian ravioli.

Our main drink is tea, tea, and more tea—as many cups a day as we can hold, just like the English. In the old days we usually drank it in the Tibetan way, mixed with yak butter; but in Darjeeling there are no yaks, and now we have it Western style, with sugar and milk. When something stronger is wanted we bring out the *chang*, our Sherpa beer. This is usually made in the household itself, each family brewing its own, and its basis can be rice or barley or one of several other grains, depending on taste and on what is available. In fact, there is only one thing that good *chang* may not be, and that is weak. We do not drink it in the usual way, as a plain liquid out of a glass or bottle, but when the fermented mash is ready we put it in a bowl, pour hot water over it, and then suck up the water —or, rather, what used to be water—through bamboo straws. Generally the bowl is not just for one person, but a big one to be drunk from by everybody present; and as the level of the *chang* goes down the host keeps pouring in more hot water—at least, until he is ready for his guests to go home.

We are a sociable people. We like talk and laughter and singing, and also our *chang*, and usually we do not stop pouring too soon, because we want our guests to stay. In fact, if they do not accept at least three drinks of *chang* or tea we consider them impolite, and our feelings are hurt. To Hindus and Moslems, who do not drink at all, our habits may very likely seem rather free and loose, but on the whole I would say we drink neither more nor less than most people who have no such taboos. For myself, I enjoy *chang*, and also many of the Western drinks I have lately had the chance to try. And I like cigarettes too. But luckily I am able to cut them all out without missing them, and this I always do before and during an expedition. Also I do not smoke or drink when I am among people to whom it might give offence for religious reasons.

Most Sherpas like to travel. We like to visit our friends and have our friends visit us, and, though we can be shy, we like to make the acquaintance of new and interesting people. Among ourselves we play games of chance, either with dice or cards. And I am afraid we are often practical jokers.[1] Most active sports and games play little part in our lives—partly, perhaps, because we have not yet had much chance to learn them, but even more because our work is such that, when it is over, we are seldom looking for more exercise. But many Sherpas, among them myself, are fond of horses and riding, and if putting a foot in a stirrup seems like too much effort there is always the Darjeeling race-

---

[1] One of the oldest and favourite jokes, on expeditions, is to hide stones in some one's pack to make it heavier. The sahibs can never see what is funny about this, and I am not sure that I can either.

track, where you can just put down a bet. Recently I
have bought a horse, and now race him there, but not, I
admit, with myself as jockey. And my friends say I am
on the way to becoming a Sherpa Aga Khan.

Many of our activities we share with our womenfolk,
who have a better standing and more freedom than most
Asian wives. In the home—as I have many times found
out—they are the absolute bosses, but their lives are not
necessarily confined to this, and often they share the men's
experiences and do what is usually considered men's work.
As I have told, Ang Lahmu, when a young girl, carried
loads in the streets of Darjeeling, and many not only do
this, but work as regular porters on expeditions and go all
the way to base camp. Most Sherpanis are small, some of
them even tiny. But their strength and endurance are
almost equal to the men's and they have been known to
carry burdens fully two-thirds as heavy as their own
weight.

Divorce is permitted and sometimes occurs. In such
cases the one who wants to leave, whether it is man or
woman, is required to pay a certain sum of money to the
other, and then he is free to go his own way. In Tibet,
from which our ancestors came, there is much practice of
both polygamy and polyandry, the latter usually taking
the form of two or more brothers having the same wife,
with the purpose of keeping their property together in
one family. But even in Solo Khumbu this is rarely done
by Sherpas, and in Darjeeling not at all. With the freedom
and equality we have between the sexes, one spouse is
about all that any man—or woman—can handle.

A great recent change among our people has to do with
children, for now at last they are being educated. In the
old days the only way a young Sherpa could learn any-

thing was by entering a monastery; and in Darjeeling, strangely, things were worse than in Solo Khumbu, because here we had no monasteries of our own—only Sikkimese and Tibetan—and very few lamas. Lately, however, the situation has become better. Since the last War many of our young people have been going to the Nepalese schools, of which there are several in Darjeeling, and in 1951 a small Sherpa school was started. As I said at the beginning of this story, my own lack of education has been a great sorrow in my life, and it means much to me that the next generation will have the advantages that I missed. My own daughters, Pem Pem and Nima, went for several years to one of the Nepalese schools, but now that I can afford it are going to the Catholic Loreto Convent, which has been in Darjeeling for many years under the direction of Irish nuns. This does not mean that they will themselves become Catholic. But they will learn to speak English fluently, meet many people of all different sorts, and have a fine education for the modern world.

With everything good, I suppose, there is also some bad. Many young Sherpas, I have noticed, know almost nothing about our old ways and customs. They can scarcely speak the Sherpa language. And I am afraid that many of their new ideas do not come from their school-books, but from the films.[1] But perhaps that is the sort of price that must always be paid when people change from an old simple life to a very different one, and at least it is better to learn and grow and make mistakes than always to go on the same.

In the previous chapter I told something about my Buddhist faith. As with myself, most of the "new"

[1] I myself have never much cared for the cinema. In fact, the only film I have been to in the last few years is—that's right—*The Conquest of Everest*.

Sherpas are religious, but not orthodox, with the love of God in their hearts, but a dislike of superstition and ritual. Since we have no monastery of our own in Darjeeling, there is no real centre for the practice of our religion, but almost all of us have a corner in our homes set aside for worship, and there are kept the candles and incense, prayer-wheels and Buddha-images, that are the important symbols of our faith. Luckier than most, I now have in my new house a whole room set aside for prayer. In it I keep the precious and holy things I brought back with me from Tibet, and there my brother-in-law, the lama Nwang La, spends many hours each day, tending the candles and incense-burners, turning the many wheels, and chanting prayers for us all. Outside, on my steep hillside lawn, I have set up several tall bamboo poles, and from them the prayer-flags flutter against the distant snows of Kangchen-junga.

As with most peoples, our principal ceremonies have to do with birth, marriage and, death. We cremate our dead —except in the case of small children, who are buried. And there are also the exceptions of those who die high in the mountains; for these too are buried, by the hand either of man or of Nature.

For important occasions, as well as for whoever would use it, we have in Toong Soong Busti a small temple. And inside it is only one thing—a great prayer-wheel, almost twice the height of a man, that almost fills the single room. A rope is attached to it, so that it may be set spinning, and when it spins it rings a gong. Often when you pass the temple you can hear it, sounding for a birth or a death, or simply because some one is there praying. *Om mane padme om*, you think. *Om mane padme om*. . . . For you know it is sounding not only for the new-born or the dead, but for all of us who are turning slowly on the Wheel of Life.

I have said that I have lived three lives. And, in a different way, the Sherpas as a people also have three—the lives of their religion, of their homes, and of their work. In the past we were all farmers and herdsmen, and in Solo Khumbu most of us still are. At the present some of us are merchants and tradesmen, and in the future, I think, we may become all sorts of things, such as doctors and lawyers, teachers and scholars. But the work for which the world knows us is as mountain men, and I believe that mountain men is what most of us will remain. Certainly, with all my heart, I hope so; for what we have received from the mountains, and given back to the mountains, is too precious ever to lose.

A Sherpa boy looks up, and he sees a mountain. He looks down, and what does he see? A load. He picks up the load and starts for the mountain, or, if not straight for it, at least up and down. That is what his life is—carrying a load up and down. It is not a strange or unpleasant thing for him, but a natural thing; and the load is not something to be handled awkwardly, to be struggled with and cursed at, but almost a part of his body. Most of its weight goes into a broad strap, that is worn not over the shoulders, but across the forehead, for long experience has taught us that this is the best way of carrying. And with it the average Sherpa can manage more than a hundred pounds in ordinary country and up to seventy or eighty on steep mountainsides. This is the way in which I myself carried loads through all my lifetime, until the big climbs of recent years. In these, as a sirdar or expedition member, I have had other responsibilities, and therefore carried less; and at really great heights I have found it better to sling a pack from my shoulders in Western style.

Many people do not seem to understand exactly what a Sherpa *does* on an expedition. Let me explain first that he is not at all like a guide in the Alps, who leads people up mountains he has climbed often before; because in the Himalayas no one knows the mountains as well as that or has ever before climbed them. Also we are not trained to teach people how to climb, and even if we were it would not matter on expeditions, because there we are out with the greatest experts in the world. In the beginning, as novices, we were a little more than load-bearers—what in the East, for long ages, have been called coolies. 'Coolie' is a name that Asians no longer like. From habit, or, perhaps, perverseness, we sometimes still use it ourselves (but never *for* ourselves, of course—always for some one else); but it has a connotation so menial and slave-like that it is greatly resented if it is used by Westerners. Among the Sherpas, however, this is no longer a problem, for it is a long time since anyone has even thought, let alone spoken, of us by that name. "The local coolies were paid off," you may sometimes read, "but the Sherpas went on." Or "The coolies descended from base camp while the Sherpas climbed higher." Over the years we have won our reputation—and our pride.

This is not to say that we are not still load-carriers. Indeed, it is part of our pride that we carry them bigger and farther and higher than any other men in the world. Unlike most simple people, we are not afraid of the mountains, and we have carried them on glaciers and icefalls, up ridges and precipices, through blizzards and avalanches, to the very last point of human endurance. Except for a few recent expeditions in Pakistan, from which we were barred for political reasons, Sherpas have set up the highest camps on every major climb in twentieth-century Himalayan history, and in many cases, after that, we have gone on with our sahibs to the top.

Nor is this all that we do. Over the years we have learned much about the methods and skills of mountaineering, until we are now able to help in other ways, such as in the finding of routes, the cutting of steps, the handling of ropes, the choosing of camp-sites. Also we consider it our duty to take care of our sahibs. We cook for them, bring them their tea, look after their equipment, and see that they are comfortable in their tents. And we do these things not because we have to, but because we want to; in the spirit not of servants, but of good companions. In return for this there have been rewards. Our pay has slowly increased. We are treated with courtesy and respect. The rank of Tiger has been established to honour those who go the highest, and some of us have been appointed sirdars, or headmen, with an authority and responsibility comparable to that, in the Army, of a regimental serjeant-major. All this is good and pleasing. Like all men, we want our work to be recognized. But the real reward, as it is the real reason, for what we do is simpler and deeper. It is that we are performing the work we want to do—that we were born to do—and that we love.

The Himalayan Club, which I have mentioned before, has over the years played an important part in the lives of Sherpas. Composed mostly of Englishmen, with also a few Indians and people of other nationalities who are interested in the high mountains, it does not itself send out climbing parties, but makes many arrangements and acts as a sort of clearing-house for almost all expeditions. A secretary of the club always lives in Darjeeling, so that he can know the Sherpas, and when an expedition writes, asking for our services, he calls us in and selects those who will go.[1] He sets the wages and other working conditions, arranges the travel, if necessary, and generally acts as business agent for both sides. When I came from Solo Khumbu to Darjeeling and was trying to get on my first Everest expedition the secretary was a Mr Kydd. Later, for many years, it was Mr Ludwig Kranek, who started the system of keeping records of the Sherpas' work. And more recently it has been Mrs Jill Henderson, the wife of a British tea-planter, who made many of the arrangements for the big post-war expeditions.

The club and its secretaries have done good work; but there has been some dissatisfaction among the Sherpas over money matters, and now we are becoming active with an organization of our own. First started back in the 1920's, it was called the Sherpa Buddhist Association, and was then concerned mostly with religious affairs. During the thirties and the War years it did little or nothing, but recently it has been revived, the word 'Buddhist' has been dropped from the title, and it concerns itself not with religion, but with all sorts of practical matters that affect our community. Various committees look after different problems and needs, many of them concerned with welfare. For instance, if an earning member of a family is ill for more than two weeks the Association pays a certain amount until he is well again. And when there is a death it contributes twenty rupees towards the cost of cremation. Also it has now begun to act as a sort of employment agency and trade union for expedition Sherpas, trying to

[1] Except, of course, when expedition members know us personally, in which case they will usually make their own selection. Also Sherpas are sometimes hired through a private agent, such as Karma Paul.

get a higher wage-scale than that set by the Himalayan Club and better compensation for men who are injured and the families of those who are killed. At the present time the Association has eighty-two members, with myself as president, and I think it can do much good work for the betterment of ourselves and our people.

Like any other men, we are concerned with such practical things. We too must feed our families, bring up our children, pay our debts, and try to set something aside for our old age. But, as I have said before, our work means much more to most of us than just the earning of a living. Perhaps it is not necessary to say it at all, but only to point at the record; for surely the things that Sherpas have done in the mountains are not things that men would do only for pay?

I think back over the years and the great ascents. In the earliest 1900's our men went on the first explorations of most of the great peaks. On Everest, in the twenties, they carried their loads up to more than 26,000 feet, which was two thousand feet higher than men had ever gone before. No one has ever suggested that Sherpas are paid to climb to the *top* of a mountain, yet twice during the thirties they went on with their sahibs to the summits of the highest peaks that had ever been scaled. The first time was on Jonsong Peak by the Tiger Lewa and Tsinabo, and the second on Kamet, again by Lewa, who made his great climb with frozen feet, and later lost most of his toes. Since then our men have been high on every big mountain that has been tried—K2, Kangchenjunga, Nanga Parbat, Nanda Devi, Annapurna, and many others—and on every one they helped to set up the top camps. On K2, in 1939, Pasang Dawa Lama climbed with the American Fritz Wiessner to within 750 feet of the top of the world's second highest mountain; and fifteen years later, with a 1954 Austrian party, he reached the top of the seventh-ranking peak, Cho Oyu. On Everest, in 1953, no fewer than seventeen of us reached the South Col, at almost 26,000 feet, and two besides myself went still higher.

I think of those Sherpas who have gone out to the mountains and not returned. For many, many of us have lost our lives, more than all the Himalayan climbers of all other nations combined. On Everest, in 1922, seven were killed; on Nanga Parbat, in 1934 and 1937, fifteen; on dozens of others, one or two or three, in storms and avalanches, from falls or freezing or exhaustion. Usually, of course, the deaths were accidents. But there have been times, too, when they came from courage and sacrifice. No Sherpa will ever forget Gaylay, who stayed with Willy Merkl on Nanga Parbat. And none will forget Pasang Kikuli on K2. Kikuli was one of our great mountain men of the 1930's, who had been on most of the big expeditions of the time, and in 1939 he was sirdar of the American expedition to that peak. This was the same attempt on which Wiessner and Pasang Dawa Lama were so nearly successful; but later, on the descent, there were all sorts of troubles, and one of the climbers, Dudley Wolfe, was left alone and sick, high on the mountain, while almost every one else was down at base camp. The other sahibs were too worn out to go up again. And the weather was turning bad. But Kikuli, with one other Sherpa, Tshering, went in a single day up the 7000 feet from base to Camp Six— probably the longest continuous climb that has ever been made on a mountain. Then the next day Kikuli, with two other Sherpas who had been at Six, went on to Camp Seven, where they found Wolfe. He was still alive, but too weak to descend, and since there was no room for them to sleep at Seven the Sherpas went back to Six for the night. The next morning, however, Kikuli led two of them up again, for he was determined to carry Wolfe down— and they were never seen again. Storms closed in; it was all the fourth Sherpa could do to get down from Camp Six to the base; and the great Kikuli and his companions had given their lives in trying to save that of another.

I think of these things, and I am proud to be a Sherpa. And I am sure that anyone who knows what we have done cannot believe that it is only for a few rupees that we go to the mountains.

11

ALL OVER THE MAP

IT is funny about letters. Though I cannot read and write, I have, over the years, received and sent far more than I can count. People in India or Europe write to me asking if I will go on this or that expedition, and after an expedition they write what they thought about it, or what their next plans are, or just to be friendly. I have the letters read to me, and then always answer, dictating to some one who can put the reply in the proper language, or, if that is not possible, using English, which can usually be translated at the other end. Certainly most of my life has had little to do with pens and typewriters, yet it is through them that many of my adventures have begun.

In the winter of 1948 I heard from my old friend Mr Gibson, of the Doon School and Bandar Punch, that he had recommended me for a certain job with the Operational Research Section of the Indian Army. And soon after I heard from the Army itself. The result was that, once that year and once the next, I went up to North-west India as a special instructor to help train the troops in the craft of mountaineering. This included not only climbing itself, but camp-making, outdoor cooking, the use and care of equipment, and, indeed, almost all aspects of living in wild country; and I found the work very interesting and satisfying. The first year's assignment was to the province of Kulu, the second to Kashmir, based on the resort of Gulmarg. And as both visits were in winter and to high country, I had a chance to do much skiing, for the first time since in Chitral during the War. For the instruction I did I received certificates from the Army. But the skiing was just for my own pleasure, and the only official records were some *Sitzmarks* in the snow.

In the spring of 1949 a sad thing happened in Darjeeling. Frank Smythe, with whom I had climbed on Everest, and who was, perhaps, the most famous of all Himalayan mountaineers, came back to the town and received a fine welcome. This time he was not part of an expedition, but was going out alone to photograph mountains and mountain flowers (at which he was very expert), and I helped him with his preparations.

Almost at once, though, it was clear to people that he was not the same as before—and this was not only a matter of age. One day he visited the studio of a well-known Darjeeling artist, Mr Sain, who was an old friend of his, and before he left Sain, as was his custom, asked him to sign his name in the guest-book. Smythe went over to it, but instead of signing at once stood for a while with the pen in his hand, looking down at the page. Then he smiled a little and said, "That's queer. For a minute I couldn't remember my own name." Bending over, he signed it, slowly and carefully. But when he came to the date he had trouble again. He wrote down *October*, thought for a few moments, and crossed it out. Then he thought again, wrote *December*, and let it stand. . . . But the month was really May.

A day or two later, walking with him on the Chowrasta, I had a shock of my own. We had been talking of something or other—I forget what—when suddenly his voice changed, and he said to me, "Tenzing, give me my ice-axe." I thought he was joking, of course, and made some sort of joke in reply. But he kept on demanding his axe, very seriously; he thought we were up in the mountains somewhere, and I realized that things were badly wrong with him. Soon after he was taken to hospital, and when I visited him there he did not recognize me, but simply lay in his bed with staring eyes, talking about climbs on great mountains. The doctors decided that he was suffering from a rare disease that affected his spine and brain, and he was flown back to England as quickly as possible. But apparently there was nothing that could be done for him there either, for a short time later he died. And so the life of one of the finest of all mountaineers came to a sad and too early end.

At last the effects of the War and of India's political troubles were wearing off a little, and there were now beginning to be more expeditions than for many years. Soon after Smythe left a Swiss party arrived in Darjeeling, led by another old friend, René Dittert, and this time they were headed for an exploration of the Nepali approaches to Kangchenjunga. They wanted me to go with them, and I would have liked to. But by this time I had already made arrangements by letter to go with H. W. Tilman to Nepal, and all I could do for the Swiss was to hire other Sherpas for them and wish them good luck.

Tilman, of course, was still another old friend—one of the best that we Sherpas have ever had. I had admired him greatly on Everest in 1938, and it was fine to be with him again, though we were both saddened by what had happened to Smythe. With four other Sherpas I went from Darjeeling down to Calcutta, where we met him and two English companions, and from there we cut back north-west towards the southern border of Nepal. Each stage of the way was different and more primitive. Through India we went by train, as far as the town of Raxaul, on the frontier. Then we rode by lorry through the jungle-covered foothill country called the *terai* to the Nepali town of Bimpedi. Beyond this there were neither rails nor roads, and we went on foot, crossing the low mountain ridges into the Valley of Nepal, while our baggage moved slowly above our heads by aerial ropeway. It was an exciting time for me, for, strange as it may seem—and close though Darjeeling is to its borders—I had not been back to Nepal since I ran away from Solo Khumbu for the second time in 1934. And it was exciting for the sahibs too, I think, for they were going into a country that was almost entirely unknown to Westerners. All through history Nepal had been tightly shut to them—even more so than Tibet, which had at least allowed a few visitors and expeditions. But now at last, while the Communists were closing Tibet entirely, Nepal was, in contrast, opening up a little, and Tilman and his friends were among the first to get in.

Nationality can be a strange thing. Though now an Indian citizen, I am also Nepalese, both by birth and by Nepal's recognition. But few people would think of calling me "a Nepali"—or, for that matter, "an Indian" —because I am of another race and religion. In Solo Khumbu we were remote from the rest of the country. What went on there did not seem to affect us; we had our own customs and ways of life, and knew almost nothing about the nation of which we were politically a part. In my later life, of course, I have learned a good deal, and I know the reasons for things that before I just took for granted. For instance, the chief reason why Nepal remained closed for so long is that for more than a century it was controlled by a great interlocking group of families called the Ranas, who had taken the power away from the kings, owned almost everything in the country, and were afraid to risk any change by admitting foreign visitors or influences. In the twentieth-century world, however, this could not go on indefinitely. Thousands of Gurkhas, the great Nepali fighting-men, went out to take part in the two World Wars, and came back with new ideas and customs. Also pressure began growing within the country and from the Indian Government. And finally, after the second War, an upheaval took place. The Ranas were put out of power; the king, who was liberal and modern-minded, regained the rights of the throne; and since then, under a new democratic form of government, Nepal has begun to open up and become a new nation.

Anyhow, we came up to the ridges on the rough trail from Bimpedi, and there was the great green Valley of Nepal, with Kathmandu at its centre. Then we came down to the city, and I was back at last—for the first time since I had run away to it as a boy of thirteen. There were many things that had not been there before, such as new buildings, electric-lights, telephone-wires, and even a few cars (which had been carried on men's backs across the passes from India). But most of it was the same as I remembered. The old crooked streets, the crowded bazaars, the Hindu and Buddhist temples, the wonderful carvings and statues; and beyond the city the bright-green rice-fields and the distant snows of the Himalayas. Since I had been to Lhasa only the year before, it was interesting to make a comparison between the two cities. They were alike, I thought, in that they were probably the two capitals in the world that had been least affected by Western civilization. But there were great differences too. For Lhasa, in its high loneliness, is all of a piece—all Tibetan, all Buddhist— while Kathmandu, as it has been for centuries, is a mixture of almost everything that can be found in the East.

Like Professor Tucci's, Tilman's expedition this year was not to climb mountains. What he was concerned with, though, was not manuscripts or works of art, but exploration of the country, and the two sahibs with him were both scientists. I had been wondering if we might go from Kathmandu towards Solo Khumbu and Everest, but we didn't. Instead, we headed in the opposite direction— west—towards a section of the country called the Lang Dang Himalaya, where I had never been before. For a few days we moved through cultivated land, with great paddy-fields and terraced hillsides. We passed villages and old forts and pagoda towers, which the Nepalese say originated here, and not in China, as most people think. Then we came to wilder country, and though, as I have said, we were not mountaineering, we still did plenty of climbing. To the north of us rose the great peaks of west-central Nepal—Annapurna, Dhaulagiri, Manaslu, and hundreds of others. And this was the first and only time that I have had a look at them.

Tilman studied the geography of the country; his two friends the flowers and minerals. And their investigations took us up and down, back and forth, around and about, for a full three months. Sometimes we would be in deep jungles, sometimes high in the mountains, working our way across great glaciers and snowy passes, and in both places, most of the time, we were breaking routes that no man had ever used before. It was during one of the glacier trips that, for the only time in my life, I became snow-blind. I had had a pair of dark goggles with me, as one must have in all snow-country, but somehow I had lost them, and one day, as we moved along a great ice-sheet, I began to feel pain in my eyes. I massaged them, I bathed them, I even tried to walk with them shut—the others did what they could for me—but it was no use. The pain grew worse, until it was almost unbearable. It was as if some one were driving lances into my eyes—long, bright lances of blinding light that plunged and twisted and tore, until I thought the eyes were going to fall right out of my head. And it went on until we were off the glacier, and for some time afterwards. Fortunately snow-blindness is only temporary and has no lasting bad effect, but I have been very careful ever since then to carry an extra pair of goggles on all expeditions.

Down in the jungle things happened to us too. Mostly it was getting lost—usually only a little, so that there was nothing to worry about, but a few times so badly that I wondered if we would ever find our way out. One time I especially remember was when Tilman, a Sherpa named Dawa Namgya, and I became separated from the others and wandered about most of the day trying to find them. By late afternoon, though, we were more lost than ever: we could not find either our companions or a village or a trail or anything, and it looked as if we would have to spend the night without food or shelter. Then we heard a sound up ahead, and came upon one of the native tribes-men of the region, who in this part of Nepal are called Limbus. Dawa Namgya and I spoke to him and gave him five rupees to lead us to his village, and he was just about to do so when Tilman came up and joined us. As I have said, Tilman, when on an expedition, was usually so hairy and shaggy-looking that we called him Balu—the Bear. His eyebrows were so big and jutting that when, in the mountains, he got snow on them they looked like the edge of a roof or the cornice on a ridge. Now in the jungle there was, of course, no snow, but he looked wild enough without it, with his long hair and beard, and more hair sprouting up from under his shirt. Like many Asians, the Limbus are almost hairless on face and body. This one had certainly not seen such a sight before, and one look was enough. Before we knew what was happening he gave a yell and disappeared, five rupees and all, and we were again as lost as ever.

When darkness came we sat down under a tree to pass the night. A little way off I could hear the sound of a stream, and once I started off to get a drink; but Tilman stopped me, because he was afraid it might be a watering-place for wild animals. The Nepali forests are full of them, including very dangerous tigers and bears, and beside a stream at night is the most likely place to meet them. So under the tree I stayed, damp outside and dry inside, and in the morning, when we went to the stream, we found that Tilman had been right, for the mud on its banks was churned up by animals' footprints.

Finally we found our companions and went on. We got lost again, and un-lost. We cut our way through tropical vines with our *kukris*, and hacked steps up ice-slopes with our axes, while Tilman made new notes on his maps and our packs became heavy with specimens. Every so often we came to a Limbu village, and as soon as the people saw Tilman there was great excitement. Sometimes they ran away, like the man in the forest. Sometimes, instead of being frightened, they were curious and crowded round him, pointing and laughing. Often when we wanted something from a village, such as food or drink, we Sherpas would go ahead, with the sahibs, and especially Tilman, keeping out of sight until we had finished our business.

But we had no real trouble with the people. And luckily none with wild animals. Our only real enemies were the leeches, and here in Western Nepal they were the worst I have ever known. In the warm low-country they were everywhere—in the mud underfoot, in the grass beside you when you sat down, on the leaves overhead waiting to drop on you as you passed. Leech-bites are not poisonous, and they do not hurt. But because they don't hurt—and, in fact, cause no feeling at all—you never know the leeches are about until you examine yourself or take off your clothes; and there they are, fastened to your flesh, big and ugly and filled like balloons with your blood. They especially like to go after the feet and ankles, and before they have swelled up are so small that they can crawl in through woollen socks or the eyelets of boots. The best way to keep them off is by rubbing yourself with salt, which they do not like. And soaking things in kerosene also helps, although the smell is then almost as bad as the leeches. Once they have fastened themselves on, they hold so tightly that you cannot just pick them off, but have to burn them or scrape them away with a *kukri*.

Luckily there were plenty of *kukris* in Nepal, and by the time the trip was over I had done so much skin-scraping that I could easily have got a job as a barber. Also I had learned many things about living in the jungle and about the country in which I had been born. . . . Tibet—Kulu— Kashmir—Nepal: I counted them off as I rode home again towards Darjeeling. You are really getting about these days, I thought. And I wondered where my travels would take me next.

It was to Garhwal. Back to Bandar Punch, "the Doon School Mountain," with my old friend Mr Gibson.

We made the arrangements by letter during the winter, and in the spring of 1950 I was off again on the now familiar route. This year there were three other climbers with the party, all of them going to the mountain for the first time. They were Major-General Williams, who was the head of the Engineering Corps of the Indian Army; Roy Greenwood, a serjeant-instructor in the Army; and Gurdial Singh, a young Indian instructor at the Doon School. Since Mr Gibson and I had last tried it in 1946 there had been several attempts on Bandar Punch, making seven in all, including our two previous ones; but nobody had yet succeeded in reaching the top. "Perhaps this will be our year," Gibson said to me, smiling. And I hoped so as much as he. Next to Everest, I knew it to be the best of all mountains, and I thought it was high time that we pulled that Monkey's Tail.

On my last two expeditions, in Tibet and Nepal, I had done no real climbing, and I was happy to be back once again at the job I loved the most. Up we went through the hills and valleys of Garhwal, along the wild rivers and up the high passes, until at last there we were at the base of the peak, just as I had been four years and thirteen years before. We set up our base camp and then the higher camps, using the same route as in 1946. But, as often happens on snow mountains, there had been many changes in the terrain, and the ridge between Camps One and Two was now much more difficult than before—narrow, and with many overhanging cornices that called for careful and delicate climbing. The weather, though, was better than on our other attempts, and, since that is the most important thing in Himalayan climbing, we were able to make good progress and set up our Camp Three at about 18,000 feet, within striking distance of the summit.

General Williams was over fifty years of age, but did wonderfully well and got to this high camp without trouble. He was also a fine companion, good-natured and considerate, and he used to tell me not to worry about him. "I'm an old codger, Tenzing," he would say, "and it doesn't matter if I get to the top. You look after the younger ones." From Camp Three we had hoped to make the summit attempt all together, but unfortunately at this point Gurdial Singh began to suffer from altitude sickness. It was obvious that he had to go down, and Mr Gibson unselfishly volunteered to be the one to take him. Meanwhile, it was agreed, the weather was too good to wait, and, while General Williams and a few Sherpas stayed as a support team at Camp Three, Serjeant Greenwood, the Sherpa Kin Chok Tshering, and I set out the next morning for the top. Our good luck continued. The weather stayed fine, and the going was not too hard. And suddenly, after several hours, we reached a bump in the ridge and stopped and grinned at each other, for there was nowhere higher to go. We were standing on the summit of Bandar Punch, 20,720 feet high, and after all these years I had grabbed the Monkey's Tail at last.

When we got back to camp we found that Mr Gibson, having got Gurdial Singh safely to the base, had come up again, and that night we had as big a celebration as our little tents would allow. Gibson still hoped personally to realize his dream of so many years, and the following day he, General Williams, and a pair of Sherpas made their try for the top. But now the weather, which had been good for so many days, turned suddenly bad. The wind rose, thick snow came down, and soon they had to turn back. The morning after was fair again; but by this time, unfortunately, our food-supply was almost gone, and we all had to go down. It was a sad disappointment for Mr Gibson, who had tried so long and so hard to climb this mountain. Yet he made no complaints. A fellow-climber had been in trouble; he had felt himself the proper one to help him; and by doing so he missed the great chance at his goal. That is the mountain way—the mountaineer's way. He was a fine gentleman, and I am proud to have climbed with him.

On the way out from Bandar Punch I had an experience that I shall not soon forget. One day we stopped for a rest by the shore of a lake called Duti Tal, and, being tired, I lay out in the warm sun and dozed off to sleep, with my hat covering my face. The next thing I knew I was half awake again, and with the strange feeling that the hat was somehow heavier than before. Reaching up, I felt to see why this was so. But it wasn't the hat I touched: it was something cool and slippery. While I slept a snake had coiled itself round the crown, and now was dozing and sunning itself too. I was wide awake now all right, and with a yell I threw hat and snake together as far away from me as I could. The other Sherpas, who had also been sleeping, jumped up, and when they saw what was going on they caught the snake and killed it. The local Garhwali porters, however, shook their heads, and told us this was a bad mistake, because a snake coming to a man of its own free will is a bringer of good luck. In fact, according to their belief, a man with a snake actually on his head is sure to become a king.

Well, perhaps. . . . But I think I would rather be a commoner with just a hatband.

12

THE NAKED MOUNTAIN

In the far west of the Himalayas, more than a thousand miles from Everest and Darjeeling, stands a mountain of danger and death. Its name is Nanga Parbat, and over the years almost as many lives have been lost on it as on all the other great mountains together.

Nanga Parbat has now been climbed. In 1953 an expedition of Germans and Austrians made the last of many attempts, and in early July, just five weeks after the climbing of Everest, an Austrian named Hermann Buhl accomplished a tremendous ascent, all alone, from the highest camp to the summit. But when I went to the mountain in 1950 it had not yet been climbed. It appeared that perhaps it would never be conquered. Already six expeditions had come to try it, and the only record they had left behind was one of terrible tragedy.

The first attempt was far back in 1895, when the famous English climber A. F. Mummery made his first and only trip to the Himalayas. With two British friends, two Gurkhas, and some local porters, he found his way to the base of the peak, and began looking for a way that might lead to the top. At first things seemed to go well, and they reached a height of about 22,000 feet; but later Mummery and the two Gurkhas set off to cross a high snowy pass and never returned. Though no one knows for sure, it is believed that they were caught and killed by an avalanche. Thirty-seven years passed before the next expedition, which was by a mixed German-American party in 1932. Trying a different side of the mountain from that taken by Mummery, they got to more than 23,000 feet, and worked out the route that has been used by all expeditions since. There they were turned back by storms and deep snow, but at least they got down off the mountain without accident.

Then in 1934 and 1937 came two German attempts— and the worst disasters in the history of the Himalayas. They were also disasters for the Sherpa people, for on both expeditions our men were with the expeditions (for the first time on Nanga Parbat), and no fewer than fifteen of them lost their lives. The tragedy of 1934 was brought on by a storm. High on the peak, the advance climbers and porters were caught in a great blizzard that raged for a week, and, though a few were able to fight their way down to safety, many were not. I have already mentioned the Sherpa Gyali, or Gaylay, who probably could have escaped, but chose instead to stay and die with the expedition leader, Willy Merkl. Four years later their bodies were found, perfectly preserved, lying together on a snowy ridge, and all the indications were that Gaylay had survived longer, but had refused to leave his chief. Three other Germans and five other Sherpas also died while struggling to get down the mountain in the storm. The body of one of the latter, Pinju Norbu, was likewise found in 1938, hanging head downward from an old rope on which he had been trying to descend a wall of ice.

In 1937 there were even more deaths—seven Germans and nine Sherpas—but at least these were quick and merciful. The expedition had set up its Camp Four in a snow-hollow below the east ridge of the mountain, and one night, while they all slept, an enormous avalanche came down and buried them. No one at the camp survived. Indeed, no one had even had a chance to struggle or move, for when a rescue-party arrived, later in the summer, they found the dead men all lying in their tents, as peacefully as if they were still asleep. All but two of the Germans were found, and their bodies taken down for burial. But at the request of the Sherpa Nursang, who was sirdar of the rescue party, our own men were left where they were found; and there they still lie, entombed on the icy slopes of Nanga Parbat.[1]

The Germans went back to the mountain in 1938 (when the bodies from 1934 were found), and again in 1939. But after the tragedies of the two previous expeditions no experienced Sherpas would go with them, and without proper porterage they had little or no chance for the top. At least, as it turned out, neither of these parties had any fatalities; and there were also none during the next ten years —for the simple reason that there were no expeditions.

But the record on Nanga Parbat was already twenty-nine deaths. And now in 1950 it was to become thirty-one.

I myself had never been to the mountain. For obvious reasons, I was not anxious to go. And it was mostly by accident that it finally happened. For some time I had been in correspondence with Captain J. W. Thornley, the officer of the Seventh Gurkha Rifles with whom I had visited the Zemu Glacier and seen the *yeti* tracks in 1946, about a big expedition he wanted to make to the most far-away parts of the Himalayas. Now at last everything

---

[1] The only Sherpa survivor in 1937 was my old friend Dawa Thondup. At the time of the accident he was down in base camp.

was arranged. With him would be two young friends—Captain W. H. Crace, of the Eighth Gurkhas, and Lieutenant Richard Marsh, of the Bengal Engineers—and the trip, as they planned it, would last for more than a year, and take us to the Karakoram Range, Western Tibet, and the borders of Russian Turkestan. It was a prospect to stir the blood of an old wanderer like myself (what Ang Lahmu thought of it I will not go into), and in August of 1950, soon after my return from Bandar Punch, I was on my way again. Besides myself, as sirdar, three other Sherpas were with the party. They were Ang Tempa, Ajiba, and Phu Tharkay.

We met Marsh in Calcutta, and started off with him across India. But right at the beginning there was already difficulty, for the area we were first going to was now in Pakistan, and there was much trouble about passports and visas. In the end, though, we got to Rawalpindi, in the North-west Provinces, and there met Thornley and Crace, who had gone ahead to make the arrangements. From Rawalpindi we went on to Peshawar, near the Khyber Pass, and from there flew to Gilgit, which was to be our real jumping-off place. Though I had travelled a great deal, this was my first time in a plane—as it was for the other Sherpas—and it was an exciting experience. I remember we were at first impatient at being tied into our seats by belts, and as soon as we could loosen them we began hurrying about and peering out of all the windows.

But it was a short trip. Soon we were in Gilgit. And there we split into two groups to continue north by foot. The first group, which was to precede the other by ten days, consisted of Marsh, myself, and twenty local porters, and, since I could speak with these men in Chitrali, the arrangement worked out well. But it was the only thing that did, for in everything else our troubles continued. Our next destination was a place called Shimshal, that lay close to the borders of Russia and Afghanistan, and our route followed an old caravan track that led through very wild country. It was even more desolate than the plateaux of Tibet, with no trees, no streams, no life of any kind— simply a great stony desert—and I found it very depressing. We got through to Shimshal all right, but no sooner were we there than both Marsh and I went down with bad diarrhœa, and had to take turns at nursing each other. Even after the worst of it was over we were still, for many days, weak and listless.

The purpose of this part of the trip was to explore the little-known frontier country where Pakistan, Afghanistan, Tibet, and Russia all come together. But now it was not just our insides that went wrong. Only a few days out of Shimshal we received a message from the Pakistani authorities ordering us to come back, because they were afraid we would come across Russian border guards and cause some sort of international incident. There was nothing to do but obey. The frontier country, we were told, was closed to us. And the Karakoram as well. Even before the expedition had really started it was being pulled down about our heads.

The part about the Karakoram was the big disappointment to me. It was one of the few parts of the Himalayas where I had never been; it contained the second highest mountain in the world—Mount Godwin Austen, or K2— and dozens of other famous peaks; and I had greatly looked forward to going there—if not to climb them (for we were too small a group for that), at least to see and know them. But there was nothing we could do. Marsh and I went back to Gilgit, and there the three sahibs made plans to go off to Nanga Parbat. The mountain stands on the borders of Pakistan and Kashmir, which then was—and still is—being disputed between Pakistan and India. The best side for climbing, which is on the north, lies in the former country, and, since we were already there, there was no political obstacle to our going to its base. For actual climbing it would be another matter: special permission is always required for attempts on big peaks. But this did not affect us, for we were not equipped even to dream of such an attempt. Or so, at least, I thought, as we headed off again from Gilgit.

The sahibs talked about what had happened and what they would do now, and gradually there began to be talk, especially from Thornley, that there might be a chance of climbing the mountain. Everything was against it, of course—the lack of permission, the smallness of our party, the terrible history of the peak; worst of all, the fact that it was now already November and would soon be full winter. But once the idea had entered the sahibs' heads they could not quite get it out. "There might be just a possibility," Thornley would say. Or, "Well, anyhow, we will go there. We will look and see."

So we went on. We reached the so-called Fairy-tale Meadow to the north of the mountain, from which all the German expeditions had started their attempts, and there at last, before us, was Nanga Parbat. The name means the Naked Mountain. But though it is a famous name, I do not think it is a good one, for the peak is anything but naked—not at all a thing of bare rock, but, on the contrary, so covered with snow and ice, cornices and glaciers, that it is almost impossible to tell its true rock-shape underneath. It might better be called the Giant Mountain, for, even to one like myself who was used to Everest, it was enormous. At 26,660 feet it actually ranks as only the ninth highest peak in the world, but on the side facing the Indus river, which flows through low plains, it is said to be the tallest of all from base to summit. Even from our side, already at an altitude of more than 12,000 feet, it appeared as great and formidable as any mountain I had ever seen.

But it is not so much size that makes Nanga Parbat terrible. It is the things that have happened there. Close to our base camp stood a tall stone shaft, and carved in it were the names of the Germans and Sherpas who had died in 1934 and 1937. When I looked up it seemed to me it was not only snow and ice that I saw, but the ghosts of all those brave men. Even on the clearest day, with the sun bright and the sky blue, a cloud seemed to move down from the heights and bring their coldness into our bones. It was a thing not of the eye or body, but of the mind. A cloud of fear. A cloud of death.

It was now late November—winter. There were only seven of us, three sahibs and four Sherpas, for our local porters had long since left us. To go on, I knew, was craziness, and yet on we went, up the skirts of the mountain. With so few of us, there were tremendous loads to carry—eighty or ninety pounds to the man—and the Englishmen carried as much as we did, using headstraps in the Sherpa fashion. They had none of them had much experience on big mountains, but they were young and strong, and had wonderful spirit. With all the trouble and, finally, tragedy that we had, this was one great thing about the expedition. There was no distinction at all between climbers and porters. We did the same work, shared the same burdens, every one helping every one else when help was needed. We were not like employers and employees, but like brothers.

Still the sahibs would not say right out that they would try to climb the mountain. They were doing scientific work, taking temperature recordings, studying snow and ice conditions. But always they wanted to go a little higher —a little higher—and at last, after many days of hard work in the deep snowdrifts, we climbed far enough above the base to set up our Camp One. Meanwhile it had grown steadily colder. Blizzards blew. The wind howled. I had been sure this would be as far as they would dare to go, but no—now that they were here, they wanted to climb still farther. Especially Thornley, who was a tremendously determined man, and seemed almost to gain strength from labour and hardship. Indeed, looking back on my lifetime in the mountains, I will say that he was perhaps the most powerful climber I have ever seen, and I believe that, given the proper conditions, he could have reached the top of Nanga Parbat, or even Everest.

But 'proper' was no word for the conditions that faced us there. And it takes more than power to conquer a great mountain. "We can go on," Thornley said, and Marsh and Crace agreed with him. But we Sherpas had no such confidence. I myself could have been persuaded to try—in fact, for a time I was, for I am a man who hates ever to turn back, and also, as sirdar, I felt it my duty to stay with my sahibs. Ang Tempa, Ajiba, and Phu Tharkay, however, said they would not go another foot higher. They spoke of the cold and the storms, of all the men who had already died on the mountain, of our probable deaths, and what would happen to our wives and children if we did not come back. "All right," I told them; "you three go down, and I will go on." But this did not satisfy them. They pleaded with me. They wept. It is a hard thing—a terrible thing—when a man has to make such a decision, for it is a matter not only of what he feels himself, but of his obligations and his loyalties. In my heart, though, I knew that the other Sherpas were right, and at last I turned back to the Englishmen. "No, I cannot go either," I told them. "It is winter now. It is too dangerous." But they were as determined to continue as the others were to go down, and so there at Camp One we separated. The sahibs gave us a note saying that, if anything happened to them, we should not be held responsible, and should be paid full wages out of funds they had set aside. And we, for our part, agreed to wait for them at the base camp for two weeks.

We went down. We waited. And after six days, to our delight, we saw that some one was descending. But it was only one of them—Marsh—and he told us his feet had become so badly frozen he had been unable to go on. Then we waited again. Hour after hour we took turns at massaging Marsh's feet, to try to restore the circulation. Day after day we watched the white slopes above us for signs of Thornley and Crace. And several times we saw them through our spyglass—following the German route up the great glacier and snow-slopes towards Nanga Parbat's eastern ridge. They set up one camp, then another, this higher one at a height of about 18,000 feet. One evening we watched them pitching their tent and preparing a meal, until darkness came, and we could see no more. That night, I remember, I had a dream, in which I saw Thornley and Crace coming towards me dressed in new clothes; and around them were many men with no faces. As I have said, I am not usually superstitious, but among my people such a dream has a very bad meaning—and, besides, on Nanga Parbat one does not need superstition to believe that the worst may happen. Through the rest of the night I tossed and worried. And in the morning, when I went out to look up again through the spyglass, the tent was gone.

It was possible, of course, that they had moved it. But not likely, during the night. We watched and waited. But we could find no tent. And no men. All day we watched the mountainside, but saw nothing, and by evening we were sure that something had gone wrong. Late into the night we held a discussion. Whether we could be of help, we knew, was very doubtful, but certainly we could not just sit there and do nothing. Finally Marsh decided that he, Ajiba, and I would try to get up the mountain, while Ang Tempa and Phu Tharkay waited at base camp. With them we made the same arrangement that the sahibs, before, had made with us—if we did not return within two weeks they were to pack up and leave.

As soon as it was light we started off. Marsh's frozen feet were still bad. But he was a brave man. He insisted on going, and also on doing his full share. And all day long we pushed upward. It was terribly hard work, for much new snow had fallen since last we had come down; no trace remained of our former tracks, and we had to force a way through drifts as high as our chests. Also, our loads were enormous, and many times we had to drop them and sink down in the snow to rest. It is impossible, I kept thinking. We cannot go on. And still we did go on. Finally, in the late afternoon, we reached a place near where the old Camp One had been and made a new one.

I had never before tried to pitch a tent on a glacier in the winter-time, and it is an experience I would not like to have again. Though we were hardly more than at the foot of Nanga Parbat, it was colder than I have ever known it to be on a mountain, and Marsh said later that the temperature had gone down to forty degrees below zero. The canvas and ropes were like pieces of iron, and our mittens so stiff we could hardly work with them; but if we had taken them off for even a few seconds our hands would have turned into stones. At last we put the tent up and crawled inside. I got out a pan and pressure cooker and started to melt snow for tea, but as soon as it dissolved it froze again into ice and cracked the pan wide open. Getting another pan, I kept stirring the snow-water, and at last we had our tea. Then, in our sleeping-bags, we lay almost on top of one another, trying to keep warm. When it grew dark the wind rose and howled. The tent shook, and snow drove through the cracks and covered us. But worst of all was the rumbling and cracking of the glacier beneath us. In winter the great masses of ice freeze even more solidly than before; as they contract and shift their weight huge crevasses suddenly open in the glacier's surface, and we were afraid that any moment one would open under the tent, and that would be the end of us.

Our own situation was bad enough. But the thought of what Thornley and Crace, up above, must be enduring was almost too much to bear. . . . If they were alive, that is. . . . Marsh lay in his bag with his arms over his face and his frozen feet pulled up to try to give them a little warmth. "Do you know what day it is, Tenzing?" he asked suddenly in a quiet voice. "No—what?" I answered. "Christmas," he said.

In the morning, if anything, it was still colder. It took hours just to make tea, open a few tins of food, and get our boots laced. Our breaths froze as they left our mouths, and left icicles hanging from our chins and noses. But at last we got out of the tent and started off again. Above it, the drifts were even deeper than below; it was less a matter of climbing than almost swimming through them, and it was hard to imagine how the others had got through—until I realized that a lot of new snow had fallen since they passed this point. In a full hour of struggling we climbed about 150 feet. In the next hour even less. By now Marsh's feet were in terrible condition, and, though he would not admit it, I could see he was almost done in. Ajiba and I, too, were getting weaker, and after a third hour we knew that it was no use. We stopped. We looked up at the miles of Nanga Parbat rising white and frozen above us. For a crazy moment I thought of shouting; but the sound wouldn't have travelled fifty yards through those masses of snow—and, besides, I hadn't the strength. Slowly we turned round and went back.

We managed to reach base camp that same evening. Ang Tempa and Phu Tharkay met us and took care of us, and after some food and warmth I was all right again. The next morning at four Ang Tempa and I left to inform the authorities what had happened, and, half running most of the distance, reached Gilgit that same day about midnight. The Army Scouts kindly offered to help us search, and a party, consisting of an Army lieutenant and eleven soldiers, returned to the mountain as quickly as possible, even using jeeps for part of the way. But it was a hopeless effort. In the short while we had been away still more snow had fallen, and this time, though there were many to help, we could not get as far as Camp One. A few days later we turned away from Nanga Parbat for good, leaving our two friends with all the others in their grave of ice.

Back in Gilgit again, we were given the use of a military plane, and flew round the mountain, looking for some final sign of them. But we could see nothing. The general belief was that they had been caught in an avalanche, like the Germans in 1937, and this is certainly possible. I myself, though, think it more likely that what happened to them was what we had feared might happen to ourselves during that terrible Christmas night at Camp One —that the glacier had suddenly opened in a great crevasse beneath their tent and swallowed them up.

Marsh's feet remained bad. For a while he could hardly walk. But I think this was nothing compared to what he felt inside. So much had been expected of the expedition; we were going to go to such interesting places and do such exciting things; but everything had gone wrong—nothing we tried had succeeded—and now it had ended with the death of his dearest friends. Sorrowfully we flew out from Gilgit, and at Amritsar, in the Punjab, we said good-bye.

"What will you do now, Tenzing?" he asked.

I tried to smile—to cheer him up a little—and I looked at Ang Tempa. He is a very small man, but thick-set, with a funny rolling way of walking, and in the early days of the expedition we had sometimes joked about his looking like a Himalayan bear. "Well, perhaps I'll put a ring in Ang Tempa's nose," I said, "and make some money showing him in the bazaars."

Marsh smiled back. Sadly we said farewell.

13

THE SACRED MOUNTAIN

IT is a Sherpa belief that the late twenties are the critical years in a woman's life, the late thirties in a man's—the age at which the best or worst things will happen to them. Now I had reached this age—I was thirty-six when I was on Nanga Parbat—and its beginnings were not good. On the Naked Mountain, for the first time, I had been on an expedition on which lives had been lost, and this next year I was to be on two more of them. Three bad-luck climbs in a row—and, though I myself was to come through them all unharmed, the signs seemed bad for me. It was not until 1952 that my fortunes took a great and sudden change. But that is a later story.

I have heard Englishmen use the expression "a feast or a famine," and that is how it is with Himalayan climbing. For years, during the War and after, there had been very few expeditions, and jobs had been hard to get. But with the beginning of the 1950's there were many each season, and, whichever one you went on, it was likely that you were missing something as good, or even better. In 1950, while I was on Bandar Punch, there had been the great French ascent of Annapurna, which was then the highest peak in the world to be climbed to the top. Many of our Sherpas, of course, had gone on this expedition, with my old friend Angtharkay as sirdar. They had done tremendous work getting their sahibs down off the mountain alive, and their stories made me wish that I too had been part of that great adventure. Also in the same year, while I was on the way to Nanga Parbat, Tilman and the American climber Dr Charles Houston had for the first time led a small party to Everest from the south, through Nepal. Though they had not been equipped to make an actual attempt, they had gone up through the Solo Khumbu country to the very base of the mountain, and started all kinds of new ideas of climbing it from this side. And I wished I had been with them too.

Now in 1951 there was another Everest expedition— this time a full-scale one led by Eric Shipton—and, though they had little hope of reaching the top, they planned to go as high as they could and work out a good southern route. I had been so many times to Everest, and I felt so much that it was *my* mountain, that I hated to miss this chance. But you cannot be in two places at the same time, and I had already signed up, through the Himalayan Club, for a different venture. This was with a French party on Nanda Devi, which I had visited, but not actually climbed on, back in 1936.

With the other Sherpas, of whom I was again sirdar, I met the expedition in Delhi about mid-spring, and soon we were on our way up to Garhwal. I had been with French Swiss in 1947, but never before with true Frenchmen, and I found them very determined and enthusiastic. The conquest of Annapurna the year before had caused great excitement in France, and turned all their climbers' thoughts to the Himalayas, and it had at first been the hope of this new group to try an even higher mountain. They had not, however, been able to get political permission for this, and so had thought up a bold and original plan for Nanda Devi. The main peak, as I have told, had been climbed in 1936 by Tilman and Odell; and in 1939 a Polish expedition had reached the top of its slightly lower neighbour, which is called Nanda Devi East. But no one had ever climbed both peaks together, and it was the Frenchmen's idea to do this—not simply by going up and down one and then the other, but by crossing from summit to summit along the high skyline ridge that connects them. Nothing like this had ever been done in the history of Himalayan mountaineering, and it would be a very difficult and dangerous undertaking.

There were eighteen of us on the expedition—eight Frenchmen, mostly from the city of Lyons, with Roger Duplat as leader; nine Sherpas, including myself; and, as representative of the Indian Army, "Nandu" Jayal (now a captain), with whom I had climbed on Bandar Punch in 1946. Also, of course, there was the usual large number of local porters for the trip in, and unfortunately we had a great deal of trouble with them about wages. But in spite of many arguments and desertions we managed to keep going, threaded our way up the deep gorge of the Rishi Ganga, and came out at last into the wonderful flower-covered "Sanctuary," at the foot of Nanda Devi.

The Blessed Goddess. The Sacred Mountain. . . .

On my previous trip to it we had not been there to climb, and I had been mostly impressed by how beautiful it was. But now it was a different matter: we were out to reach, not only one, but both of its peaks; and, while it was still beautiful, it was also, I could see, very big and formidable. Especially impressive was the part of the mountain which would be the key to the whole climb—the great ridge of snow joining the two peaks, which the Frenchmen planned to traverse. Nanda Devi's main summit is 25,660 feet high, the east summit about 24,400, and the white saw-edge between them dipped nowhere to less than 23,000—and was more than two miles in length! Certainly it was a tremendous job that we had picked for ourselves, and I did not have too much confidence in our success.

But the French were optimistic, and the leader, Duplat, who was a very excitable and impatient man, seemed almost to think that the whole thing could be done in a few days. We did not move as fast as that, of course, but, still, faster than on almost any expedition I can remember, and very soon, with good weather, we had a chain of higher camps above our base. This was on the slopes of the main peak; for it had been decided to ascend this one first, make the traverse of the ridge from the higher to the lower summit, and then come down the side of the east peak. Only two men would make the final ascent and crossing— Duplat himself and a young companion named Gilbert Vignes. Both were good men, especially Vignes, who, although only twenty-one, had already made many famous ascents in the Alps, and was the best rock-climber I have ever seen. But there is little rock on Nanda Devi. There is much snow—and great distances. And I could not help feeling that their plan was reckless.

From Camp Three, where most of the expedition was gathered, Duplat and Vignes, with several Sherpas, worked their way higher, and set up a fourth camp at about 23,600 feet. Then the Sherpas came down, the two climbers spent the night there, and the next morning— June the 29th—set out for the top. With them, besides the usual mountaineering equipment, they carried a light tent and considerable food, for they expected to spend the next night somewhere out on the skyline ridge.

Meanwhile arrangements had been made to meet them when they descended Nanda Devi East, and the men assigned to this job were Louis Dubost, one of the climbers, Dr Payan, the expedition physician, and myself. A few days before the summit attempt we had left the others, crossed over beneath the mountain, and climbed up the far side of Nanda Devi East to a high pass called Longstaff Col.[1] There we set up our tents and waited, and on the morning of June the 29th, through our glasses, we could see two tiny specks moving up the slopes of the main peak a few miles away. Against the snow we were able to follow them very high—almost to the summit—but then they moved out of our sight, and we did not see them again. That same day we did not expect them, for they planned to bivouac on the skyline ridge; but the next morning we climbed up from the col towards the east peak, to meet them coming down. The morning passed— and they did not come. Then the afternoon passed—and they did not come. With the glasses we searched the mountain above us, but saw no sign of them. We shouted, but there was no answer. And when darkness came we had to return to our camp.

It had been arranged with the rest of the expedition that if, for some reason, Duplat and Vignes were to turn back and descend the way they had gone up we would be signalled to that effect, so that we could come down our-selves. But there had been no signal that day. And there was none the next. By this time we knew that something

[1] Named after Dr Thomas Longstaff, one of the early British explorers of the region.

had gone very wrong, and Dubost, Dr Payan, and I had to make up our own minds what to do. Just to go on waiting there on the col was demoralizing—and useless. We must either go down or up.

Dubost and I went up.

Leaving Dr Payan (who was not a high climber) in charge of the camp, we worked our way up the steep slopes of Nanda Devi East, past the point which we had reached before, always higher and higher. We had had plenty of supplies on the col, and we carried heavy loads with us, including a tent, for we were determined to go as far as was humanly possible. All that day we climbed, and then made a camp. All the next day, and made another camp. Altogether we made three of them above the col, and without them we would have got nowhere, for the going was terribly slow. Most of the time we were on a ridge—the opposite ridge of the mountain from the one on which Duplat and Vignes were to have made their traverse—and as we climbed it grew ever steeper and narrower, and was plastered with ice and loose snow. We were not the first on this route. It was the way the Polish climbers had gone when they went up the mountain twelve years before, and several times we came upon ropes and pitons of theirs, still fixed in the ice. But these were now too old and worn to be safe, and we had to make our own way—up over great humps and spires; along the thin meeting-point of two mile-high precipices; always over loose footing that we thought at any minute would crumble beneath us. Often in recent years people have asked me, "What is the hardest, most dangerous climb you have ever made?" They expect me to say Everest, but it is not Everest. It is Nanda Devi East.

By now Dubost and I knew there was no chance of

finding the missing men—at least, not alive. But still we kept on. And, though the steepness was terrible, and the danger of a fall never absent, at least the weather held fine. On July the 6th, exactly a week after Duplat and Vignes had last been seen, we left our third camp and made our try for the top; and we knew it would be the only try, for now our supplies were running out. The ridge continued as it had been before. If anything, it was even worse, even steeper. We slipped. We struggled. We balanced on knife-edges, and lost our balance and caught it again. We did everything but fall down the mountain, and I still cannot understand why we didn't do that. But at last blue sky began showing, not only around us, but in front of us, above the ridge; and then there was no more ridge at all. We were at its top. On the top of the mountain. For the second time Nanda Devi East had been climbed, and for myself it remains, next to Everest, the highest peak on which I have gone to the summit.

It had been a hard and good victory. The view on that clear day, spreading off across the great mountains to the plains of Tibet, was one of the finest I have ever seen. But it was not of victory or view that we were mostly thinking. In front of us, on the far side of the peak from that which we had climbed, the summit ridge connecting the two Nanda Devis twisted away into space—a narrow, jagged ribbon of snow and ice, rising and falling, rising and falling, for two long miles, until it rose for the last time to the main summit of the mountain. For a long time we studied it through our glasses. We tried to cover every yard, every foot, of those two miles. But we could see nothing. Nothing except the snow and ice, the terrible steepness on either side, and beyond the steepness two oceans of blue air. It was hard to believe that anyone could have clung to the ridge for even a few minutes, let alone move along it for hour after hour.

There was nothing to do. We turned to go down again. On the descent there was even more danger of slipping than on the way up, and we moved very slowly. But at last we arrived at the col, where Dr Payan was waiting for us, and the next day we continued on down and rejoined the rest of the expedition at base camp. They too had seen nothing of Duplat and Vignes after they had passed out of sight near Nanda Devi's main summit. They had not become worried as soon as we had, because they thought, or at least hoped, that they were over with us on the far side of the mountain. But when we had been so long in returning they realized that something must have gone wrong. The stronger of the other climbers had tried to follow the tracks up towards the main summit, but had been unable to get far. And since then they had just waited. It was a little consolation that Dubost and I had reached the top of the east peak—at least, the expedition had not been a total failure—but this did not mean much compared to the loss of their two companions.

What had happened to Duplat and Vignes? As with Thornley and Crace on Nanga Parbat—as with any men who disappear on a mountain—one can only guess. My own belief is that they reached the main summit of Nanda Devi, for they were very close when we last saw them, and there seemed to be no great difficulties in the way. But once they had passed the summit and begun the traverse of that two-mile ridge, they must have found it a very different matter; and I think that what happened is that they slipped and fell—probably down the far side of the mountain, which is the steeper, and on to the glacier far below.

Anyhow, they were gone. They had been brave men and fine climbers. But, like Thornley and Grace—like so many other men before them—they had held a great mountain too lightly, and they had paid the price.

Two expeditions—four deaths. That was enough, it seemed. But the bad luck was not yet over. That same year came another expedition, and another death.

This was in the autumn of the year, after the monsoon. And the place was the Kangchenjunga region, north of Darjeeling. Like the earlier expeditions I had gone with to the area, this one was not directed at any one big mountain, but was rather a general exploring party. And it was a very small one. In fact, there was only one sahib—Mr George Frey, a Swiss, who was Assistant Trade Commissioner for his Government to India, Pakistan, and Burma. There was myself, as sirdar, and a few other Sherpas. Frey, though an excellent climber, had nothing very ambitious in mind, and it was the last sort of expedition on which one would expect an accident.

Everything started off well. The weather was fine. Reaching the high country, we made many trips round and between the peaks, exploring the great Yalung Glacier, near Kangchenjunga, and crossing the difficult Ratong Gap between Nepal and Sikkim—which was only the second time that this had ever been done. Part of our trip took us near the places where, years before, a Swiss-Sherpa party and the young American Farmer had disappeared during their unsuccessful attempts on Kangchenjunga; and we searched for traces of them, but without finding any. Then we made attempts on several smaller mountains near by, and were very successful, reaching the top of most of them, and leaving our names in tin-cans for the benefit of anyone who might some day follow us. And finally, before turning home, we decided to try our luck on a slightly higher summit called Kang Peak.

As the Himalayas go, there was nothing very big about it. Alongside Kangchenjunga, its 19,000 feet gave it the size of a midget. But, seen by itself, it was quite impressive, and, since it had never been climbed, it seemed just the right sort of prize for a small party such as ours. So we moved over to its base, selected our route, and pitched camp. Until now everything had gone just as it should have, and I can think of no reason why I should have worried. But during that next night I had a bad dream. I know I have spoken of my dreams before, and perhaps some readers will be impatient with me. But I must tell the truth. I *did* have the dream, and it was bad, and the next day bad things happened—just as they had happened the year before after my dream on Nanga Parbat. This time, in my sleep, I did not see anyone I knew. There was just myself and a strange woman who was giving away food, and I was very hungry, but she gave me nothing. That was all. But according to Sherpa beliefs such a dream is a bad one, and I was worried; and in the morning, when I told my companions about it, the other Sherpas were worried too. But Frey just laughed and made some joke about it, and then he said, "Come on; it's time to start."

Perhaps I should have refused. It is hard to tell about such things. Some of the other Sherpas refused to go, but I did not, and finally three of us began the climb—Frey, the Sherpa Ang Dawa, and myself. At first the going was easy enough, following a long snow-slope into which we could kick good steps, and not so steep that we needed a rope between us. But after a while the angle grew a bit sharper, and the snow harder, and I stopped and put on my steel-spiked crampons, so as to have a steadier footing. "Aren't you going to put yours on?" I called up to Frey, who was in the lead. "No, I don't need them," he answered. And we continued climbing. Once again there is the question of whether I should have done otherwise, such as arguing or urging more strongly. But Frey, as I have said, was an excellent climber. He had had much experience in the Alps, had certainly been in much more difficult places than where we were now, and seemed to be having no trouble. We continued smoothly and easily —he first, myself second, Ang Dawa third—still unroped, and with perhaps fifteen feet between us; and, looking round, I judged that we were at about 17,000 feet, with only another 2000 to go to the top of Kang Peak.

Then Frey slipped. Just how or why I could not tell. But one moment he was climbing steadily above me, and the next he was plunging down. At first it looked as if he were going to fall right on top of me and carry me along with him, but actually he was a little to one side, and as he came by I dug in and lunged and tried to hold him. It was hopeless, though; there was too much weight and momentum. His body struck my outstretched hand, there was a quick, sharp pain in one finger, and then he was past me— past Ang Dawa, below me—falling, and tumbling down the mountainside, until he came to rest on a flat place about a thousand feet below.

It was the first time in all my climbing that I had ever seen a fall. But others, who had had the experience, had told me what it was like—that for a few minutes you are just numb; you cannot move; you cannot feel or think of anything except that in the next instant you will fall your-self. And that was the way it was now with Ang Dawa and me. At first we just hung there, frozen, as if we were part of the mountain. The accident had happened so quickly it was almost impossible to believe it, and I had the feeling that if I looked up Frey would still be there above me, as he had been before. But he wasn't there. He was a little speck on the whiteness far below. And at last I went down to Ang Dawa. He was very shaken, and at first said he could not get down; but after another wait he was better, and we began the descent, going very slowly and carefully, because we knew that in our shocked condition we might easily lose our balance. About half-way down I saw a small dark object in the snow, and, going after it, found that it was Frey's camera. Then we continued on to where he himself lay; he was dead, of course, for no man could have survived such a fall.

On our backs we managed to get him down the rest of the way, and when we neared the camp the other Sherpas, who had been waiting there, came up and helped. The next day we buried him—not in the glacier itself, where he would have been carried away by the moving ice, but under the rocks of the moraine beside it, with a pile of stones as a permanent marker. Then we sadly started back for Darjeeling. It was not until we were on our way that I realized that the finger I had hurt in trying to catch Frey was broken—the first time I had suffered more than a bump or a scratch in all my years of mountaineering.

So here I was in my late thirties, I thought. In the 'critical' age. And though I had come through all right myself, I had been on three expeditions in a row on which lives had been lost. . . . Nanga Parbat, Nanda Devi, Kang Peak. . . . "And now what?" I wondered, and was a little afraid. For I had two years of my thirties still to go.

14

EVEREST WITH THE SWISS: SPRING

NANGA PARBAT, Nanda Devi, Kang Peak. Kashmir, Garhwal, Nepal, and even Tibet. I had been all over the map. I had climbed many mountains, seen many sights, lived through many experiences. But one thing had been missing—Chomolungma, the Great One. It was five years now since I had even seen it, on that strange, quick trip with Denman; fourteen since I had climbed high on its walls to win my rank as a Tiger. Sometimes I wondered if I would ever get back to it, or if the gods, for reasons of their own, were going to keep me for ever from this mountain that was closest to my heart.

But the gods were kinder than that. I was to go back again—and again, and again. And the last years of my 'critical' late thirties were to be the great years of my life.

It was a new Everest to which I returned. For the post-war expeditions were no longer approaching it from the north, but from the south, and to climb a mountain from a different side is almost like climbing a different mountain. But while it was in one way new, in another it was old—older, for me at least, than the peak I had approached four times from Tibet and Rongbuk. For the southern route to Everest leads through Solo Khumbu and the country of my childhood; and, while I had never tried climbing from this side, it was the side I knew best of all in my memories and dreams. Now, after eighteen long years, I would see my mother again. I would stand beside her again in the steep pastures beyond Thamey and look up at The Mountain So High No Bird Can Fly Over It. In two different ways I would be coming 'home.'

It was politics that had brought about the change of route. By now the Chinese Communists were well established in Tibet, and it was impossible for any Western expeditions to enter; but at the same time Nepal had had its own quieter revolution, and was slowly opening up to the outside world. In 1950, as I have mentioned, H. W. Tilman and the American Dr Charles Houston made their way from Kathmandu through Solo Khumbu to the southern base of Everest. Then the next year Eric Shipton led a full-scale expedition there to test the chances of actually climbing from that side. Neither party had got very high. Tilman and Houston had not been equipped to try even a partial ascent; Shipton and his men had been stopped by a great crevasse in an icefall that sweeps down to the Khumbu Glacier. And the first group, at least, agreed with Mallory, who had looked down on this route from near the Lho La many years before, that it was much more difficult than the old northern route, and very likely impossible.

Still, with Tibet closed, it was the only way there was. As far as the non-Communist world was concerned, Everest had to be climbed from the south, or not at all.

Now, in 1952, there was also to be something else new on Everest besides the route. All through its climbing history it had been entirely a "British mountain." The only men of other Western nations who had come even close to it were Dr Houston and a Dane named Larsen, who in 1951 had made a half-circuit of the peak from Khumbu to Rongbuk; and none but Englishmen had ever set foot on the mountain itself. Now, however, there was to be a change—a great change. For while Tibet, in the old days, had allowed only the British to enter, newly opened Nepal was prepared to welcome climbers from many countries. And the first of the newcomers were the Swiss.

It was a great day for me when the news reached Darjeeling. There was one letter direct to me from Switzerland, another to Mrs Henderson, the secretary of the Himalayan Club. And they asked for me as sirdar. Not only would I be going back to Everest at last, but I would be doing it with the people with whom I enjoyed climbing most of all. I did not know all the expedition members, of course; but I had met the leader, Dr Wyss-Dunant, in Darjeeling a few years before, two of the climbers—René Dittert and André Roch—were old friends from Garhwal in 1947, and I was sure that I would like the others just as well. "Would I go?" the letters asked. And they might as well have asked if I would eat or breathe. The way I behaved about the house for a few days, Ang Lahmu and the girls must have thought I was possessed by devils.

The Himalayan Club handled the financial arrangements, but I was entrusted with the selection of the other Sherpas, of whom the Swiss wanted thirteen from Darjeeling, and planned to hire another ten in Solo Khumbu. I soon found, though, that there were not many as anxious as I was to go back to Everest. For one thing, there had been troubles on the Shipton expedition of the year before. Many of the Nepali porters who had been on the expedition claimed they had not received their full wages; there had been difficulties about a lost, or perhaps stolen, camera;

and no *baksheesh* had been given out at the end of the climb. I said, "Perhaps so. Still, what has that got to do with the Swiss?" But many seemed to blame what had happened on the mountain. They did not want to go back to the mountain. Everest was too big, too dangerous; it was impossible to climb by the southern route. Even the great Tiger Angtharkay, who had been the 1951 sirdar, was not going back this time. And he bet me twenty rupees that the Swiss, like Shipton's men, would never get past the great crevasse in the Khumbu Icefall.

Nevertheless I was finally able to get thirteen good men, and in the early spring—'expedition time' for all climbing Sherpas—we were off to meet our sahibs in Kathmandu. Besides those I had known before, there were six other climbers in the party, plus two scientists, and they seemed to me both a strong team of mountaineers and a fine group of men. Dittert and Roch had both been on other Himalayan expeditions since I had gone with them in 1947, and were now experienced veterans, and the others were the best of the French-Swiss mountaineers from the region round Geneva. Most noted of all, perhaps, of these mountaineers was Raymond Lambert, who, though I was now only meeting him for the first time, was soon to become my companion of the heights and the closest and dearest of my friends. "Look, I have brought a bear with me," Dittert said, introducing him. And Lambert shook hands, big and grinning, so that all of us liked him right from the start. Almost at once I noticed that his boots were strangely short and cut-off in appearance, and soon I learned why. Many years before he had been caught in a great storm in the Alps, had suffered frostbite, and had lost all the toes of both his feet. But this had not kept him from continuing as one of the greatest of Swiss guides; and it was not to keep him from going on almost to the summit of Everest.

In Kathmandu there was much work to be done with the tons of food and equipment that had been brought from Switzerland, and this we did on the new airfield near the city, where the loads were divided up and issued to the Nepalese porters who would carry them to Solo Khumbu. As usual, there was some trouble with the porters about wages. But this time it was not bad trouble, and I like to think I was at least partly responsible. For I refused to take the share which sirdars often get from the wages of men they employ, which made it possible for them to receive their full pay without any extra cost to the expedition. Anyhow, we were able to leave on March the 29th, which was the day we were supposed to. Part of my job as sirdar was to decide who carried what, and I followed the system that from long experience I have found the best. Each day the porters who were ready to leave first were given the current rations and kitchen equipment, so that at the end of the march the evening meal might be quickly prepared. Those who went next took the tents and personal effects which would be needed overnight. And the last ones to go carried the stores and equipment that would not be needed until we reached the mountain. If these lagged on the trail it was of no great matter; but it is no good on a trek if most of a party arrives at a camping-place and then has to wait for hours for its food and shelter.

It is about 180 miles from Kathmandu to Namche Bazar, and the trip took sixteen days. Mostly our direction was towards the east, then for the last few days towards the north, but always it was up and down, up and down, as we crossed the ridges and deep valleys that make up almost all of Nepal. On the old Tibetan route to Everest pack-animals had been used nearly to the base of the mountain, but here this was not possible. Mostly, the trail itself would have been all right for animals—indeed, it was one of the main travel routes between Nepal and Tibet—but at the bottom of every valley was a river, and no horse or mule could manage the hanging and swaying plank bridges that are the only way across them. This is the chief reason why, through all the centuries, the Nepalese have carried their loads on their own backs. And even to-day any travellers through the country must do the same.

Up and down—up and down. Each day it was like crossing a small mountain range, with another one ahead for the next. But it was not all climbing and load-carrying. As we went we made our plans for Everest, and also we got acquainted with each other, with the other Sherpas, like myself, becoming very fond of the Swiss. Dittert, who was to lead the expedition on the higher parts of the mountain, was a jolly and lively man, and it was hard for anyone to be in bad humour when he was about. He hopped about so much that we called him Khishigpa—the Flea. Lambert he had introduced to us as a bear, and, as with Tilman, the name stuck. Lambert sahib became Balu sahib. He knew none of the Eastern languages, and only a few words of English, so that our conversations were mostly with the hands; but after a while we grew to understand each other very well.

As we marched on the country began to change. It was still up and down, up and down, but more up than the other, and soon the paddy-field country was behind us, and we were passing through forests and fields of barley and potatoes. Also the people were changing. They were no

longer Hindu, but Buddhist; no longer Nepali, but
Mongolian. On about the tenth day we began bearing
north into the Sherpa country—first through the lower
region of Solo, and then on up the wild stream of the
Dudh Kosi towards Khumbu and Namche Bazar. These
were exciting days for me—approaching not only Chomolungma, but my old home as well. All about me I saw
things that I remembered from long ago, and I hardly
knew whether to shout for joy or to weep for old memories. When at last we reached Namche there was a great
reunion, not only for myself, but for all the Sherpas who
had been long away, and I am afraid that for a little while
the expedition had to get along without us. The news of
our coming had, of course, gone before us, and it seemed
that every Sherpa in the world was there, ready to welcome
us and celebrate. Even my mother, though now very old,
had come on foot from Thamey; and I said, "Ama la, here
I am at last," and, after eighteen years, we held each other
and cried a little.

But there was more to laugh about than cry about. So
much to see and hear and learn and tell. In her arms my
mother carried one of her grandchildren. With her were
my three sisters, and all about were in-laws and cousins,
nephews and nieces, whom I had either not seen since
I was a boy or who had not even been born when I left
home. They brought gifts. They brought food and
chang. And so did almost all the people of Khumbu.
Surely we needed no excuse to celebrate; but by a happy
chance the day after our arrival was both the Nepali New
Year and the Easter Monday of the Western sahibs, and
we all joined together in singing, dancing, and drinking
chang. Later I had the chance to look round Namche, and
most things were just as I remembered them. But there

had been a few changes, and the most important, I think, was that there was now a school. It was only a small one, of course, with one teacher, and the work must have been hard, because the Sherpa language has no written form and the teaching had to be in Nepali. But I was happy to see that there was a school at all, and I thought, That is a good sign for the future of our people.

There was only one day for reunion, celebrating, and sightseeing. Then it was back to work. The Nepali porters who had come with us from Kathmandu were paid off and started their return trip. According to plan, ten of the best Khumbu Sherpas joined those of us who had come from Darjeeling for high-altitude work on the mountain, and what seemed like half the rest of the people joined up to carry the big loads as far as base camp. These included not only men, but women, and among the Sherpanis were my youngest sister, Sona Doma, and my niece, Phu Lahmu, who was the daughter of one of my deceased brothers. Many of the other Darjeeling Sherpas also had relatives with them, and it was a sort of great family party that started out for Thyangboche Monastery and the mountains beyond.

At Thyangboche the lamas gave us a fine welcome. But I am not sure how much the sahibs enjoyed it, for it included the serving of much Tibetan tea, which is full of salt and rancid yak butter, and I have seldom seen a Westerner who could get much of it down. But Lambert was the hero of the day. Or perhaps he just has a "Tibetan stomach." For while the others sipped and gagged and struggled hard not to offend their hosts, he not only drank all of his, but then, grinning, took the cups of his companions and emptied them too. Later that day every one was waiting for him to be sick, but it never happened.

"*Quel espèce d'homme!*" the others murmured, in admiration and gratitude.

At the monastery we were already at more than 12,000 feet, but beyond it we entered the real mountains. Following the route of Tilman and Houston and of the 1951 Shipton party, we forked eastward from the Dudh Kosi, climbed up steep valleys between the beautiful peaks of Taweche and Ama Dablam, and reached the snout of the Khumbu Glacier, that descends from the high passes to the south-west of Everest. During this part of the trip we could see little of Everest itself, for it is mostly hidden by the great walls of its southern neighbour, Lhotse, and its western one, Nuptse, and all that showed was its very summit, usually streaming its white snow-cloud in the cold blue sky. The lower part of the glacier was about the highest point I had been to while tending yaks as a boy. On the far side of the mountain I had, of course, been much higher, but from now on everything on our present route would be new to me.

One evening there was great excitement in camp, for the two Swiss scientists returned from a day's exploring and said they had found mysterious footprints. The next day some of the rest of us went to the place—a strip of soft snow along the glacier at about 16,000 feet—and, sure enough, there they were—the tracks of a *yeti*, just as I had seen them on the Zemu Glacier, near Kangchenjunga, in 1946. They were clear and firm, and even the sahibs, who, like all Westerners, were made unhappy by things they did not understand, admitted they were unlike the prints of any animal they knew. The scientists measured them carefully, and found they were $11\frac{1}{2}$ inches long and $4\frac{3}{4}$ inches wide, while the length of each pace was exactly 20 inches. There was only a single line of them; they seemed to begin nowhere and faded out into nowhere; and, though the scientists did much searching, no *yeti* was found, nor even any more footprints. I wish I could tell more. I wish I knew more. But I do not.

On April the 22nd we established our base camp on the Khumbu Glacier at 16,570 feet. From here most of the local Sherpas went back to Namche, but the Swiss kept about thirty of them—besides the ten for the high climbing —to help carry firewood and provisions to the next camp. Straight ahead of us now, to the north, the glacier ended in a great wall of snow and ice. And at the top of the wall was the pass of the Lho La, which separated us from Tibet, and from which in 1938 I had looked across to this side of the mountain. But it was not at the Lho La that we looked now. It was off to the right—the west—where a great tumbled mass of ice, known as the icefall, plunged down to the glacier through a narrow passage between the walls of Everest and Nuptse. Here was where Tilman and Houston had looked and shaken their heads; where Shipton and his men had tried and failed; where we must now try—and succeed—if we were to get into the Western Cwm and then on to the heights of the mountain.

We had some bad weather on the glacier. But it never lasted too long, and we made progress. From the base we went up and across, and set up Camp One near the foot of the icefall, and from there the Swiss began searching for a way up through the steep tangle of ice. For this they divided into two teams—Dittert, Lambert, Aubert, and Dr Chevalley in one, Roch, Flory, Asper, and Hofstetter in the other—which took turns in the hard work of finding a route, cutting steps, and fixing ropes. Dr Wyss-Dunant, who was older than the rest, would stay at base camp and

Camp One, in charge of operations there, while Dittert would become leader of the high climbers. During this stage my own job as sirdar was to see that the Sherpas got the loads to the higher camps, as they were established—up and down, up and down again, safely and on schedule.

It went slowly in the icefall. It was like finding your way through a white jungle. And it was dangerous too, for everywhere there were ice-towers that might collapse on you and deep, snow-hidden crevasses into which you might fall. The Sherpas who had been with Shipton the year before did not seem to remember the way at all; or perhaps there was no way to remember, because the icefall keeps changing all the time. The sahibs tried this way, then that way. They came up against unclimbable ice-walls and uncrossable chasms. They turned back, tried a third way, went on, cutting steps, fixing ropes, and we Sherpas followed with the loads. In a sheltered place half-way up the icefall we pitched Camp Two. And above this it was even harder. But we kept working our way higher. There were no accidents. And at last we were getting close to the level of the Western Cwm. "We are almost there," the sahibs kept saying hopefully. And Lambert, who now not only looked like a bear, but worked like ten of them, would turn and grin and use his favourite expression—"Ça va bien! (It goes well!)"

Then, almost at the top, we came to what we knew we would find, and were worried about—the great crevasse just below the entrance of the cwm that had stopped Shipton's party the year before. It was a frightening thing all right—so wide no man could jump it, so deep you could not see its bottom, and stretching all the way across the icefall from the walls of Everest to those of Nuptse. What was to be done? What could be done? The Swiss walked

Longstaff Col, Nanda Devi

A Sherpa gazing at One of the Unnamed Peaks at the Approach to Nanda Devi

Crossing a River during the Swiss Expedition of 1952

With Lowe on the South Col

On Everest with Raymond Lambert

Sherpas crossing a Bridge above Camp Three in 1953

The Final Ridge

Sherpas crossing a Bridge above Camp Three in 1953

Camp Four, 1953

I think the South Col of Everest must be the Coldest and Loneliest Place in the World

The Final Ridge

"*The Dream comes True*"

From the Top of the World
I felt like a mother hen with her chicks.

With Hillary back at Camp after the Climb

"The Road to Victory"

Victory Drive
Here I am at Bagdogra, in Bengal.

Smiles of Victory
Hillary and myself a few days after the climb.

Hunt, Hillary, and Myself wearing Medals presented to us at Delhi

Two to Whom I owe Much.
Ang Lahmu and Mitra.

"The Happiness comes Late

"*Wearer of a Coat with Rows of Medals*"

"Zindabad !"

back and forth along the rim. They examined every yard of it. They spent hours trying to find a way to get across, but they had still not succeeded when it began to grow late, and they had to go back to Camp Two. The next day they went up again. After another long search they had the idea that it might be possible to swing across on a rope, and Asper, the youngest in the party, made the try. It was no good, though. From a rope fastened to the lower rim of the crevasse he was able to swing the whole way across, but he could not get a hold either with his fingers or his axe on the smooth ice of the far side, and each time he swung back against the lower wall with a crash.

After a while he had to give up. But the Swiss continued their efforts, for if they were stopped here like Shipton it would be the end of all their hopes and dreams. And at last they found a way. In one section of the crevasse they saw, about sixty feet down, a sort of shelf or platform, by which a man might be able to cross over to the farther wall, and the wall at this particular point did not look too steep to be climbed. Once more it was Asper who made the attempt. His companions lowered him carefully to the platform, he managed the crossing all right, and then, as they had hoped, he succeeded in hauling and hacking his way up until he came out on the upper rim. At that altitude the work had been so exhausting that for several minutes he could only lie there in the snow, trying to regain his strength and breath; but once he was all right again, *everything* was all right. For with one man across there was no longer any problem. The rope between him and the others was made secure. Other ropes were thrown over. A whole rope bridge was built. And soon what had looked like an impossible crossing was the easiest sort of operation for both men and loads.

It was a great victory. We were almost as happy as if we were already standing on the summit of Everest. For now we had gone farther than anyone before us and were the first of all men to enter the Western Cwm. Aha, Angtharkay, I thought, that's twenty rupees you owe me! But I am sorry to say that I have not yet collected it.

The sahibs went on to establish Camp Three, and the loads came up behind them. There were two and a half tons altogether to be brought from the base into the cwm, and at forty-five pounds a load, which at this altitude was all that could safely be carried, this meant about 125 separate porter-trips. Now it was I, not Dittert, who was the flea, going up and down, up and down, seeing that the routes and schedules were right. But I had fine help from the other senior Sherpas—among them Sarki, Ajiba, and my old friend Dawa Thondup—and even the youngest and most inexperienced of our boys did everything that was expected of him.

To give an idea of how complicated it all was, I will quote a few lines from Dittert sahib's notes:

1st May. Twelve Sherpas to go up to Camp II. Six of them to sleep at II with Aila and Pasang, who are already there. Thus eight Sherpas this evening at II. The other six to come down again to I, where Sarki and Ajiba will rest for to-day.

2nd May. Six Sherpas to go up to II, Sarki and Ajiba Sherpas at II to take up the first units to Camp III.

3rd May. Four Sherpas to ascend to II. Ten Sherpas to ascend from II to III.

And so on, day after day.

We were now at almost 20,000 feet, and some of the Swiss were beginning to feel the thinness of the air—especially Asper and Roch, who had worked very hard at the first crossing of the crevasse. One evening, I remember, they were sitting round talking about it, and some one said there was no need to worry about it: every one felt bad until they were acclimatized—even the Sherpas.

"Except this one," some one else said, pointing at me.

"Oh, him! He's got three lungs."

"The higher he goes the better he feels."

They laughed. And I laughed too. But the strange thing was that the last part of it, at least, was true. It had always been true in the mountains that the farther I went the more strongly I went, the better I felt in my legs and lungs and heart. What it is that makes this so I do not know. But it is there. As surely as the mountains are there. And it is this, I think, that has made possible what I have done; that has given me not only the strength, but the will, to go on; that has made my life in the high places not only a thing of work and struggle, but of love. Looking up on that evening through the cold, darkening air, I felt inside me a wave of strength, of warmth, of happiness. And I thought, Yes, I feel well. And it is going well. . . . I looked at Lambert. "*Ça va bien*," I said, smiling. . . . Perhaps this time—this time at last—we would go on and on until the dream came true.

There we were in the cwm, where no man—no living thing except an occasional bird—had ever been before. It was a deep, snow-filled valley, about four and a half miles long and two miles wide, with Everest on the left, Nuptse on the right, and the white walls of Lhotse rising straight ahead. Once you are really close to a mountain, it is hard to see much of it, and it was that way now with Everest, with its whole upper part lost in the sky above us. But we knew which way we must go to get there, for there was only one possible way—along the length of the cwm to the foot of Lhotse, and then up the steep snow-slopes on its left to the great saddle called the South Col which joined the peaks of the two mountains. After that .. . But that was something we hardly dared think about. The first thing was to get to the col.

For three weeks we lived and worked in the Western Cwm. But the Swiss did not call it that. They had a better name for it—the Valley of Silence. Sometimes, of course, the wind would howl. Once in a while there was a great roaring as an avalanche fell from the heights above us. But mostly there was only a great snowy still-ness, in which the only sounds were our own voices, our own breathing, the crunch of our boots, and the creaking of the pack-straps. We set up Camp Four, our advance base, near the middle of the cwm, and Camp Five near the foot of Lhotse. Every few days there was a storm that kept us pinned down in our tents; but mostly we were able to move according to schedule, and this was of the greatest importance. For, like all spring Everest expedi-tions, we were in a race with the monsoon, and we had to be not only up, but down and off the mountain, before it struck.

Camp Five was at about 22,640 feet, the South Col more than three thousand higher. The route selected for reaching it slanted upward from the head of the cwm, followed a deep couloir in the ice, and then ran along a great out-cropping of rock which the Swiss named the Éperon des Genevois, or Geneva Spur. As in the icefall, there had to be much reconnoitring, much trying and failing, long days of step-cutting and rope-fixing, in which sahibs and Sherpas both took their turns. By this time I was working mostly with Lambert. There was nothing official about it; no one had ordered it that way. It had just seemed to happen.

And I was happy about it, for we got along fine and made a strong team. By the beginning of the last week in May all the preparations had been made. A supply-dump had been established half-way up to the col; some of the climbers had gone still higher, almost to the top of the Geneva Spur; and now we were ready to try for the col itself. The team that was chosen to make the first effort— and also, if we got there, the first attempt on the summit —consisted of Lambert, Aubert, Flory, and myself, and with us went the Sherpas Pasang Phutar, Phu Tharke, Da Namgyal, Ajiba, Mingma Dorje, and Ang Norbu. My own job was now a double one. As from the beginning, I was still sirdar of the Sherpas, with the responsibility of seeing that they got their loads to their destination; but now I was also one of the climbing team and a real expedition member. It was an honour I was well aware of—the greatest honour that had ever been paid me—and in my heart I swore that I would prove myself worthy.

We made one start on May the 24th, but were turned back by bad weather. Then we set off again the next day, and this time kept going. We followed steps that had already been cut, and our loads were not heavy; so for a while we made good time. But after an hour we had our first bad luck when Ajiba had a sudden attack of fever, and there was no question but that he had to go back. Luckily we had not gone so far that he was unable to do it alone, and while he descended the rest of us divided up his load and went on. Towards midday we reached the supply-dump at the half-way point, and here we added to our loads many of the things that had already been brought. These included tents, food, fuel, and oxygen cylinders, but we were just carrying the oxygen, not using it. We had only enough with us to use near the very top of the mountain, where it might not be possible to live without it.

We moved on for another four hours—eight altogether since we had left the cwm. The 25,680-foot peak of Nuptse, behind us, was now no higher than we were; we were already well up alongside the rocks of the Geneva Spur; the col was not far away. But the sun was sinking, and it was getting terribly cold. After struggling on a little farther Ang Norbu and Mingma Dorje stopped, dropped their loads, and said they were going down, because they were exhausted and afraid of frostbite. I began to argue with them; but the sahibs said, "No, they have done their best. Let them go." And they were right. When a man has done his best—and when he is in such a position as we were—he himself must be the only judge of what he will do, and to make him do otherwise may result in his injury or death. So the two of them went down. Again the rest of us shared out the extra loads; but we could carry only a small part of them, and the bulk we had to leave to be brought up later. Suddenly something whipped past my face. It was Aubert's sleeping-bag, that had somehow got loose during the repacking. The wind carried it like a great wobbling bird far out into space.

We went on for another hour. And another. Then it grew dark, and, though we were very close, we knew we could not reach the South Col that day. Stopping, we dug out a platform in the steep snow and ice and set up two tents. The three sahibs crawled into one; Pasang Phutar, Phu Tharke, Da Namgyal, and I into the other. The wind rose, and many times seemed about to carry us away. But we managed to hold ourselves down, and I succeeded, after many attempts, in making some hot soup. Then we tried to sleep, but it was too cold. In the tiny tent we lay almost on top of one another, trying to get some warmth into our bodies, and the night seemed to go on for ever. Then at last it was morning again—and a clear morning. We looked up, and the col was very close. To-day we would reach it.

Only four of us started up—Lambert, Aubert, Flory, and myself. Phu Tharke and Da Namgyal went down to bring up the loads that we had had to leave below, and Pasang waited for them at the bivouac. The three Swiss and I moved up again—and up—but this time it was not for too long, and at about ten o'clock there came a great moment. The ice and rock flattened out before us; we had reached the top of the Geneva Spur, and there before us, at last, was the South Col. Indeed, it was not only before us, but *below* us, for the top of the spur is about 500 feet above it, on the Lhotse side, and we now had to go down to it just then. While the sahibs continued, taking my pack with them, I turned and descended the way we had come, to meet the three other Sherpas and help them carry up the loads. I had hoped to meet them part of the way down, but this didn't happen, and I had to go all the way to the bivouac. Phu Tharke and Da Namgyal had come back all right with the loads from below, but had made no start to go farther, and Pasang Phutar, who had stayed at the bivouac all along, was lying in his tent and moaning.

"I'm ill," he told me. "I'm ill and going to die."

"No, you're not," I answered. "You're going to be all right. You're going to get up and carry a load to the South Col."

He said he couldn't. I said he must. We argued, and I swore at him, and then I began slapping and kicking him to prove to him he wasn't dead. For it was a different thing now from when the others had turned back below. If the loads did not get up to the col the three sahibs there would surely die. And if I left Pasang where he was he too would die—and this time not only in his imagination. He was ill, yes. He was exhausted and miserable. But he could still move. And he had to move.

"Come on! Come on, Jockey!" I yelled at him. ("Jockey" was what we all called him, because he was little and often used to ride horses at the Darjeeling race-track.) And at last I got him up and out of the tent. We slung on our loads and started off. We climbed and crawled and staggered and pushed and pulled, and at last the four of us got up to the top of the spur, and then down to the col. By this time Phu Tharke and Da Namgyal were almost as done in as Pasang, and all they could do was get their tent up and creep inside. Luckily, though, my own "third lung" was still working fine; so, since there was still much food and equipment left at the bivouac place, I went down alone twice more and brought it all up. Now at last we had everything with us that we were supposed to have, and could make our attempt for the top.

I have been in many wild and lonely places in my life, but never anywhere like the South Col. Lying at 25,850 feet between the final peaks of Everest and Lhotse, it lacks even the softness of snow, and is simply a bare, frozen plain of rock and ice, over which the wind roars with never a minute's stop. We were already almost as high as any mountain that had ever been climbed, but above us Everest's summit ridge rose up and up, as if it were another mountain in itself. The best route seemed to lead first up a long slope of snow, and then out on to the ridge itself; but how it would go we would not be able to tell until we

got there. And the very top we could not even see, because
it was hidden behind the snowy bump of a slightly lower
south summit.

Night came. The wind howled. Lambert and I shared
a tent, and did our best to keep each other warm. It was
not quite so bad a night as the one before—but bad enough
—and in the morning it was plain that the other three
Sherpas were finished. Jockey was still talking about
dying, and by now seemed really very ill; and the others
were not much better off. The Swiss knew that if we were
to have any chance of reaching the summit we must set up
still another camp—the seventh—on the ridge above us,
and they offered Phu Tharke and Da Namgyal special
rewards if they would try to make the carry. But the two
refused. Not only their bodies were worn out, but their
spirits too; and, besides not being willing to go higher
themselves, they begged me not to do it. I was as determined one way, however, as they were the other, and
finally things were worked out in the only possible manner.
We got Jockey to his feet, tied him tightly on the rope
between Phu Tharke and Da Namgyal, and the three of
them started down, while the three sahibs and I made our
preparations to go up. Without the others to help with the
loads we could not carry nearly as much as was needed for
Camp Seven, and our prospects for success looked slim.
But there was nothing we could do about it.

So we started off—Aubert and Flory on one rope,
Lambert and I on another. We climbed and climbed,
hour after hour, up from the col along the steep snow-slope
to the base of the south-east ridge, and then on up the
ridge itself. The weather was clear, and the mountain
itself now protected us from the west wind; but the going
was very slow, both because of the altitude and the prob-

lems of finding a safe route. We had only one tent with us, which I carried, and enough food for one day, and each of us also carried a small tank of oxygen, this being the first time in my mountain experience that I had ever used it. But the oxygen did not do us much good, because the apparatus would work only when we were resting or standing still, and not when we were actually climbing, which, of course, was when we needed it most. Still we kept going. To 27,000 feet, and then farther. Now I have broken my own record, I thought. We are higher than I was at Camp Six, on the other side of the mountain, in 1938. . . . But there were still almost two thousand feet to go.

At about 27,500 feet we stopped. We had gone as far as we could that day. As I have said, we were travelling very light, and I think it had been the sahibs' intention only to reconnoitre that day, dump the tent and a few supplies, and then come back up again when more porters were available. But the weather was almost perfect. Lambert and I were not too tired. I saw a small, almost level place where the tent could be pitched, pointed to it, and said, "Sahib, we ought to stay here to-night." Lambert smiled at me, and I could tell he had been thinking the same thing. Aubert and Flory came up behind us, the three talked it over, and it was decided that the first two would go down while Lambert and I stayed there. And in the morning, if the weather was still good, we would make our try for the top.

Aubert and Flory dumped their few things. "Take care of yourselves," they told us—and there were tears in their eyes. Like Lambert and me, they were in good shape. It could have been they, instead of us, who stayed there, and they would have had as good a chance of success. But there was only the one tent and very little food, and they made the sacrifice without complaint. That is the mountain way.

They went down. They became tiny specks and disappeared. Lambert and I pitched the little tent, gasping and stumbling with the exertion; but as soon as we stopped working we felt better again, and the weather was so fine that we were able, for a while, to sit outside in the fading sunlight. With our different languages, we could not talk much. But there was no need to talk. Once I pointed up and said in English, "To-morrow—you and I." And Lambert grinned and said, "*Ça va bien!*" Then it grew dark and colder, and we crawled into the tent. We had no stove, but we were not hungry, and all we ate was a little cheese, which we washed down with snow that I melted over a candle. Also we had no sleeping-bags, and we lay close together, slapping and rubbing each other to keep the circulation going. This worked better for me, I think, than it did for Lambert, for I am of normal size, while he is so big and husky that I could warm only a small bit of him at a time. Still, it was not himself but me that he was concerned about—and especially that I should not get frostbitten feet. "For me it is all right," he said. "I have no toes. But you hang on to yours!"

There was no sleep. But we did not want to sleep. Lying still, without any bags to protect us, we probably would have frozen to death. So we just slapped and rubbed, rubbed and slapped, and slowly, slowly the hours passed, until at last there was a faint grey light in the tent. Stiff and cold, we crawled out and looked about; and what we saw was not good, for the weather had worsened. It was not wholly bad—there was no storm—but the clearness was gone, clouds filled the sky to the south and west, and the wind, rising, blew sharp grains of ice into our faces.

We hesitated a few moments, but, as usual, there was no need for words. Lambert jerked his thumb at the ridge with a wink, and I nodded, smiling. We had gone too far to give up. We must make our try.

It seemed to take hours to get our crampons fastened on with our numb hands. But at last we were on our way. Up—up—very slowly, almost creeping—three steps and a stop, two steps and a stop, one step and a stop. We had three tanks of oxygen between us, but, as before, they were of no use while we were moving, and after a while we dropped them to relieve ourselves of the weight. Every twenty yards or so we changed places in the lead, so as to share the harder work of breaking the trail, and also so that one of us could rest and breathe deeply while letting the other pass. An hour went by. A second and a third hour. Mostly, the climbing itself was not too hard, but we had to be very careful of our route, for on one side of the ridge was a great precipice, and on the other a cornice of snow overhanging a whole ocean of space. Then at times the ridge steepened, and we had to cut steps; and at this sort of climbing Lambert was wonderfully good, because his short feet, with no toes, allowed him to stand on the tiniest places, just like a goat.

Another hour passed. It seemed like a day—or a week. The weather was growing still worse, with waves of mist and wind-driven snow. Even my "third lung" was beginning to have trouble, my throat was dried up and aching with thirst, and some of the time, in the steep snow, we were so tired that we had to crawl on all fours. Once Lambert turned and said something, but I could not understand him. Then, a while later, he spoke again; under his goggles and thick wind-cream he was grinning; and this time I understood him all right.

"*Ça va bien!*" he was saying.

"*Ça va bien!*" I answered back.

It was not true. It was not going well, and we both knew it. But that was how things were between us. When things were good it was *ça va bien!* And when they weren't it was *ça va bien* just the same.

At a time like this you think of many things. I thought of Darjeeling, of home, of Ang Lahmu and the girls. I thought of Dittert and his second team of climbers now coming up below us, and that if we didn't get to the top, perhaps they would do better. I thought, No, we ourselves will get there—and can do it! But if we do it, can we get down again? I thought of Mallory and Irvine, and how they had disappeared for ever, on the other side of the mountain, at just about the height we must be at now. . . . Then I stopped thinking. My brain went numb. I was just a machine that moved and stopped, moved and stopped, moved and stopped.

Then we stopped and did not move again. Lambert stood motionless, hunched in the wind and driving snow, and I knew he was working things out. I tried to work them out too, but it was even harder to think than to breathe. I looked down. We had come—how far? About 650 vertical feet, Lambert reckoned later; and it had taken us five hours. I looked up. And there was the south summit about 500 more feet above us. Not *the* summit. Just the south summit. And beyond it . . .

I believe in God. I believe that in men's hardest moments He sometimes tells them what to do, and that He did it then for Lambert and me. We could have gone farther. We could perhaps have gone to the top. But we could not have got down again. To go on would be to die. . . . And we did not go on. We stopped and turned back. . . .

We had reached an altitude of about 28,250 feet—the nearest men had ever come to the top of Everest, the highest anyone had ever climbed in the world. But it was still not enough. We had given all we had, and it was not enough. We turned without speaking. We descended without speaking. Down the long ridge, past the high camp, along the ridge again, along the snow-slope. Slowly —slowly. Down—down—down. . . .

That was all for Lambert and me. The next day, with Aubert and Flory, we went down from the col to the Western Cwm, while the second team of four Swiss and five Sherpas, under Dittert, went up past us to try their luck. At first they did better than we, getting from the cwm to the col in a single day's climbing; but there their luck left them. Altitude sickness struck both sahibs and Sherpas. The wind grew stronger, and the cold deeper. And after three days and nights they had to come down, without having been able even to start an ascent of the summit ridge.

Well, it had been a great effort.

And I had made a great friend.

15

EVEREST WITH THE SWISS: AUTUMN

B UT it is autumn," Ang Lahmu said.
"Yes, it is autumn."
"You have never gone before at this time of year."

"No, never before."

"Then why are you going now?"

"Because we must try again," I said. "We must try everything."

For many years there had been talk of going to Everest in the autumn. During the winter, of course, it could not be dreamed of. In the summer there were the storms and avalanches of the monsoon. But in the autumn it was at least a possibility, and there were those who thought the weather might be even better than in the spring. The idea was never tried out, though, until in 1952, by the Swiss. They could not wait until the next spring, because for them there would be no next spring: for 1953 the Nepali Government had promised Everest to the British. So if the Swiss were to have another chance it must be now—again in 1952—while they alone had permission to go to the mountain. Back at home that summer they talked things over and made their decision. Yes, they would try again. . . .

Only two sahibs from the spring expedition were able to come back—Dr Gabriel Chevalley, who was now the leader, and Raymond Lambert, whom I do not think they could have kept away if they had tied him up and sat on him. Besides them, there were four new climbers—Arthur Spöhel, Gustave Gross, Ernest Reiss, and Jean Busio—and a climber-photographer, Norman Dyhrenfurth, the son of the famous Swiss Himalayan explorer, who was now an American citizen. Also, I was asked to come too, this time not only as the sirdar of the Sherpas, but as a full expedition member, and it was an honour I was proud to accept. As before, I collected my Sherpa team in Darjeeling—many of them the same men who had been with us in the spring—and by early September we were back in Kathmandu.

In membership the party was a little smaller than the first one, but in amount of equipment it was bigger, for the Swiss had run short of some items in the spring, and this time, with the likelihood of even colder weather, they wanted to be fully prepared. As a consequence, it was a procession of almost four hundred men—sahibs, Sherpas, and Nepali porters—who set off for the mountain; and if I have talked before of a brigade going off to war, this was like a whole army. I have never yet seen an expedition get under way without some sort of mix-up or disappointment, and this time it had to do with Dyhrenfurth. Having an American passport, he had had trouble in getting his Nepali visa, and was still in India waiting for it to come through. The Sherpa Ang Dawa was assigned to wait for him in Kathmandu for two weeks, and then, if Dyhrenfurth got in all right, the two would come along after us.

Through the middle and end of September we marched

up and down, up and down again, across the hills of Nepal. The monsoon, which had been late in starting, was also late in ending, and most of the time the weather was terrible, with more rain and mud than I have ever seen in my life. Because of this a good many men fell ill, including Dr Chevalley. And as we approached Solo Khumbu things got really bad. For now we were reaching higher altitudes; there was not only wetness, but bitter cold; and the Nepali porters, who did not have expedition clothing, had a hard time of it. On the fourteenth day we crossed a high pass, at almost 13,000 feet, called the Shamung-Namrepki-La, which in the old days used to be called "the pass where your hat touched the sky." And here the weather was as bad as on a real mountain in a storm. Several of the Nepalese collapsed, and later two of them died—which made a sad beginning for the expedition.

As a result, many of the other porters left. But we sent ahead to Khumbu for Sherpa helpers, and by the end of the month, when we reached Namche Bazar, the monsoon was over and the sky was blue and clear. Once more we Sherpas had a reunion with our families and friends in our home country. I visited my mother and sisters. There were dances and feasts and bowls of *chang*. Then, as before, we hired many local Sherpas to take the place of the Nepalese, and we and our loads moved on towards the mountain. I do not think I have seen the top of Everest clearer than in those days, with its black rock swept almost clean of snow by the wind, and its white plume streaming out into the sky.

Again base camp was pitched near the head of the Khumbu Glacier, and we began working our way up through the icefall. It had changed a lot over the summer, so that we had to find a new route; but with the experience we had already had with it it was not so difficult as before. Also we were prepared for the crevasses. From Namche Bazar we had brought up a supply of logs and timber, which we used as bridges over the big cracks in the ice; and for the great crevasse near the head of the icefall, which had given us so much trouble in the spring, we had a long wooden ladder that made everything easy. The rope bridge we had used before was still there where we had fixed it, but because of the snowfall during the summer it was now several feet down in the crevasse.

While we were in this stage of things Dyhrenfurth and Ang Dawa caught up with us, making the party complete. But in another way we were really never complete, for this time, more than on any previous expedition, some one was always ill. For a while the worst off was the Sherpa Ang Norbu, who had some sort of infection that made a great swelling in his neck. Dr Chevalley had been filling him full of penicillin, but this did not seem to do much good, and he decided to operate. So the mess tent at Camp One was turned into a sort of hospital, and Reiss, Spöhel, and I had the job of holding Ang Norbu down while the doctor cut into his neck. I cannot say it was something I much enjoyed: it was hard to believe that so much blood and pus could be inside just one man. But the main thing was that the operation was a success, and after a few days Ang Norbu was all right again.

Above the icefall we came out into the Western Cwm, or Valley of Silence. Only it was not so silent now, but filled day and night with the sound of the wind. Sometimes we were not actually in the wind: we would only hear it as a roaring on the peaks far above us. But then it would come down. It would hit us, not like moving air, but like some sort of terrible wild animal let loose by the gods, and until it stopped we could not move or work or do anything except barely keep alive. All the time, of course, we were getting higher. All the time it was getting later in the autumn. Our equipment was excellent. Our boots, especially—almost knee-high and made of reindeer-hide—were the best I had ever seen, and no one suffered frostbite. But already we were wondering, with the wind and cold so bad down there in the cwm, if it would be possible to live at all higher up.

Still, by the end of October we were in Camp Five, near the foot of the Lhotse face, and ready to begin the fight for the South Col. It was the plan to follow roughly the same route as in the spring—up the ice-slopes and couloirs to the Geneva Spur—and, dividing into teams, we went to work cutting steps and fixing ropes. But we had hardly started when, on October the 31st, there was an accident. Dr Chevalley and Spöhel, with several Sherpas, were on a steep slope not far from Camp Five, roped together in four teams of three men each. Suddenly there was a rumbling up above, and a mass of loose ice came tumbling down on them. It was not a big avalanche—just a few fragments that had broken off higher up the slope—and not the sort of thing that would usually be very serious. As it was, eleven of the twelve men were all right. They pushed in as close to the slope as they could and ducked their heads, so that the worst that happened was a few pieces of ice bouncing off their shoulders. But the Sherpa Mingma Dorje, who was on a rope with Ajiba and my young nephew Topgay, must have looked up at just the wrong moment, for he was hit full in the face. A moment later he was hanging limp on the rope, with the other two holding him up, moaning softly and with his face full of blood.

On the steep ice it was impossible to move quickly, and it took a while for the other ropes to manœuvre into position where they could help him. Finally Dr Chevalley and Spöhel, with their Sherpas, were able to do so, and they were slowly getting Mingma Dorje down towards Camp Five—when a second accident happened. This was to the fourth rope, consisting of the three Sherpas Aïla, Norbu, and Mingma Hrita, and started when one of them, perhaps upset by the first accident, missed his footing and slipped. Anyhow, in the next instant all three were falling head over heels down the slope, and did not stop until they reached level ground about two hundred yards below.

Again it took a while before help could be brought. The others still had to work their way down slowly with Mingma Dorje. But at last every one was at the bottom, Dr Chevalley administered first aid to the injured, and they were laid out on air-mattresses, which were brought up from Camp Four. Of the three who had fallen Mingma Hrita had a broken collar-bone, Aïla and Da Norbu only bad bumps and bruises. They would probably not be of much further use to the expedition, but they would be all right. Mingma Dorje, however, was in a bad way, for it was now discovered that it was not only his face that had been struck by the falling ice. A sharp sliver had gone into his body between the neck and collar-bone, piercing his lung. And a few hours later, in spite of all Dr Chevalley's efforts, he died.

Along with most of the rest of the party, I had been at Camp Four when the accidents happened. But the sad news was soon brought down, and we went up quickly. All the Sherpas, of course, were badly upset; but the Swiss, if anything, were even more so, for they took their obligations to their porters very seriously, and felt a deep responsibility. Indeed, they asked me to talk with the men and report back to them, and said that if the majority, in view of the tragedy, wished to go no farther they would abide by this decision. So far into the night we Sherpas discussed the situation. No one, to be sure, was very happy. Some were very pessimistic about our chances. But in the end they all agreed that they could not let their sahibs down. They would go on as far as they could. The next day the three injured men were taken down towards base camp, and Mingma Dorje was buried in the moraine at one side of the cwm between Camps Four and Five. Above him we raised a tall monument of stones, and at its foot placed a wooden cross, carved with his name and the date. Then we said good-bye to our friend—the first man to die on Everest since the lone climber Maurice Wilson in 1934.

The first thing that was decided was that a new route must be found to the South Col. Even in the spring there had been worry about ice-falling in the couloir below the Geneva Spur; and now it had happened—a comrade had been killed—and we were not going to risk any more lives needlessly. So for long days and weeks we worked on a different approach—no longer straight up from the cwm to the col, but over to the right, on the great snow-slopes of the Lhotse face, where the danger of avalanches seemed less great. One thing we had learned on the first expedition was that the climb from cwm to col was too much to be made in a single day. Even if we had stayed on the old route we would have set up a new camp at about the half-way point; and on the new route, which was considerably longer, we decided to establish two. So once again came the hard, drudging work of all big mountain-climbs—the searching-out of a way, the cutting of steps, the fixing of ropes, the carrying-up of the heavy loads. Altogether we attached almost 2500 feet of fixed rope on this section of the mountain, and slowly the two little camps (Six and Seven) took shape on the white walls above.

We kept going. We climbed always higher. Lambert and I, of course, were again working as a team, and much of the time we were out in front clearing the trail. We were both in good condition—"*Ça va bien! Ça va bien!*" —and during much of the work we used oxygen, for which our apparatus was much better than it had been in the spring. But men could work, or even live, only for a short time at such heights. And in such wind—such cold. For day by day now it was getting more wintry. There were no clouds or snow-storms, as before the monsoon. The sky stayed brilliantly clear. But the coldness was so deep that it bit through even our warmest clothing into our flesh and bones. And worst of all, as the autumn advanced, the days got shorter and shorter. Even before two in the afternoon the sun would disappear behind the summit ridge of Nuptse, and from then on until well into the next morning there was no minute of relief from the icy bitterness.

We would come down, go up, come down again. One night at Camp Four, in the cwm, a terrible windstorm arose, and Ajiba and I, who were sharing a tent, were hardly able to keep it from blowing away. Then, hearing a feeble cry from outside, we managed to struggle out, and found that Norman Dyhrenfurth's tent, which was next to ours, had gone down completely. At this time Dyhrenfurth was one of those on the sick list. He had both laryngitis and a high fever, and had lost so much strength that he could not now get out from under the collapsed canvas that lay on top of him. Ajiba and I wrestled with it, and finally got it up again, but not until the tent, and us with it, had almost blown away across the cwm.

By this time the weather was having a bad effect on almost all of us—not only physically, but in our spirits. Some of the Sherpas had lost all heart for their work, and could think of nothing but getting down out of the wind and the cold; and sometimes I had to have long arguments, and even get angry, before I could get them to do their jobs. Also, some one was always getting ill, or pretending to get ill; the base camp on the glacier was like a hospital; and at one time we were so short of men on the Lhotse face that I had to go all the way down there to bring some back with me. At the base there was much talk about a *yeti* that had been seen a few days before by one of the low-level porters, near the place where we had found tracks during the spring expedition. According to the man, the *yeti* was between four and five feet tall, had heavy brown hair, and walked upright on its two hind legs. It had a pointed head, broad cheek-bones, and big jaws, which it opened menacingly, staring at the man from close range and looking as if it were going to charge. Instead, though, it had suddenly made a sort of hissing noise, turned, and run away, and that was the last that had been seen of it. I talked to the porter who claimed to have had this experience, and saw no reason to disbelieve his story. In fact, it helped confirm the opinion I have already given that the *yeti* is some form of big mountain ape.

But we were having problems enough on Everest without getting mixed up with *yetis*. "Come on! Come on!" I told the men at base camp. "We have a mountain to climb. Get going!" Finally, I had a fair number rounded up, and led them back through the icefall and cwm to continue work on the Lhotse face.

In another week or so everything was ready. The steps and ropes. The high camps and equipment. But if we were to get to the South Col—and higher—we must do it quickly, for it was already past the middle of November, and soon it would be full winter. For the first attempt a party of ten was assigned, with Lambert as leader, Reiss and myself as the other climbers, and the seven Sherpas who were in the best condition to help with the loads. These were Ang Tempa, Pemba Sundar, Ang Nyima, Ang Namgyal, Goundin, Pemba, and Topgay. Most of them were young and inexperienced, but they had withstood the wind and cold better than many of the older men; and I am proud to say that the youngest of all was my nephew Topgay, who at the time was only seventeen years old.

From the cwm we climbed to Camp Six. From there to Seven. Then on November the 19th we went on towards the col. The going here was not terribly steep, for at Camp Seven we were already high on the Lhotse face, and the rest of the route was mostly a diagonal traverse across to the top of the Geneva Spur and the col beyond it. But our progress was slow, because we were now breaking fresh trail, and several times the porters had to wait while Lambert, Reiss, and I went ahead to cut steps and string ropes. We had started off at about nine in the morning. At four-thirty in the afternoon we gained the high point of the climb at the top of the spur, and a little while later reached the col itself—for the second time in one year. It was getting dark, and the cold and wind were indescribable. For what seemed like hours more we staggered round, trying to set up our camp near the still-visible remains of the spring one; and when at last two tents were up the seven Sherpas piled into them and disappeared. There was no use trying to argue with them. Lambert, Reiss, and I had had the benefit of oxygen on the climb. They had not, and they were done in. So the two sahibs and I worked away at the other three tents until we had them up and secured. Then it was our turn for shelter and rest. Almost all our food was frozen like stone, but I managed to heat up some chocolate and pass it round. Then came another night at the last limit of the earth.

Above the cwm we had been using a double thickness of tents, one inside another, but up here even this hardly helped; and the two tents rubbing together in the dry, icy wind filled the tiny sleeping space with sparks of electricity that crackled round our heads. Lambert had a small thermometer, and it went down to thirty below zero. He estimated later that the wind had been about sixty miles an hour—not only in gusts, but in a steady gale. It was hard even for him to say, "*Ça va bien!*" Then at last morning came, and the gale was still blowing; but nevertheless we made ready to move on. We *had* to move, or else freeze to death. For breakfast we succeeded in making a little tea; that was all. Then we started off. The other Sherpas wanted to go down, not up, and one could scarcely blame them; but only one of them—Goundin—was actually ill, and the others finally agreed to try to go higher. With the two extra camps on the Lhotse face, the col camp was now Number Eight. On their backs they carried the equipment for the small Camp Nine that we hoped to set up on the summit ridge.

But on their backs was where Camp Nine stayed. It was already eleven-thirty before we were organized to leave. It took us almost another hour just to cross the col and begin the ascent of the snow-slope that leads up to the ridge. Flattened against a wall of ice were the remains of an eagle, and, though we were scarcely flying, it was all we could do to keep from being flattened out ourselves. Using our oxygen, Lambert, Reiss, and I went a little ahead of the others. Six months before, even with bad oxygen apparatus, the Bear and I had had little trouble with this part of the climb. But now, though the apparatus was good, it was of little help. The wind was too much. The cold was too much. Under our three pairs of gloves our fingers had lost all feeling. Our lips, then our noses, then our whole faces, began turning blue. Behind us the line of struggling Sherpas had almost ceased to move at all. There was only one sane—one even possible—thing to do. That was to turn back, and we knew it. But for Lambert and me it was a terrible decision. For this was our second try; it had become the hope of our lives that we could climb Everest together; and if we turned back now, who could tell if we would ever have another chance? Left to ourselves, we might have tried to go on. I do not say that we would have—or could have. Only that we *might* have; the desire was so strong. But there were the staggering Sherpas behind us. There was Reiss beside us, grimly shaking his head. We stopped, and for a few moments stood where we were, crouched over like animals against the fierceness of the wind. If it had not been so cold that the tears would have frozen before they left the eyes I think that I might have wept. I could not look at Lambert, and he did not look at me. Silently we turned and started down.

The Swiss later chose a word for what had happened to us. They said we had been "purged" from the mountain. And in that purging—once we had turned back—there was never the slightest hope that we could get back up again. At the very point where we gave up, about a thousand feet above the col, we dumped most of the equipment that we were carrying. At the col camp itself we stopped only long enough to pick up Goundin (who would have been dead of cold if he had stayed there much longer), and left behind almost another three hundred pounds of gear that we had carried up so painfully the day before. Nothing mattered now except to get down out of that hell that was so close to heaven. We were in a race with the cold and the wind—and with death.

We spent that night, almost prostrated, at Camp Seven, where we were met by Dr Chevalley. And the next day we got down to Camp Five, in the cwm. There was no talk of another try; I do not think any of us would have had the strength to climb another ten feet upward. All that was in our minds was to get down, down and away from the cold, where a man could breathe, where he could eat and sleep, where he could warm his hands and his feet and his bones. And at last we did it—along the cwm, down the icefall, and on to the glacier, which, after where we had come from, seemed almost like the plains of India. Miraculously there had been no serious frostbite, and no one lost so much as a single finger or toe. Or perhaps it had not been a miracle, but rather the fine quality of our clothes and equipment. Anyhow, there we all were— except poor Mingma Dorje. We had been purged. We had been routed. But we were still alive.

In Namche Bazar I saw my mother and sisters again. After the news of Mingma Dorje's death had reached the village one of my sisters had become worried about me, and, with her children, had climbed all the way to Camp One, at the foot of the icefall, carrying a basket of things that she thought I might need. I had not seen her then, because I was high on the mountain, but now I thanked her with all my heart. "I'll see you all again next year," I told my family, trying to be cheerful. But what the next year would bring I, of course, had no idea.

By early December we were on the homeward trip through the hills of Nepal. Everest sank away behind us, wrapped in winter storms. "I am sick at heart," Dr Chevalley wrote in his diary as he thought about our second failure; and we all felt much the same. But mixed with our sadness, I think, was also a certain quiet pride, for we knew that in the conditions we had faced no men could have done more than we did. We marched on. It rained and rained. Then, to make everything wrong, I sprained my ankle, in the first 'accident' I had ever had on an Everest expedition, and for the rest of the way I had to hobble along using two ski-poles as crutches.

All day long we were soaked to the skin. My ankle ached, and I began to feel feverish. If Everest was still my dream it was only a bad one.

16

IT MUST BE NOW

IN Kathmandu we were received almost as if we had succeeded instead of failed. The King himself presented me with the Nepal Pratap Bardhak medal, which was a great honour. But by now I was so ill I hardly knew what was happening. Partly it was malaria, and my fever was high; but even more, I think, it was the strain of two big expeditions in one year. As always, the Swiss were wonderful to me. They flew me out from Kathmandu to Patna, in Northern India, and there I stayed for ten days at the Holy Family Hospital, which is run by American Catholic missionaries.

After leaving me there the Swiss went on home to Europe. The other Sherpas were returning by train to Darjeeling. And I was alone in the hospital. Some of the time my fever was so high I was delirious, and I thought I was back on Everest, fighting the wind and the cold. Then it would pass, and I would lie motionless in bed for hours, too weak even to open my eyes or raise my hand. . . . Yes, it was too much, I thought. Two expeditions. The wind and the cold. And, most of all, being two things at once— a sirdar and a climber. That was too much, both in the work and the responsibility. . . . I lay there, and there was only weakness in my mind and body. Then the fever would come again.

When I left the hospital I had lost sixteen pounds. And a few days later, when I reached Darjeeling, my wife and family were shocked to see me. "You must rest now," Ang Lahmu said. "This whole year you must rest and get back your health." And I think that then at the beginning I just nodded and said nothing, for I hadn't the strength for anything else.

But now it was already 1953. The story of the two Swiss expeditions had become known throughout the world, and I was receiving letters from many countries asking me to go on climbs during the coming spring. Even while I was still in the hospital in Patna a letter had come from a Major Charles Wylie inviting me to go back to Everest with a new British party, of which he would be transport officer; and now, in Darjeeling, Mrs Henderson, of the Himalayan Club, urged me to go with them. "You have been with the English so often," she said. "And they want you so much." But Ang Lahmu was against it, and I was too tired and weak to make a quick decision. Mrs Henderson was patient and understanding, and for a week sent me milk and Ovaltine to help me get back my strength.

I rested. And I thought. I thought about the Swiss and their two great efforts, and of how proud and happy I had been to be with them. Of all the *chilina-nga* I had met— and by now there were many—I liked the Swiss the best, and I think that if they ever come back to Solo Khumbu they will find the trails lined with Sherpas holding welcoming bowls of *chang*. Dearest of all things to my heart would have been going back with them to Everest—to climb high into the sky again with my friend Lambert, and this time, perhaps, to reach our goal. But the Swiss were not going back. They had had their chance, and now in 1953 it would be the British. If they failed the Nepalese Government had promised permission to the French for 1954. It would be three years before the Swiss would have another try, even if some one did not get to the top before then.

And there was certainly a good chance that some one *would* get to the top. In our spring try Lambert and I had come very close. With better oxygen equipment or better weather we would have done it. And now the British were coming with the strongest possible expedition. In 1952, while we were on Everest, a group of them under Shipton, with a few New Zealanders added, had climbed on the near-by mountain Cho Oyu, to gain practice and test new equipment. They would profit greatly from the Swiss pioneering of the route. Most important of all, they would be prepared to make a tremendous effort, for they had always considered Everest *their* mountain, and now it seemed to be slipping away from them. Before them had been the Swiss. Waiting for the next turn would be the French, and then the Swiss again. In the late autumn of 1952 travellers in Solo Khumbu who had come down over the Nangpa La from Tibet had reported that there had been a Russian expedition from Rongbuk, on the north side, at about the same time that we were on the mountain. And the Russians, very likely, might soon be trying again. Certainly the circle was drawing tighter round the top of the highest mountain, and it seemed almost sure that if the British did not win it now they would lose it for ever.

And for myself?

I did not know any of the climbers who would be going this year. In the beginning Eric Shipton led the expedition, but later Colonel John Hunt, of the British Army, who had lived and climbed much in India, but whom I had never met, became the leader. With him would be the best pick of English mountaineers, and two New Zealanders (these would be new *chilina-nga* for me!), one of whom, Edmund Hillary, had been on both the 1951 Everest reconnaissance and the Cho Oyu expedition of 1952. I thought about the trouble there had been in 1951 about *baksheesh* and the payment of the Nepali porters, and I mentioned this to Mrs. Henderson. "But that's one of the reasons it's so important that you go," she answered. "No one can handle the men like you, and if you are with them there will be no such troubles."

"I will decide soon," I told her.

And still I thought about it.

In this story, everywhere, I have been honest, and I will continue to be so. In all honesty, then, I would rather have gone back to Everest with the Swiss. In spite of the way some people have tried to twist things, this does not mean that I dislike the British. I have climbed more with the British than with any other people, and been happy with them; and some of them—men such as Mr Gibson, Major Osmaston, Major White, Mr Tilman, Mr Smythe, Lieutenant Marsh—I have counted among my close and dear friends. But it is still true that the English in general are more reserved and formal than the men of most other countries whom I have known; and especially is this so, I think, with people not of their own race. Perhaps this is because they have so long been rulers in the East, or perhaps it is only something in their own nature. But it is a thing which we Sherpas have had much chance to observe, since we have climbed, in recent years, with men of so many nations. With the Swiss and the French I had been treated as a comrade, an equal, in a way that is not possible for the British. They are kind men; they are brave; they are fair and just, always. But always, too, there is a line between them and the outsider, between sahib and employee, and to such Easterners as we Sherpas, who have experienced the world of 'no line,' this can be a difficulty and a problem.

Yes, that is true, I thought. But how important is it? You have been happy with the British before, and you can be happy again. And, besides, you would not be going to a reception or tea-party, but back to Everest. . . . Everest —your life, your dream. . . . What will happen if you wait for the French or the Swiss? How will you feel if the British climb it and you are not with them? For you, no less than for them, it may be now or never.

You think. Your head spins. You make up your mind, change it, make it up again. I am almost thirty-nine, I thought. I am getting near the end of my 'critical years.' How much longer will I be able to climb high? Or am I already unable, after the strain and sickness I have just been through? I have been to Everest how often? Six times, including Denman. This would be the seventh, and, as with most people, that is held a lucky number among Sherpas. In our dice games, as in the *chilina-ngas*', seven is good. A group of seven is considered good for an undertaking, and seven children as the best number in a family. My mother had seven sons. This would be my seventh trip to Everest. . . .

But I was worried about my health. After a little while at home I was no longer ill, but still weak and underweight, and what would another big expedition—the third in only a little more than a year—do to me? Like the Swiss, the British wanted me both as sirdar and as a climber, and I had already decided that the combination was too much. But how else could I go? I thought about it all so much that I could hardly sleep at night. If it kept up much longer this way I would be ill all over again. So one day I left Toong Soong Busti, went to Mrs. Henderson, and said simply, "Yes, I will go." What I could not tell her—what I find it hard to say even now in the right words—is that I would go because I *had* to go.

Saying yes to Mrs Henderson was one thing, but with Ang Lahmu it was another. "You are too weak," she argued. "You will get ill again, or you will slip on the ice and fall and kill yourself."

"No, I will look out for myself," I told her. "Just like I always have."

"You take too many risks."

"I am paid for climbing. They don't pay me for play. I must do what I am paid for."

"You are a daredevil," Ang Lahmu said. "You care nothing about me or the children, or what happens to us if you die."

"Of course I care, woman. But this is my work—my life. Can't you understand that? You are in charge of the household here, and I don't interfere with that; but when it is a question of Everest no one can interfere with me."

"But you are mad. You will kill yourself on this mountain. You will die."

"All right, I will die." By this time I was getting angry. "If I die I would rather do it on Everest than in your hut!"

I suppose all husbands and wives sometimes talk like that to each other. We got angry, made up, then got angry again. But at last Ang Lahmu saw that I was determined, and she said, "All right; you win."

So that part was settled. But I, no less than she, was concerned about money and how things would go for my family, whether or not I came back. By the old standards I was now being paid very well. My basic salary would be 300 rupees a month, as against 100 to 125 for the regular climbing Sherpas; and if I was killed my family would get 2000 rupees compensation, which was twice as much as with the Swiss, and four times as much as had been usual before that. But things had changed greatly in the world, the cost of living was much higher, and even this would not mean any real security. I talked over my problems with Rabindranath Mitra, a young, well-educated Bengali, who owned a printing-press in Darjeeling, and who, during the past two years, had become my close friend and adviser. And he said that if anything happened to me he would see that a fund was raised to help my family.

Meanwhile I was trying hard to get myself back into good condition. As I had done for many years past, before big expeditions, I got up early in the morning, filled a knapsack with stones, and took long walks up and down the hills round the town. I did not smoke or drink, and kept away from parties, which I usually enjoy. And all the time I was thinking, planning, hoping about what would happen on this, my seventh trip to Everest. "This is the time you must do it," I kept telling myself. "You must do it or die." . . . And then: "Yes, that is all very well, but you cannot do it alone. There must be some one to go with you. On a great mountain you do not leave your companions and go to the top alone. And even if you did, and came back alive, no one would believe you. . . . This time there will be no Lambert. Who will there be?

There will be somebody, and we will go to the top together. We will get there. We *must* get there. I must get to the top or die. . . ."

With Mrs Henderson I picked the Sherpa team of twenty men, which was the number the British wanted. It was a strong team, with most of the men veterans of Everest, either from the Swiss expeditions or from the reconnaissance in 1951. The oldest was my lifelong friend Dawa Thondup, who, though he was now in his late forties and had no objections to a few drinks when he could get hold of them, was still one of the best of all mountain men.[1] And the two youngest were my nephew, Topgay, who had reached the South Col the year before, and a second nephew, Gombu (the son of my sister, Lahmu Kipa), who I was also confident would make a fine high-climber. Remembering the troubles in 1951, and also what Mrs Henderson had said, I told the men there were to be no difficulties or arguments about money matters; no *baksheesh* was to be expected or demanded; and if they had any complaints they should come to me, and I would do my best to satisfy every one. So there I was—a sirdar again, with all a sirdar's problems—and soon, too, I would be a climber as well, and doing the double job that had worn me out with the Swiss. But that was the way it had to be. For a chance to climb Everest I would have been willing to take on any job from dish-washer to *yeti*-keeper.

March the 1st had been set as the day for us to leave Darjeeling, and as it drew near there was much preparation and excitement. Many Sherpanis were coming with us, to go as far as Namche Bazar or even the base camp, and they

---

[1] He was ill, and could not come when the rest of us left Darjeeling, but he joined us later at base camp.

say that after we left Toong Soong Busti was like a de-
serted village. Because the Swiss had got so close the year
before there was much more talk than usual about the
possibility of reaching the top of Everest, and our send-off
was a great one. When I visited the homes of friends to
say good-bye to them they placed the ceremonial scarves
called *khadas* round my shoulders. My friend Mitra (whom
I call Robi Babu) gave me a small Indian flag to take with
me—"to put in the right place," as he said. And my
younger daughter, Nima, gave me a red-and-blue stub of
pencil which she had been using at school, and which I
promised also to put in the "right place," if God willed it
and was good to me. Then it was good-bye. And I was
glad that my leave-taking from my family was in our own
home, and not in a public place, for I do not like displays
of emotion at such a time.

Once more we made the familiar trip—first down to the
plains, then west by train to Raxaul, and from there up
into Nepal. And I think we must have been a colourful
crowd, because we were wearing clothes and carrying
equipment that came from the many expeditions we had
been on before. When we reached Kathmandu some of
the British were already there, and others were arriving
at the same time as ourselves. Besides Colonel Hunt,
Major Wylie, and Hillary, whom I have already mentioned, there were seven other climbers—Tom Bourdillon,
Dr Charles Evans, Alfred Gregory, George Lowe (who,
like Hillary, was from New Zealand), Wilfrid Noyce,
George Band, and Michael Westmacott. Also there were
Dr Michael Ward, the expedition doctor, Griffith Pugh,
a scientist who was to make various tests on us, and Tom
Stobart, who would make a moving picture. Finally
there would be James Morris, the correspondent of *The*

Times, which had put some money into the expedition, but he had not yet arrived at this time.

The British gave us a warm welcome, but unfortunately there were difficulties almost straight away. And here I must say again, as I have said before, that in telling about such troubles I am trying only to be honest, to say what truly happened, and not in any way to make complaints or accusations. It is a Sherpa saying that in a big house there is bound to be some trouble from time to time, and certainly I have never been on a big expedition where everything went smoothly from beginning to end. One thing about this 1953 expedition that made it different from the others was that afterwards it had so much publicity. All sorts of people started twisting the facts for their own purposes, and events sometimes ended up sounding very different from what they really were. In his own book of the expedition Colonel Hunt (now Brigadier Sir John) refers to these various troubles hardly at all; and perhaps he is right, for his is an official account, he is writing as an Englishman for Englishmen, and certainly none of our difficulties were of any importance compared to the climbing of Everest. But each man must tell his story—as he lives his life—from his own point of view. And my story is not 'official.' I am not an Englishman, but a Sherpa. I must tell what I, not some one else, saw and experienced, or my book will have no honesty and no value.

Anyhow, the first difficulty arose on the same day we reached Kathmandu, and it had to do with the Sherpas' sleeping quarters for that night. These were in a garage, formerly a stable, in the grounds of the British Embassy (the climbers being in the Embassy itself), and, especially because there were no toilet facilities, the Sherpas didn't like it at all. I cannot say that I blamed them, for it is a long time since our people have risen above a 'coolie' standard of living; so I presented their complaints to the English, and for a time considered going myself to a hotel, as a form of protest. But it was too late to change the arrangements that night. And, besides, I was interested in quieting the trouble, not making it worse. So I told the Sherpas, "It is only for one night. Let's make the best of it." And after some more murmuring they agreed. They all went to sleep there, and I with them, though I had been offered a room of my own. But the next morning most of them showed their displeasure by using the road in front of the garage as a latrine. This made the Embassy staff really angry, and they were given a lecture; but I don't think anyone was listening very hard.

It was at this time that I had the first of many experiences with the Press that I was to have from then on. As I have said, part of the money for the expedition had been put up by *The Times*, and the British members were not supposed to give information to other newspapers. But word of the garage incident, of course, soon got round, and since I was bound to no such agreement, I was soon almost surrounded by journalists. I told them that what had happened was of no importance; but what you say is one thing, what appears in a paper—I do not mean *The Times*—can be quite another, and I am sorry to say that my statements were twisted to make further trouble. No less than a mountain itself, the Press can raise a man high and drop him down low. That was one of the lessons I was to learn painfully from the climbing of Everest.

A few hours later, though, both the Press and the garage were behind us, and we were taken out in a lorry to Bhadgaon, a few miles east of Kathmandu, where the gear for the expedition was being assembled. Then followed the

usual busy time, dividing up the loads, assigning them to
the hundreds of Nepali porters, and making all the arrangements that are necessary to get a big caravan under way.
Before this happened, however, there was more trouble.
For now it turned out that the Sherpas were not going to
be issued with any of their expedition clothing or equipment, except sleeping-bags, until they reached Solo
Khumbu, and they didn't like this any better than they
had liked the garage. "Why is this?" they demanded.
"On other expeditions we have been given our things
straight away, and we want them this time too." But
Colonel Hunt felt that if they were not issued until later
they would be in better condition for use on the mountain, and once again I found myself in the middle, trying
to make peace. "Why do you make such a fuss over little
things?" I said to the Sherpas. "If you were given all your
things here you would have to carry them yourselves.
This way they are divided up among the Nepali porters."

So at last we got going. As with most large expeditions,
we went in two sections, a day apart, with myself in charge
of transport for the first and Major Wylie for the second.
Major Wylie was a fine man, who spoke Nepali fluently
and was very good with the local porters; but both he and
I had our hands full on the trip in, because we had got off
on the wrong foot, and there was almost constant complaining and grumbling. Now it was about one thing,
now about another. For a while it was mostly about food,
for the British were eating mostly tinned rations that they
had brought with them, but buying local food for the
Sherpas, and the Sherpas thought they should be eating
the same as the sahibs. In some things I thought they were
right. In others I thought they were wrong—and I told
them so. What got me angriest was when they didn't

actually say anything, but just mumbled and grumbled, for it is in my nature to speak out what is on my mind, and I like others to do likewise.

"Come on! Come on! Stop fussing about all these little things," I would tell them. "We have a mountain to climb!"

Up and down we went—up and down—across the hills and valleys and rivers. And in spite of the troubles the mountains were working their usual magic for me, for with every day I was feeling better. For a while I was afraid it had been a mistake for me to come: that my illness had left me too weak to climb high. But now I knew that I was going to be all right, and I gave thanks to God. As I thought of Everest and the great days ahead of us the complaints of my companions sounded like the cackling of so many hens.

My own personal relations with the British were quite satisfactory. True, there was not the informal, easy comradeship there had been with the Swiss. I did not share a tent with one of them, as I had with Lambert, and there was not much joking and horseplay between us. But Colonel Hunt was a fine man and an excellent expedition leader; Hillary, with whom I was already spending much time, was quiet and friendly; and all the others were pleasant and considerate to me. "All right; they are not like the Swiss," I told the grumbling Sherpas. "Why should they be? They are different people. Think more of the mountain and less of your little complaints, and everything will go well."

We arrived in Namche Bazar on March the 25th, and once more there was the big welcome, the songs and dances, the flowing *chang*. Again my mother and family came from Thamey to see me, and when she met Colonel

Hunt she blessed him and the expedition. But, like Ang Lahmu back in Darjeeling, she was worried that I was risking myself on Everest too often, and begged me to be careful. "Don't fret, *ama la*," I told her. "This time we may get to the top, and then I won't have to go back any more." And I hoped with all my heart that it would be so.

From Namche we marched on to the Thyangboche Monastery, which was to serve us as a sort of preliminary base. And here we had our biggest and last trouble about the expedition arrangements. This time it was again about equipment and clothing; for the British, in now issuing them to the Sherpas, announced that most of the things were not theirs to keep, but were only to be used on the mountain and then returned. This caused the worst storm we had had yet. On all previous expeditions, including the earlier British ones, there had been no conditions attached to the gear that was given out, and most of the Sherpas said they would absolutely not go on if that were not done this time as well. Colonel Hunt explained his point of view. He thought it a good idea not to hand out the things as outright gifts at the beginning, but to present them later as a reward for good work. But the Sherpas did not like this idea at all. They considered the clothing and gear as part of their normal pay, and were not going on unless they received it in that way.

This was the worst time I had on the whole expedition. Along with Major Wylie, who was also doing his best to make peace, I felt like the middle of a sandwich pressed between two slabs of bread. Each side thought I was working for the interests of the other side, and the Sherpas especially seemed to think I was being paid big money by the British to argue against them. Half the time I wished

I was just an ordinary Sherpa, and not in the middle of all the arguments. And once I was so fed up I said to Major Wylie, "Look, I have my Swiss equipment with me and will use that. Give my British equipment to the others, and perhaps that will keep them quiet."

But something like that was obviously not going to solve the problem. Instead, the discussions and arguments went on, and at last a sort of compromise was reached, to which all the Sherpas agreed, except two. These were Pasang Phutar ("The Jockey") and Ang Dawa, and they left the expedition there at Thyangboche and started back home. Pasang, who had been my assistant sirdar, was a capable and intelligent man, and in some ways I was sorry to see him go. But he was also quite a politician; throughout the trip he had been at the centre of most of the complaints and difficulties; and on his departure, with Ang Dawa, things quietened down almost immediately. I don't mind saying that I drew a deep breath of relief, for I have always hated small bickerings and resentments while one is engaged on a great adventure. When people are going to a mountain they should forget the molehills. When they are involved in a big thing they should have big hearts to go with it.

I watched Jockey and Ang Dawa go down the trail towards Namche and the outside world. I turned and watched the other Sherpas, no longer standing about resentfully, but pitching into their work with the gear and the loads. Then I looked up past them to what lay ahead— to the hills and valleys and glaciers and great peaks beyond; to Ama Dablam and Taweche, Nuptse and Lhotse, rising like towers before us; to Everest—old Chomolungma— behind them, with its white plume streaming out against the sky. And as I looked all the rest was gone. The troubles and arguments and bickerings meant nothing.

Nothing in the world meant anything, except Everest. Except the challenge—and the dream.

"All right, let's get at it!" I shouted.

And I thought, Yes, at it. Up it. Up it this time—the seventh time—to the top.

It must be now. . . .

17

FOR THE SEVENTH TIME

SHERPAS working. Sherpas talking. Part in our own language, part in Nepali, with a little English. . . .
"Ready to go now?"

"*Ah chah*. O.K."

"But *husier*—be careful. It's a *bara sapur*—long trip."

And off we go. Up the glacier. Along the moraines.

"Still *ah chah*?"

"No, not *ah chah*. *Toi ye!* Damn it [always with a big spit]! My load is crooked."

"*Kai chai na*. It doesn't matter."

"*Toi ye* [with a spit]! It does matter. I must stop. *Kuche kuche*. Please."

"*Ap ke ukam*. Have it your own way. Here, I'll help you. . . . Is it *ah chah* now?

"Yes, *ah chah*. *Thuji chey*. Thank you."

"Let's get going, then. But *husier!* It gets steep here."

"Too steep. *Toi ye!*"

Then more spitting. More climbing. More glacier and moraine, and at last the next camp.

"*Shabash!* Well done! We've done it."

"For that day's work we should have *baksheesh*."

"Or at least a bowl of *chang*."

"With some *chang* we could toast ourselves. . . . *Tashi delai!* Here's how!"

"*Tashi delai* to you! To all of us!"

"*Sherpas zindabad!* Long live the Sherpas!"

From Thyangboche we did not go at once to Everest. It was part of Colonel Hunt's plan that we first get acclimatized and have some practice with our equipment, so we split into three groups and went off separately on near-by mountains. The party I was with consisted of Hunt, Lowe, Gregory, and five Sherpas, and for about a week we worked out of a camp at about 17,000 feet on the Nuptse Glacier, climbing, cutting steps, trying out the oxygen equipment, and generally preparing ourselves for the real job ahead. Then we went back to Thyangboche and, along with the other parties, began working our way up the Khumbu Glacier towards our regular base camp, which would be near the foot of the great icefall.

Since Pasang Phutar had left things were much better between sahibs and Sherpas, but there was still a certain amount of complaint and argument. Some of it was about food. Some was about the weight of the loads on the practice climbs, which the British set at sixty pounds per man, but which the Sherpas said was too heavy; and after some discussion I succeeded in getting them reduced to fifty pounds. Then I had a little argument of my own about the necessity of carrying up timber to be used as bridges over the crevasses in the icefall. The sahibs had brought with them from England a long, light metal ladder that could be taken apart in sections, and they thought this was all that was needed. But I pointed out that there would be many, many crevasses; it would waste much time always to be moving the ladder back and forth, and with the timber we could build a permanent usable route. The chief objection of the British was that this would make added expense for the extra local Sherpas who would be needed to carry up the timber. But when I made a strong point of it they were reasonable and agreed.

Indeed, from here on there was almost no trouble between sahibs and Sherpas, and the relations became excellent. The expedition was a very big one; it was run on almost military lines, and there is no doubt that most of our men would have preferred more ease and informality. But even those who had done the most complaining had to admit that the expedition was very well run. Hunt —whom we called Colonel Sahib—sometimes was inclined to run things as if we were part of an army, but was always fair and considerate. Major Wylie, as I have said, was an excellent transport officer. And the other climbers, as we came to know them, were all good, kind men. The things I have said about our small difficulties have been only to set the record straight on matters over which there has been much loose talk, and not at all to put blame on our good friends and comrades in adventure. No man could have been happier than I when the difficulties were at last behind us, for, as sirdar-climber, I had always been in the middle, and it had not been a happy position.

Base camp, of course, was a very busy place, with all the loads arriving and being sorted out and tents going up everywhere. With all the people about—not only those of us actually with the expedition, but also hundreds of local Sherpas and Sherpanis—it sometimes seemed not like a camp at all, but a small city. Work began almost at once on the icefall, with Hillary leading the party that was finding the way; but at this stage I myself was mostly busy with Major Wylie, working on the tons of equipment and seeing that all the people concerned did their proper jobs. One of the very efficient things about the expedition was that every one had his special assigned job —some on the icefall route, some with the loads, others with the oxygen or radio or photography or medical work. At this time the doctors began giving examinations, and unfortunately one of the veteran Sherpas, Gyaltsen, was found to have a small heart-murmur and was not allowed to climb any higher. Along with the Jockey and Ang Dawa, this made three men we had lost; but by this time Dawa Thondup had joined us, and we had also taken on several of the Solo Khumbu Sherpas. Altogether now there were about forty porters who would go higher than the base camp, and it was expected that about two-thirds of them would continue on above the Western Cwm.

Mail came up to us about once a week, and I received letters from Ang Lahmu and my friend Mitra. They were not such as to make me very happy, for the meeting that had been arranged to raise a fund for my family had turned out to be all talk and no action, and Ang Lahmu, in particular, was worried about the future. Money, money, I thought. It can follow you all the way to the top of the highest mountain. But what could I do now? Nothing at all. And I was not going to let it worry me. Though it may sound hard and selfish, that is one thing I am grateful for: that on a mountain I can put away all other thoughts —of the world, the problems of living, even of home and family—and think of nothing, care for nothing, except what lies ahead. There in base camp and in the days to come only one thing, of all things, mattered to me. And that was Everest. To *climb* Everest.

There is no point, I think, in my going into all the details of the next few weeks. Colonel Hunt has already done

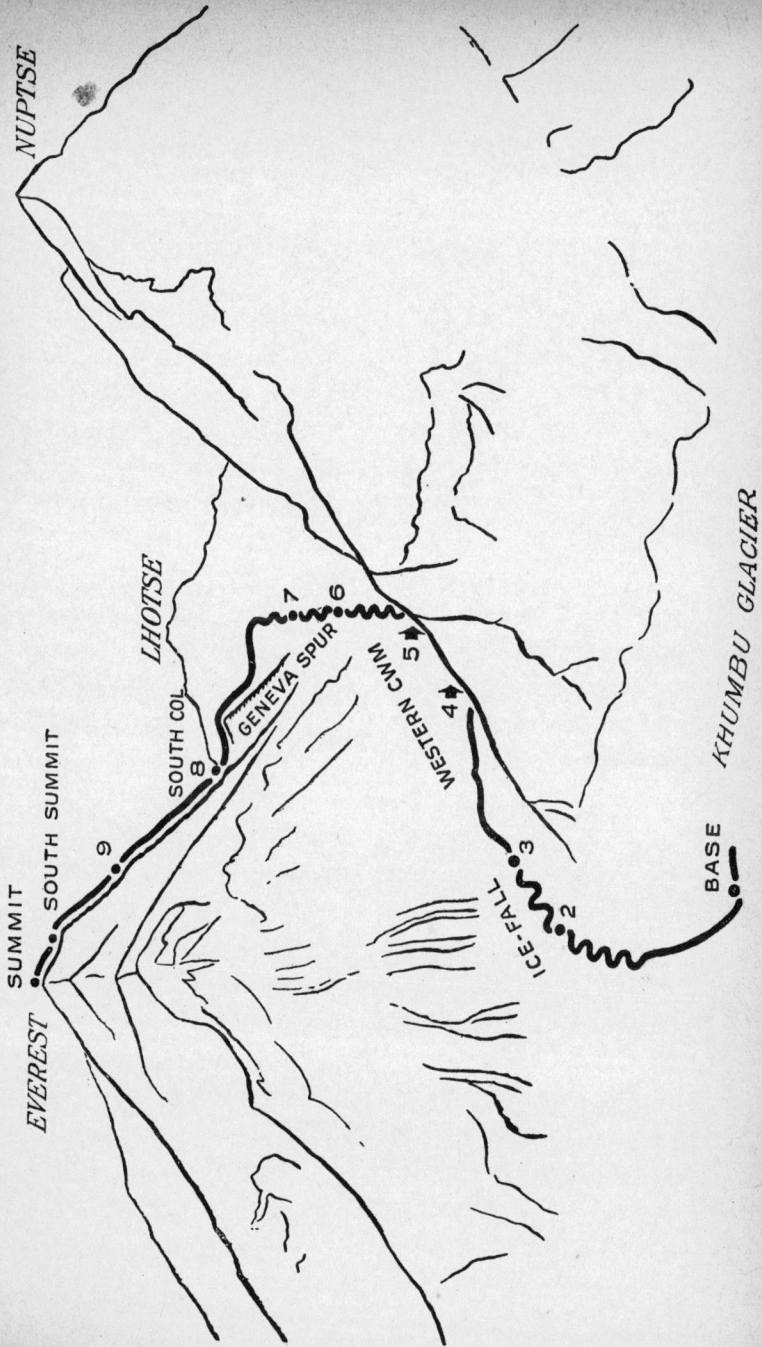

The Road to Victory

that in his fine book. A route up the icefall was found—again different from those of the earlier expeditions, because the ice was still always changing. Flags on tall poles were set up to mark the way. Steps were cut, ropes fixed, the ladder and timber bridges put in place across the crevasses, and long lines of Sherpas carried the loads up to Camp Two, in the icefall, and Camp Three, at the foot of the cwm. The weather was as usual for the middle of spring—generally clear in the morning, with cloud and some snow in the afternoon. But there were no really bad storms, nor the terrible wind and cold that we had had in the past autumn. The schedule was arranged so that different teams took turns at the hardest work, and also that every one should come down regularly from the higher camps—not only to the base, but even farther down the glacier to a place called Lobuje, where there was a stream and some vegetation and the men could regain their strength quickly in the lower altitude. I think that much of the success of the expedition lay in the fact that there was time to do such things, while the Swiss had always been forced to hurry on.

Meanwhile Colonel Hunt had been working out his plan for the upper part of the mountain, and one day at base camp he announced how it would be. Before the expedition started I had been promised my chance at the top if I were in good physical condition, and a few days before, in an examination by the doctors, I had been found fitter than anyone. So I was to have the chance, as I had hoped and prayed. The three others chosen for the two summit attempts were Dr Evans and Bourdillon, who would climb as one team, and Hillary, who would be my partner in the second, and just how we were to operate I shall explain later. If neither succeeded, still a third team would be organized; but this would involve much difficulty and reorganization, and every one hoped it would not be necessary.

I was as happy as I think a man can be, but many of the other Sherpas, when the plan was told to them, felt otherwise. They had no desire to climb to the top themselves, and could not see why I should want to. "You are mad, *Au* Tenzing," they told me. (*Au* means "uncle," which was what they were calling me now. And I suppose it was friendly and respectful, but it made me feel a little old.) Anyhow, that is what they kept saying. "You are mad, *Au* Tenzing. You will get yourself killed, and then how will we show our faces to *Anie* [Aunt] Ang Lahmu?"

"Stop worrying like old women," I told them. "I'll be all right."

"But even if you are all right—if you get to the top and come down—still it is no good. You will be taking the livelihood away from all of us."

"What are you talking about?"

"If Everest is climbed there will be no more expeditions. There will be no more jobs."

"It's you who are mad," I said. "If Everest is climbed the Himalayas will be famous all over the world. There will be more expeditions and jobs than ever."

Anyhow, I was not wasting any more time arguing.

From now on I was teamed with Hillary the whole time. We were not supposed to do the heaviest jobs, and so wear ourselves out, but only to get ourselves in the best condition; and, while the others did the work up ahead on the Lhotse face, we kept going up and down between base camp and the Western Cwm, carrying light loads, practising with the oxygen, and helping the younger novice

Sherpas on the steep route through the icefall. How many times we went back and forth I can hardly count, but once, I remember, we went all the way from the base to Camp Four and back again in one day, and we certainly could not have done that if we had not been going strong. Hillary was a wonderful climber—especially on snow and ice, with which he had had much practice in New Zealand —and had great strength and endurance. Like many men of action, and especially the British, he did not talk much, but he was nevertheless a fine, cheerful companion; and he was popular with the Sherpas, because in things like food and equipment he always shared whatever he had. I suppose we made a funny-looking pair, he and I, with Hillary about six feet three inches tall and myself some seven inches shorter. But we were not worrying about that. What was important was that, as we climbed together and became used to each other, we were becoming a strong and confident team.

One example of how we could work together happened while we were still on the icefall. Late one afternoon we were coming down, just the two of us, from Camp Two to Camp One, roped together, with Hillary ahead and myself second. We were winding our way between the tall seracs, or ice-towers, when suddenly the steep snow under his feet gave way, and he fell into a crevasse. "Tenzing! Tenzing!" he shouted. But fortunately there was not too much rope between us, and I was prepared. Jamming my axe into the snow and throwing myself down beside it, I was able to stop his fall after about fifteen feet, and then, with slow pulling and hauling, managed to pull him up again. By the time he was out of the crevasse my gloves were torn from the strain; but my hands were all right, and, except for a few bruises, Hillary was unhurt. "*Shabash*, Tenzing! Well done!" he said gratefully. And when we got down to camp he told the others that "without Tenzing I would have been finished to-day." It was a fine compliment, and I was pleased that I had done well. But it was certainly nothing out of the ordinary. Mishaps are sure to happen on a mountain, and climbers must always be ready to help each other.

In the cwm we pitched our third, fourth, and fifth camps near where the Swiss had had theirs the year before. In the autumn, when we were hurrying to get off the mountain, they had left a great deal of food and equipment at Camp Four, and after digging about a bit in the snow I was now able to find it. Indeed, during the whole climb we made much use of things left behind by the Swiss—from stacks of firewood at the base camp to half-used oxygen-tanks high up near the summit. Besides such items as we found in this way, I myself had a good deal of personal gear from the year before; for, though the British equipment was excellent, I had become used to the Swiss, and in general preferred it. This was especially true of the high reindeer-boots, which kept my feet wonderfully warm and had a waterproof canvas covering, which the English boots lacked, and also of my Swiss tent, which by now had come to seem almost like a small movable home.

While Hillary and I were busy in the cwm and the icefall other teams of sahibs and Sherpas were working on the route up to the South Col. This was much the same one we had taken in the autumn, after the death of Mingma Dorje—first up the Lhotse face and then across towards the top of the Geneva Spur—and, as the Swiss had done, the British established two camps on the way. Altogether this took about three weeks, and, of course, the higher the advance parties climbed the slower was their progress. As always on the upper mountain, the altitude began to affect some of the men badly, and two of them, Michael Westmacott and George Band, finally had to come down and stay down. Both were fine climbers. In fact, I considered Westmacott, in a technical way, the best on the expedition. But an interesting point is that they were the youngest two of the Englishmen, and I have often noticed that young men on their first high climbs, no matter how strong and able they may be, usually have a much worse time than older men who have had experience at great altitudes.

The man has never been born, of course, who does not have some difficulties on a peak like Everest. There is the threat of exhaustion, of freezing. There is the constant struggle for air. There are headaches and sore throats and nausea and loss of appetite and sleeplessness, and at the higher altitudes all the British had to take sleeping-pills to get any rest at all. Perhaps because of that famous "third lung" of mine I was luckier than most. Certainly I could not have *run* up the mountain, any more than the others, but it was still true, as it had been so often before, that the higher I got the better I felt. To keep busy, always busy: that was the secret of how I kept warm and healthy. Caring for the equipment; keeping the tents in order; boiling snow-water for hot drinks. And when there was nothing else to do I would just knock my hands and feet against ice or rock. Anything to keep active—to keep the blood going against the weakness of the high altitudes. It was partly because of this, I think, that I never had headaches or vomiting. And I never took sleeping-pills. For a sore throat, which would sometimes begin, I found it helpful to gargle with warm water and salt. Up very high one never has an appetite—indeed, you have to force yourself to eat—but because of the thin dryness of the air there is often a terrible thirst. For this, in my experience, it is very bad to eat snow or drink cold snow-water, for this seems only to make the throat drier, and often sore. Tea, coffee, or soup are all much better. And, best of all, on this 1953 climb, was the powdered lemon-juice that we mixed with sugar and warm water. On the upper mountain we drank so much of it that I began calling us "the lemon-juice expedition."

The work on the Lhotse face went on, and Camps Six and Seven were established on the way to the South Col. Sometimes storms would blow up, and everything would have to stop. Sometimes things would go wrong, and Colonel Hunt would swear fluently in Hindi. But mostly the going was good, and by May the 20th the advance-party was ready to move on to the col itself. This consisted of Wilfred Noyce and sixteen Sherpas, who were already at Camp Seven; but on the morning of the 21st, when they were supposed to climb the last stretch, those of us who were in the cwm below, watching through binoculars, saw only two of them start off. These, we guessed rightly, were Noyce himself and his head Sherpa, Annullu; but what had gone wrong with the others we did not know, and we were very worried.

By now Band and Westmacott had had to go down. Major Wylie, with a few Sherpas, was at Camp Six, ready to carry loads up to Seven. At Camp Four, the advance base in the cwm, there were seven of us—Colonel Hunt, Dr Evans, Bourdillon, Lowe, Gregory, Hillary, and myself. But we were the two summit parties, with the support-team that was to help us up, and Hunt did not like to see us wear ourselves out just a few days before we were to make our great effort. Still, some one had to go up to see what was wrong, and it was decided that it would be Hillary and myself. "If the Sherpas are having trouble," I said, "it is my job to go. I will talk to them and get them started all right." And, since Hillary was glad to go too, we soon started off. It was the first time either of us had been higher than the cwm, and, though it meant hard extra work, we were both happy to be on the real mountain at last. Using oxygen, we climbed strongly and steadily, and by late afternoon reached Camp Seven, high on the Lhotse face.

Noyce and Annullu were there, after having gone up to the col and come back. So were Wylie and his party, who had come up from Camp Six. And so were the Sherpas who should have gone up with Noyce, but hadn't. Some of them had headaches and sore throats, and all, of course, were tired, but no one was really ill, and it had mostly been fear of the mountain that had kept them from going on. Now that Noyce and Annullu had done so well, however, much of that fear was gone, and after I had been with them awhile—encouraging them, massaging them, and giving them hot drinks—they agreed to make the try the next day. That night nineteen of us were piled into the few tents at Camp Seven, and we were hardly comfortable. But at least there had been no real breakdown, and in the morning all of us started up. It had been the plan that Hillary and I would go no farther than Seven; but as long as we had come this far we wanted to do the job right, and so, following the route of Noyce and Annullu, we led the way up to the col. Then that same day we went all the way back to Camp Four in the cwm, having climbed almost five thousand feet up and down in about thirty hours.

We were tired, of course, but not worn-out; after a

little rest we were all right. And now the last fight for the summit was ready to begin. According to the plan, Bourdillon and Evans were to go up to the col first, together with Colonel Hunt and several Sherpas, who would be their supporting team. Then a day later, while they were making their try for the top, Hillary and I would go to the col, helped by Lowe, Gregory, and another group of Sherpas, and if Bourdillon and Evans had not reached the goal we would then make our effort. There has since been much talk and confusion about which was the "first" team and which was the "second," and I shall try to make this as clear as I can. Bourdillon and Evans were obviously the first, as far as time is concerned. They would leave from Camp Eight, on the South Col, and climb as high as they could—all the way, if possible; but there were about 3300 feet between col and summit, no half-way camp was to be set up for them, and it would be a marvellous feat if they could go to the top and back in one day. They *might* be able to do it: no one knew. But they were not specifically *expected* to do it. Colonel Hunt called their try a "reconnaissance assault," and said he would be well satisfied if they could get to the south summit and have a close look at the last stretch beyond it.

Then, if they could go no farther, Hillary and I would have our turn. But for us another camp—the ninth— would be set up on the summit ridge, as high as men could carry it, and we would make our try from there, with a much greater advantage. So if Bourdillon and Evans were first in one way we were first in another—in terms of what was expected of us. If we failed it might, after reorganization, be possible to make still another attempt; but as far as present plans went ours would be the great effort. After the expedition was over there were stories in certain newspapers that I was upset because I did not have the first chance at the top. But this is wholly untrue. My chance was as much "first" as anyone's. If anything, Hillary and I would have the better opportunity. And it seemed to me that the plan was in all ways sound and sensible. You do not climb a mountain like Everest by trying to race ahead on your own, or by competing with your comrades. You do it slowly and carefully, by unselfish teamwork. Certainly I wanted to reach the top myself; it was the thing I had dreamed of all my life. But if the lot fell to some one else I would take it like a man, and not a cry-baby. For that is the mountain way.

So on May the 23rd the Bourdillon–Evans party started up from the cwm. And on the 25th we followed after them—Hillary and myself, Lowe and Gregory, with eight of the best Sherpas. On the Lhotse face we met those who had set up the South Col camp on their way down, and they wished us luck; but no one knew if we would ever have a chance at the summit, for on the next day the others would be making their try. Round the haft of my ice-axe I had wound four flags. Two of them—of Britain and the United Nations—had been brought by the expedition. One—of Nepal—had been presented to us in Kathmandu. And the fourth was the Indian flag that Robi Mitra had given me in Darjeeling. "Is it all right if I take it too?" I had asked Colonel Hunt a few days before. And he had said, "Yes, that's a fine idea." So there I was with my four flags, but where they would end up no one could tell. Bourdillon and Evans also had flags with them, and they were now high above us on the mountain.

As on our first time up to the col, Hillary and I used oxygen for most of the way. There were two types of apparatus on the expedition—the so-called "closed circuit," with which you breathed pure oxygen, and the "open circuit," in which the oxygen was mixed with the surrounding air. Bourdillon and Evans had the closed type, Hillary and I the open (which we had been using since the beginning); and, though ours did not make breathing as easy while you were actually using it, there was less bad effect when you had to turn it off, and in general it seemed more dependable. Besides this equipment for climbing, we also, at the higher camps, used what we called "night oxygen." Taking the apparatus into the tents with us, we would set them at a lower rate of flow and breathe from them on and off through the night, when we felt close to suffocation or were unable to sleep.

Again we spent a night at Camp Seven, but this time it was not so crowded, for every one else was now either above or below us. In the morning it was clear, and soon after we started off we saw, high above us and just a little below the south summit, two tiny specks that we knew must be Bourdillon and Evans. Then they disappeared, and we went on with our own climbing—across the snow-slopes of the upper Lhotse face, up along the Geneva Spur to its highest point, and finally down the few hundred feet from there to the South Col. The only person at Camp Eight, when we arrived, was the Sherpa Ang Tensing, whom we called Balu—the Bear.[1] He had been one of the two Sherpas attached to Colonel Hunt, but that morning had felt too ill to go with the others when they climbed on still higher. He told us that they had left early: Bourdillon and Evans together, to go as far as they could, and Colonel Hunt with the remaining Sherpa, Da Namgyal, to carry up supplies for the highest camp that

[1] What with Lambert, Tilman, Ang Tempa, and now Ang Tensing, we had plenty of 'bears' on our expeditions.

might later be used by Hillary and myself. He had not seen them since, and, in fact, knew less than we did, for we had at least seen the two specks up near the south summit.

We did not have to wait long. Only a little while after we reached the col we saw Colonel Hunt and Da Namgyal coming down the snow-slope from the south-east ridge, and we hurried out to meet them. They were terribly tired. In fact, the Colonel Sahib collapsed for a few minutes, and then I gave him lemon-juice to drink and helped him into a tent. When he had rested a little he told us that they had climbed to about 27,350 feet, which was some 200 feet higher than where Lambert and I had camped the year before. He had hoped to go still farther —to 28,000 feet if possible—but this had been their limit, and there they had dumped the stores for Camp Nine. This included the oxygen-tanks they themselves had been using on the way up, and their coming down without any oxygen at all was one of the reasons why they were in such bad shape. While they lay in their tents I brought them more lemon-juice and then tea, and slowly their strength returned. One of my happiest memories of the expedition is of Colonel Hunt looking up at me from his sleeping-bag and murmuring, "Tenzing, I will never forget this."

Then we waited again—for Bourdillon and Evans— and this wait was a long one. Part of the time I took care of the Colonel and Da Namgyal, and the rest of it I stood outside, looking up towards the summit and wondering what was happening. Once, when I was in his tent, Hunt said, "It would be fine if they did it for the Queen's coronation"; and I thought, Perhaps that is why the two Englishmen went first, instead of Hillary and me. But then straight away I said to myself, "No, that is foolish thinking. There is no 'first' or 'second,' and Hunt has just now almost killed himself carrying up supplies for Hillary and me. There is no 'first' or 'second,' but only Everest—and *some one* must climb it." Then I went outside and looked up again, waiting and wondering.

As always, the col was cold and windy, and the camp was a terribly lonely place among the broken stones and ice. We had pitched it in the same place where the Swiss had been the year before, and round about us were old tent-frames and packs and oxygen-tanks that looked as if they had been left by ghosts. Our own camp consisted of four tents, of which three were for sleeping, and altogether about 750 pounds of food and equipment had been carried up from below. This, of course, had been mostly the work of the Sherpas, and I was proud of them as I thought now of what they had done. Before the expedition was over seventeen of them reached the col, six of them twice, carrying loads that averaged thirty pounds, and without the help of oxygen. "Where would we be without them?" I asked myself. And the answer was easy: "Down at the base of the mountain." Now most of those who had come up with us were getting ready to go down again, for they had done their job, and there was not room at the camp for so many to sleep. It was interesting that among them were the oldest on the expedition—Dawa Thondup—and one of the youngest two—my nephew Topgay. The others were Annullu, Ang Norbu, and Da Tensing (yes, there were several Tensings—and with different spellings), and with them went Da Namgyal and Tensing Balu, who had come up with the first party. "Good-bye. Good luck. . . . *Husier!* Be careful! . . . It will be *ah chah*. O.K." Then they were gone. Besides myself, there were now only three Sherpas left on the col—Ang Nyima, Ang

Tempa, and Pemba, who had been specially chosen to help Hillary and myself up to Camp Nine.

We waited—looked up. Waited—looked up. And then at last, in the middle of the afternoon, we saw two figures coming down the snow-slope towards the camp. They have not done it, I thought. It is still too early for them to have got to the top and back. As before, with Hunt and Da Namgyal, we hurried out to meet them, and they too were so tired they could hardly speak or move. No, they told us, they had not reached the top. They had reached the south summit, only a few hundred feet below it, and the highest point to which men had ever climbed. But that had been the limit for them. Like Lambert and myself the year before, they might have been able to go on all the way, but surely would never have returned alive. Night would have come. Death would have come. And they had known it and turned back. Now in their tent we made them warm and gave them lemon-juice and tea. They were so thirsty that each of them drank about two quarts of liquid, and for a while we simply let them rest. But later, when some of their strength had returned, I asked them all sorts of questions about what they had done and seen, and how the route was, and what the problems were. "Tenzing, I'm confident you and Hillary will do it," said Evans. "But it's hard going, and will take four or five hours from the high camp. It's dangerous too—very steep and with cornices—and you must be careful. But if the weather's good you'll do it. You won't have to come back again next year."

He and Bourdillon answered all our questions. They were worn-out, sick with exhaustion, and, of course, terribly disappointed that they had not reached the summit themselves. But still they answered our questions.

They did everything they could to advise and help us. And I thought, Yes, that is how it is on a mountain. That is how a mountain makes men great. For where would Hillary and I have been without the others? Without the climbers who had made the route and the Sherpas who had carried the loads? Without Bourdillon and Evans, Hunt and Da Namgyal, who had cleared the way ahead? Without Lowe and Gregory, Ang Nyima, Ang Tempa, and Pemba, who were there only to help us? It was only because of the work and sacrifice of all of them that we were now to have our chance at the top.

Ten of us spent the night on the col, huddled together in the three sleeping-tents. It was the plan that we start off early the next morning, but in the darkness the wind grew even stronger than usual, and when light came it was roaring like a thousand tigers. It was hopeless even to think of going up. All we could do was wait and hope the storm would blow itself out, and luckily we had enough food to last for at least one extra day. About noon the wind dropped a little, and, though by now it was too late to go higher, Bourdillon and Evans prepared to go down. Colonel Hunt had intended to stay on the col until Hillary and I made our attempt, but Bourdillon was in such bad shape that he decided he had better go with him to help him; and Ang Tempa, who had been feeling ill, went with them too.

"Good luck. Take care of yourselves," Evans told us as he left. "Remember, if you get to the top you can take it easy next year."

This left six of us at Camp Eight—Lowe and Gregory, Ang Nyima and Pemba, Hillary and myself. While the hours dragged by we lay in our tents, trying to keep warm and drinking great quantities of tea and coffee, soup and lemon-juice; and later I got out some salmon, biscuits, and fruit, and, though no one was hungry, we forced ourselves to eat a little. All the time I listened to the sound of the wind against the canvas of the tents. When it was loud I would be worried, and when it was softer I would feel better. Every so often I would go out and stand in the wind and the cold, looking up at the top of the mountain above us.

Then came the second night, and the weather was still bad. We lay close together in our sleeping-bags, breathing the "night oxygen," and the sahibs took pills to help them sleep. I lay in the darkness, listening to the wind, and I thought, It must stop. It must stop, so that to-morrow we can go up. I have been seven times to Everest. I love Everest. But seven times is enough. From here we must go on to the top. It must be this time. It must be now. . . . An hour passed, and another. Slowly. Slowly. I dozed a little, awoke, and dozed again. Half waking and half sleeping, my mind moved about in the darkness. . . . So many men have died on Everest, I thought. Like on a battlefield. But some day a man must win. And when he wins . . . My thoughts moved on. Suddenly I was thinking of Professor Tucci, and how he once told me he would introduce me to Pandit Nehru. Now if I got to the top it might really happen. Then I was thinking of Solo Khumbu, my old home, my father and mother. I thought of their faith in God and their prayers for me, and then I myself was praying, to God—and to Everest. After that I was not thinking at all any more, but dreaming. I dreamt of yaks playing about in a pasture, and then of a big white horse. It is a Sherpa belief that to dream of animals is good. And that is what I dreamed of. Somewhere behind the yaks and the horse was another dream. A tall white dream in the sky. . . .

18

THE DREAM COMES TRUE

MAY the 28th. . . . It had been on the 28th that
Lambert and I had made our final effort, struggling
up as far as we could above our high camp on the
ridge. Now we were a day's climb lower; a day later. A
year later.

When it first grew light it was still blowing, but by
eight o'clock the wind had dropped. We looked at each
other and nodded. We would make our try.

But a bad thing had happened during the night: Pemba
had been ill. And it was clear that he could not go higher.
The day before we had lost Ang Tempa, who had been
one of those supposed to go up to Camp Nine, and now,
with Pemba out of it, only Ang Nyima was left of the
original Sherpa team of three. This meant that the rest
of us would all have to carry heavier loads, which would
make our going slower and harder; but there was nothing
we could do about it. A little before nine Lowe, Gregory,
and Ang Nyima started off, each of them carrying more
than forty pounds and breathing oxygen, and about an
hour later Hillary and I followed, with fifty pounds
apiece. The idea of this was that our support party would
do the slow, hard work of cutting steps in the ice, and then
we would be able to follow at our own pace, without tiring

ourselves... Or perhaps I should say without tiring ourselves *too much*.

We crossed the frozen rocks of the col. Then we went up the snow-slope beyond, and up a long couloir, or gully, leading towards the south-east ridge. As had been planned, the fine steps cut by the others made the going easier for us, and by the time they reached the foot of the ridge—about noon—we had caught up with them. A little above us here, and off to one side, were some bare poles and a few shreds of canvas that had once been the highest camp for Lambert and me; and they brought back many memories. Then slowly we passed by and went on up the ridge. It was quite steep, but not too narrow, with rock that sloped upward and gave a good foothold, if you were careful about the loose snow that lay over it. About 150 feet above the old Swiss tent we came to the highest point that Colonel Hunt and Da Namgyal had reached two days before, and there in the snow were the tent, food, and oxygen-tanks which they had left for us. These now we had to add to our own loads, and from there on we were carrying weights of up to sixty pounds.

The ridge grew steeper, and our pace was now very slow. Then the snow became thicker, covering the rocks deeply, and it was necessary to cut steps again. Most of the time Lowe did this, leading the way with his swinging axe, while the rest of us followed. But by two in the afternoon all of us, with our great loads, were beginning to get tired, and it was agreed that we must soon find a camping-place. I remembered a spot that Lambert and I had noticed the year before—in fact, that we had decided would be our highest camp-site if we had another chance at the top—but it was still hidden above us, and on the stretch between there was no place that could possibly have held a tent. So on we went, with myself now leading—first still along the ridge, then off to the left, across steep snow, towards the place I was looking for.

"Hey, where are you leading us to?" asked Lowe and Gregory. "We have to go down."

"It can't be far now," I said. "Only five minutes."

But still we climbed; still we didn't get there. And I kept saying, "Only five minutes. . . . Only five minutes."

"Yes, but how many five minutes are there?" Ang Nyima asked in disgust.

Then at last we got there. It was a partly level spot in the snow, down a little from the exposed ridge and in the shelter of a rocky cliff, and there we dropped our loads. With a quick "Good-bye—good luck" Lowe, Gregory, and Ang Nyima started down for the col, and Hillary and I were left alone. It was then the middle of the afternoon, and we were at a height of about 27,900 feet. The summit of Lhotse, the fourth highest peak in the world, at which we had looked up every day during the long expedition, was now below us. Over to the south-east Makalu was below us. Everything we could see for hundreds of miles was below us, except only the top of Kangchenjunga, far to the east—and the white ridge climbing on above us into the sky.

We started pitching the highest camp that has ever been made. And it took us almost until it was dark. First we chopped away at the ice to try to make our sleeping-place a little more level. Then we struggled with frozen ropes and canvas, and tied the ropes round oxygen-cylinders to hold them down. Everything took five times as long as it would have in a place where there was enough air to breathe; but at last we got the tent up, and when we crawled in it it was not too bad. There was only a light wind, and inside it was not too cold to take off our gloves. Hillary checked the oxygen-sets, while I got our little stove going and made warm coffee and lemon-juice. Our thirst was terrible, and we drank them down like two camels. Later we had some soup, sardines, biscuits, and tinned fruit, but the fruit was frozen so hard we had first to thaw it out over the stove.

We had managed to flatten out the rocks and ice under the tent, but not all at one level. Half the floor was about a foot higher than the other half, and now Hillary spread his sleeping-bag on the upper half, and I put mine on the lower. When we were in them each of us rolled over close against the canvas, so that the weight of our bodies would help hold it in place. Mostly the wind was still not too bad, but sometimes great gusts would come out of nowhere, and the tent would seem ready to fly away. Lying in the dark, we talked of our plans for the next day. Then, breathing the "night-oxygen," we tried to sleep. Even in our eiderdown bags we both wore all our clothes, and I kept on my Swiss reindeer-boots. At night most climbers take off their boots, because they believe this helps the circulation in the feet; but at high altitudes I myself prefer to keep them on. Hillary, on the other hand, took his off and laid them next to his sleeping-bag.

The hours passed. I dozed and woke, dozed and woke. And each time I woke I listened. By midnight there was no wind at all. God is good to us, I thought. Chomolungma is good to us. The only sound was that of our own breathing as we sucked at our oxygen.

May the 29th. . . . On the 29th Lambert and I had descended in defeat from the col to the cwm. Down—down—down. . . .

At about three-thirty in the morning we began to stir. I got the stove going and boiled snow for lemon-juice and coffee, and we ate a little of the food left over from the night before. There was still no wind. When, a little while later, we opened the tent-flap everything was clear and quiet in the early-morning light. It was then that I pointed down and showed Hillary the tiny dot that was the Thyangboche Monastery, 16,000 feet below. "God of my father and mother," I prayed in my heart, "be good to me now—to-day."

But the first thing that happened was a bad thing. Hillary's boots, lying all night outside his sleeping-bag, had frozen, and now they were like two lumps of black iron. For a whole hour we had to hold them over the stove, pulling and kneading them, until the tent was full of the smell of scorched leather and we were both panting as if we were already climbing the peak. Hillary was very upset, both at the delay and at the danger to his feet. "I'm afraid I may get frostbitten, like Lambert," he said. But at last the boots were soft enough for him to put on, and then we prepared the rest of our gear. For this last day's climbing I was dressed in all sorts of clothes that came from many places. My boots, as I have said, were Swiss; my wind-jacket and various other items had been issued by the British. But the socks I was wearing had been knitted by Ang Lahmu. My sweater had been given me by Mrs Henderson, of the Himalayan Club. My woollen helmet was the old one that had been left to me by Earl Denman. And, most important of all, the red scarf round my neck was Raymond Lambert's. At the end of the autumn expedition he had given it to me and smiled and said, "Here, perhaps you can use it some time." And ever since I had known exactly what that use must be.

At six-thirty, when we crawled from the tent, it was still clear and windless. We had pulled three pairs of gloves on to our hands—silk, wool, and windproof—and now we fastened our crampons to our boots, and on to our backs slung the forty pounds of oxygen apparatus that would be the whole load for each of us during the climb. Round my axe were still the four flags, tightly wrapped. And in the pocket of my jacket was a small red-and-blue pencil.

"All ready?"

"*Ah chah*. Ready."

And off we went.

Hillary's boots were still stiff, and his feet cold, so he asked me to take the lead. And for a while that is how we went on the rope—up from the camp-site to the south-east ridge, and then on along the ridge towards the south summit. Sometimes we found the footprints of Bourdillon and Evans and were able to use them; but mostly they had been wiped away by the winds of the two days before, and I had to kick or chop our own steps. After a while we came to a place I recognized—the point where Lambert and I had stopped and turned back. I pointed it out to Hillary, and tried to explain through my oxygen-mask, and as we moved on I thought of how different it was these two times—of the wind and the cold then and the bright sunshine now—and how lucky we were on this day of our great effort. By now Hillary's feet were feeling better, so we changed places on the rope; and we kept doing this from then on, with first one of us leading the way and then the other, in order to share the work of kicking and chopping. As we drew near to the south summit we came upon something we had been looking for—two bottles of oxygen that had been left for us by Bourdillon and Evans.

We scraped the ice off the dials, and were happy to see that they were still quite full. For this meant that they could be used later for our downward trip to the col, and meanwhile we could breathe in a bigger amount of what we were carrying with us.

We left the two bottles where they were and climbed on. Until now the climbing—if not the weather—had been much the same as I remembered from the year before —along the steep, broken ridge, with a rock precipice on the left and snow cornices hiding another precipice on the right. But now, just below the south summit, the ridge broadened out into a sort of snow-face, so that the steepness was not so much to the sides as straight behind us, and we were climbing up an almost vertical white wall. The worst part of it was that the snow was not firm, but kept sliding down, sliding down—and we with it—until I thought, Next time it will keep sliding, and we will go all the way to the bottom of the mountain. For me this was the one really bad place on the whole climb, because it was not only a matter of what you yourself did, but what the snow under you did, and this you could not control. It was one of the most dangerous places I had ever been on a mountain. Even now, when I think of it, I can still feel as I felt then, and the hair almost stands up on the back of my hands.

At last we got up it, though, and at nine o'clock we were on the south summit. This was the highest point that Bourdillon and Evans had reached, and for ten minutes we rested there, looking up at what was still ahead. There was not much farther to go—only about 300 feet of ridge —but it was narrower and steeper than it had been below, and, though not impossible-looking, would certainly not be easy. On the left, as before, was the precipice falling away to the Western Cwm, 8000 feet below, where we could now see the tiny dots that were the tents of Camp Four. And on the right were still the snow cornices, hanging out over a 10,000-foot drop to the Kangshung Glacier. If we were to get to the top it would have to be along a narrow, twisting line between precipice and cornices—never too far to the left, never too far to the right, or it would be the end of us.

One thing we had eagerly been waiting for happened on the south summit. Almost at the same moment we each came to the end of the first of our two bottles of oxygen, and now we were able to dump them here, which reduced the weight we were carrying from forty to only twenty pounds. Also, as we left the south summit, another good thing happened. We found that the snow beyond it was firm and sound. This could make all the difference on the stretch that we still had to go.

"Everything all right?"

"*Ah chah*. All right."

From the south summit we first had to go down a little. Then up, up, up. All the time the danger was that the snow would slip, or that we would get too far out on a cornice that would then break away; so we moved just one at a time, taking turns at going ahead, while the second one wrapped the rope round his axe and fixed the axe in the snow as an anchor. The weather was still fine. We were not too tired. But every so often, as had happened all the way, we would have trouble breathing, and have to stop and clear away the ice that kept forming in the tubes of our oxygen-sets. In regard to this, I must say in all honesty that I do not think Hillary is quite fair in the story he later told, indicating that I had more trouble than he with breathing, and that without his help I might have suffocated. In my opinion our difficulties were about the same—and luckily never too great—and we each helped and were helped by the other in equal measure.

Anyhow, after each short stop we kept going, twisting always higher along the ridge between the cornices and the precipices. And at last we came to what might be the last big obstacle below the top. This was a cliff of rock rising straight up out of the ridge and blocking it off, and we had already known about it from aerial photographs and from seeing it through binoculars from Thyangboche. Now it was a question of how to get over or round it, and we could find only one possible way. This was along a steep, narrow gap between one side of the rock and the inner side of an adjoining cornice, and Hillary, now going first, worked his way up it, slowly and carefully, to a sort of platform above. While climbing he had to press backward with his feet against the cornice, and I belayed him from below as strongly as I could, for there was great danger of the ice giving way. Luckily, however, it did not. Hillary got up safely to the top of the rock, and then held the rope while I came after.

Here, again, I must be honest and say that I do not feel his account, as told in *The Ascent of Everest*, is wholly accurate. For one thing, he has written that this gap up the rock-wall was about forty feet high, but in my judgment it was little more than fifteen. Also, he gives the impression that it was only he who really climbed it on his own, and that he then practically pulled me, so that I "finally collapsed exhausted at the top, like a giant fish when it has just been hauled from the sea after a terrible struggle." Since then I have heard plenty about that "fish," and I admit I do not like it. For it is the plain truth that no one pulled or hauled me up the gap. I climbed it myself, just as Hillary had done; and if he was protecting me with the rope while I was doing it, this was no more than I had done for him. In speaking of this I must make one thing very clear. Hillary is my friend. He is a fine climber and a fine man, and I am proud to have gone with him to the top of Everest. But I do feel that in his story of our final climb he is not quite fair to me: that all the way through he indicates that when things went well it was his doing, and when things went badly it was mine. For this is simply not true. Nowhere do I make the suggestion that I could have climbed Everest by myself; and I do not think Hillary should suggest that he could have, or that I could not have done it without his help. All the way up and down we helped, and were helped by, each other—and that was the way it should be. But we were not leader and led. We were partners.

On top of the rock-cliff we rest again. Certainly, after the climb up the gap, we are both a bit breathless, but after some slow pulls at the oxygen I am feeling fine. I look up; the top is very close now; and my heart thumps with excitement and joy. Then we are on our way again. Climbing again. There are still the cornices on our right and the precipice on our left, but the ridge is now less steep. It is only a row of snowy humps, one beyond the other, one higher than the other. But we are still afraid of the cornices, and, instead of following the ridge all the way, cut over to the left, where there is now a long snow-slope above the precipice. About a hundred feet below the top we come to the highest bare rocks. There is enough almost level space here for two tents, and I wonder if men will ever camp in this place, so near the summit of the earth. I pick up two small stones and put them in my pocket to bring back to the world below. Then the rocks too are beneath us. We are back among the snowy humps. They are curving off to the right, and each time we pass one I wonder, Is the next the last one? Is the next the last? Finally we reach a place where we can see past the humps, and beyond them is the great open sky and brown plains. We are looking down the far side of the mountain upon Tibet. Ahead of us now is only one more hump—the last hump. It is not a pinnacle. The way to it is an easy snow-slope, wide enough for two men to go side by side. About thirty feet away we stop for a minute and look up. Then we go on. . . .

I have thought much about what I will say now—of how Hillary and I reached the summit of Everest. Later, when we came down from the mountain, there was much foolish talk about who got there first. Some said it was I, some Hillary. Some that only one of us got there—or neither. Still others, that one of us had to drag the other up. All this was nonsense. And in Kathmandu, to put a stop to such talk, Hillary and I signed a statement in which we said "we reached the summit almost together." We hoped this would be the end of it. But it was not the end. People kept on asking questions and making up stories. They pointed to the "almost" and said, "What does that mean?" Mountaineers understand that there is no sense to such a question; that when two men are on the same rope they are *together*, and that is all there is to it. But other people did not understand. In India and Nepal, I am sorry to say, there has been great pressure on me to say that I reached the summit before Hillary. And all over the world I am asked, "Who got there first? Who got there first?"

Again I say, "It is a foolish question. The answer means nothing." And yet it is a question that has been asked so often—that has caused so much talk and doubt and misunderstanding—that I feel, after long thought, that the answer should be given. As will be clear, it is not for my own sake that I give it. Nor is it for Hillary's. It is for the sake of Everest—the prestige of Everest—and for the generations who will come after us. "Why," they will say, "should there be a mystery to this thing? Is there something to be ashamed of? To be hidden? Why can we not know the truth?" . . . Very well: now they will know the truth. Everest is too great, too precious, for anything but the truth.

A little below the summit Hillary and I stopped. We looked up. Then we went on. The rope that joined us was thirty feet long, but I held most of it in loops in my hand, so that there was only about six feet between us. I was not thinking of "first" and "second." I did not say to myself, "There is a golden apple up there. I will push Hillary aside and run for it." We went on slowly, steadily. And then we were there. Hillary stepped on top first. And I stepped up after him.

So there it is—the answer to the "great mystery." And if, after all the talk and argument, the answer seems quiet and simple I can only say that that is as it should be. Many of my own people, I know, will be disappointed at it. They have given a great and false importance to the idea that it must be I who was "first." These people have been good and wonderful to me, and I owe them much. But I owe more to Everest—and to the truth. If it is a discredit to me that I was a step behind Hillary, then I must live with that discredit. But I do not think it was that. Nor do I think that, in the end, it will bring discredit on me that I tell the story. Over and over again I have asked myself, "What will future generations think of us if we allow the facts of our achievement to stay shrouded in mystery? Will they not feel ashamed of us—two comrades in life and death—who have something to hide from the world?" And each time I asked it the answer was the same: "Only the truth is good enough for the future. Only the truth is good enough for Everest."

Now the truth is told. And I am ready to be judged by it.

We stepped up. We were there. The dream had come true. . . .

What we did first was what all climbers do when they reach the top of their mountain. We shook hands. But this was not enough for Everest. I waved my arms in the air, and then threw them round Hillary, and we thumped each other on the back until, even with the oxygen, we were almost breathless. Then we looked round. It was eleven-thirty in the morning, the sun was shining, and the sky was the deepest blue I have ever seen. Only a gentle breeze was blowing, coming from the direction of Tibet, and the plume of snow that always blows from Everest's summit was very small. Looking down the far side of the mountain, I could see all the familiar landmarks from the earlier expeditions—the Rongbuk Monastery, the town of Shekar Dzong, the Kharta Valley, the Rongbuk and East Rongbuk Glaciers, the North Col, the place near the north-east ridge where we had made Camp Six in 1938. Then, turning, I looked down the long way we ourselves had come—past the south summit, the long ridge, the South Col; on to the Western Cwm, the icefall, the Khumbu Glacier; all the way down to Thyangboche, and on to the valleys and hills of my homeland.

Beyond them, and around us on every side, were the great Himalayas, stretching away through Nepal and Tibet. For the closer peaks—giants like Lhotse, Nuptse, and Makalu—you now had to look sharply downward to see their summits. And, farther away, the whole sweep of the greatest range on earth—even Kangchenjunga itself—seemed only like little bumps under the spreading sky. It was such a sight as I had never seen before and would never see again—wild, wonderful, and terrible. But terror was not what I felt. I loved the mountains too well for that. I loved Everest too well. At that great moment for which I had waited all my life my mountain did not seem to me a lifeless thing of rock and ice, but warm and friendly and living. She was a mother hen, and the other mountains were chicks under her wings. I too, I felt, had only to spread my own wings to cover and shelter the brood that I loved.

We turned off our oxygen. Even there on top of the world it was possible to live without it, so long as we were not exerting ourselves. We cleared away the ice that had formed on our masks, and I popped a bit of sweet into my mouth. Then we replaced the masks. But we did not turn on the oxygen again until we were ready to leave the top. Hillary took out his camera, which he had been carrying under his clothing to keep it from freezing, and I unwound the four flags from around my axe. They were tied together on a string, which was fastened to the blade of the axe, and now I held the axe up, and Hillary took my picture. Actually he took three, and I think it was lucky, in those difficult conditions, that one came out so well. The order of the flags from top to bottom was United Nations, British, Nepalese, Indian; and the same sort of people who have made trouble in other ways have tried to find political meaning in this too. All I can say is that on Everest I was not thinking about politics. If I had been I suppose I would have put the Indian or Nepalese flag highest, though that in itself would have been a bad problem for me. As it is, I am glad that the U.N. flag was on top. For I like to think that our victory was not only for ourselves—not only for our own nations—but for all men everywhere.

I motioned to Hillary that I would now take his picture. But for some reason he shook his head; he did not want it. Instead he began taking more pictures himself, around and down on all sides of the peak, and meanwhile I did another thing that had to be done on the top of our mountain. From my pocket I took the package of sweets I had been carrying. I took the little red-and-blue pencil that my daughter, Nima, had given me. And, scraping a hollow in the snow, I laid them there. Seeing what I was doing, Hillary handed me a small cloth cat, black and with white eyes, that Hunt had given him as a mascot, and I put this beside them. In his story of our climb Hillary says it was a crucifix that Hunt gave him, and that he left on top; but if this was so I did not see it. He gave me only the cloth cat. All I laid in the snow was the cat, the pencil, and the sweets. "At home," I thought, "we offer sweets to those who are near and dear to us. Everest has always been dear to me, and now it is near too." As I covered up the offerings I said a silent prayer. And I gave my thanks. Seven times I had come to the mountain of my dream, and on this, the seventh, with God's help, the dream had come true.

"*Thuji chey*, *Chomolungma*. I am grateful. . . ."

We had now been on top almost fifteen minutes. It was time to go. Needing my axe for the descent, I could not leave it there with the flags; so I untied the string that held them, spread the flags across the summit, and buried the ends of the string as deeply as I could in the snow. A few days later planes of the Indian Air Force flew round the peak, taking photographs, but the fliers reported they could see nothing that had been left there. Perhaps they were too far off. Or perhaps the wind had blown the flags away. I do not know.

Before starting down we looked round once more. Had Mallory and Irvine reached the top before they died? Could there be any sign of them? We looked, but we could see nothing. Still they were in my thoughts, and, I am sure, in Hillary's too. All those who had gone before us were in my thoughts—sahibs and Sherpas, English and Swiss—all the great climbers, the brave men, who for thirty-three years had dreamed and challenged, fought and failed, on this mountain, and whose efforts and knowledge and experience had made our victory possible. Our companions below were in my thoughts, for without them too —without their help and sacrifice—we could never have been where we were that day. And closest of all was one figure, one companion—Lambert. He was so near, so real to me, that he did not seem to be in my thoughts at all, but actually standing there beside me. Any moment now I would turn and see his big bear face grinning at me. I would hear his voice saying, "*Ça va bien,* Tenzing! *Ça va bien!*"

Well, at least his red scarf was there. I pulled it more tightly round my throat. "When I get back home," I told myself, "I will send it to him." And I did.

Since the climbing of Everest all sorts of questions have been put to me, and not all of them have been political. From the people of the East there have been many that have to do with religion and the supernatural. "Was the Lord Buddha on the top?" I have been asked. Or "Did you see the Lord Siva?" From many sides, among the devout and orthodox, there has been great pressure upon me to say that I had some vision or revelation. But here, again—even though it may be disappointing to many—I can tell only the truth; and this is no, that on the top of Everest I did not see anything supernatural or feel anything superhuman. What I felt was a great closeness to God, and that was enough for me. In my deepest heart I thanked God. And as we turned to leave the summit I prayed to Him for something very real and very practical—that, having given us our victory, He would get us down off the mountain alive.

We turned on our oxygen-sets. We started off. And, though we were anxious to get down as quickly as possible, we went slowly and carefully, because we knew that we were more tired than before, that our reactions were less sure, and that most accidents on mountains happen when men are tired and careless on the way down. Kick-step, kick-step we went in the steep snow, mostly using the track we had made on the climb up. When we got to the rocky cliff and the gap beside it we got down with little trouble. In fact, I just let go and jumped for part of the way. Then we were on the ridge again, kicking and sliding, and in an hour we had reached the south summit. Through this part of the descent Hillary went first and I second, holding the rope tight when there was any danger. And, though we were both tired, we were not exhausted. The thing that bothered us most was thirst; for the water in our flasks had frozen, and to have eaten snow would have made it only worse for our mouths and throats.

At the south summit we rested a little. Then came the

steep snow-wall just below it, and, even more than on the
way up, it was dangerous and terrifying. In front of me
Hillary was at the same time trying to go down and to hold
himself back, and his knees were so bent that his buttocks
often touched the snow. Above him, I was every moment
gripping the rope and bracing myself in case he should
slip, for beneath him here was nothing but the Kangshung
Glacier, 10,000 feet below. In the end, though, we got
down all right. Now the worst was behind us. A little
farther on we picked up the two oxygen-bottles that had
been left by Bourdillon and Evans; and the timing of this
was just right, because our own supply was now almost
gone. At about two o'clock we reached the high tent,
where we stopped and rested again, and I heated some
sweet lemon-juice over the stove. This was the first drink
we had had for hours, and it was like new life pouring
down into our bodies.

Then we went on down from Camp Nine. Along the
ridge, past the old Swiss tent, down the big couloir of the
snow-slope that led to the South Col. Here we were
sometimes able to use our old steps, but in other places the
wind had wiped them out, and it was so steep that, even
with our crampons, we had to cut new holds to keep from
sliding off. Here we changed places, and I went first on
the rope, hacking and chopping for what seemed like
days instead of hours. But by now we could see the tents
on the col and little moving dots around them. Slowly
the tents and the dots grew bigger. And then at last we
came down on to the easier snow, just above the col, and
George Lowe, in the lead of those below, came up to meet
us. He threw his arms around us, gave us hot coffee to
drink, and then, with the help of the others, led us down to
the camp.

Gregory had gone down earlier that day. But Noyce had come up with the Sherpa Pasang Phutar,[1] and now they and Lowe did everything possible to make us warm and comfortable. Lowe had given us coffee. Now Noyce brought us tea. And he must have been excited and tipped the stove while he was making it, for it was full of kerosene; but it didn't matter—it didn't matter at all—and I thought, as I was drinking it, It tastes as sweet as buttered milk, because it is mixed with love and kindness. The others were asking us questions, of course. But just then we could answer only a few. We had to rest. It was getting dark and cold, and we crept into our sleeping-bags —Hillary in one tent with Lowe and Noyce and I in another with Pasang. I lay still, with my "night oxygen," and tried to sleep. I felt *ah chah*—O.K. But tired. It was hard to think or feel anything.

The real happiness, I thought, will come later.

[1] This was another Pasang Phutar—not the one called Jockey who had left the expedition at Thyangboche.

19

"TENZING ZINDABAD!"

Yes, the happiness came. And later other things too.
But first the happiness.

The next day the weather was again fine. The sun
was shining. And though we were, of course, still tired,
and a little weak from our three days at such great heights,
it was with joy and peace of spirit that we made the long
descent from the South Col. The sahibs left most of their
things at Camp Eight, but I carried three or four bags of
equipment, a flask, and also one of Lowe's two cameras,
which he had forgotten in the excitement. On the way
we kept meeting our friends who had been waiting for us
below. At Camp Seven were Major Wylie and several
Sherpas. Below Camp Six Tom Stobart came up to meet
us with his moving-picture camera. And at Camp Five
were several more Sherpas, including Dawa Thondup and
my young nephew, Gombu. At each meeting there was
much talk and excitement, and at Five the Sherpas gave
us tea, and insisted on carrying my load for me the rest of
the way down.

Then at Camp Four, the advance base, we met the main
part of the expedition. As we descended the long snow-
slope of the cwm they came out to meet us, and at first we
gave no sign of what had happened. But when we were

about fifty yards away Lowe could keep the secret no longer. With one hand he made the 'thumbs-up' sign, and with the other he waved his axe towards the summit, and from that minute on I think there has never been such excitement in the history of the Himalayas. Even with their boots and in the thick snow they came almost running towards us. Hunt embraced Hillary and me. I embraced Evans. Everybody embraced everybody. "Is it really true? Is it really true?" Hunt kept saying over and over again. And then he hugged me again in joy. Anyone who had seen us then could never have thought about distinctions between sahibs and Sherpas. We were all mountaineers together, who had climbed our mountain.

For hours then we drank and ate and rested—and talked and talked. It was a wonderful evening—the happiest, I think, of my whole life. But, although I did not know it then, certain things had already begun to happen which were later to cause much difficulty and misunderstanding. A short while before a false report had gone out over the Indian Wireless News that we had failed in our attempt. Now the true report was sent—by runner to Namche Bazar and then by radio from there to Kathmandu. But it was sent in code, and only to the British Ambassador, Mr Summerhayes, who forwarded it to London, but did not inform anyone else for more than a day. The idea, I believe, was for Queen Elizabeth to have the news first, and for it to be made known the next day as a special feature of her coronation. For the British the timing was perfect, and there was a wonderful celebration. But for many Easterners it was quite the opposite, for they did not receive the news until a day later—and then from the other side of the world. This was true even for King Tribhuvana of Nepal, in whose country Everest stood.

At the time, as I say, I knew nothing about all this. I myself could have sent the news straight away by Sherpa runner to Namche Bazar, and perhaps things would have worked out differently. But I asked myself, "Why should I?" I was working for the British. As we Sherpas say, I was "eating their salt." They had run the expedition; why should they not handle this in their own way? So I sent no message, and I told the other Sherpas not to break the news until it was official. Later there was loose talk that I had been bribed by the British to do this, and even that I had been bribed to say that Everest had been climbed, when it really had not been. To the first of these accusations I can say only that it was completely untrue. The second is so ridiculous that it is not worth answering.

When I say I sent no message I mean no public one, to be announced at once. Now for the first time in weeks and months I was able to think of something besides climbing—besides getting to the top. My mind turned to my loved ones who were waiting for me at home, and that night at Camp Four one of my friends wrote a note for me to Ang Lahmu. "This letter is from Tenzing," it said. "Myself along with one sahib reached summit Everest 29th May. Hope you will feel happy. Cannot write more. May I be excused." And at the bottom I myself signed my name.

I spent only one night at Camp Four. Half of it was celebration, half rest. The next morning my only thought was to get down off the mountain, and in one day I descended the cwm and the icefall, all the way to base camp, with the Sherpa Ang Tshering and my nephew Gombu. Now I am free, I kept thinking. I have been freed by Everest. And, luckily, I could not know yet how wrong I was. At base camp, too, I stayed only one night, and then, in another single day, I went thirty-five miles down the glacier and valleys to Thamey, to see my mother. I told her we had had success, and she was very happy. Staring up into my face, she said to me, "Many times I have told you not to go to this mountain. Now you don't have to go again." All her life she had believed that there was a golden sparrow on the top of Everest, and also a turquoise lion with a golden mane; and when she asked me about them I was sorry to have to disappoint her. But when she asked if I had seen the Rongbuk Monastery from the top I was able to say yes—and this pleased her.

I had come to Thamey alone. Now I spent two days there with my mother and my younger sister, who lived with her, and it was the first time since I had been a child that I had been so long in my native village. All the people came to see us, the *chang* flowed, and I am willing to admit that, as the English say, I "broke training." Then, remembering my duties to the expedition, I collected a hundred men to serve as porters on the return trip to Kathmandu, and left with them for Thyangboche. Before going I asked my mother if she would like to come with me and live in Darjeeling; and she said, "Yes, I would like it. But I am too old. I would be too much trouble to you." Though I tried to persuade her, she would not come, and once again I had to bid my *ama la* good-bye. But on the way from Thamey to Thyangboche I met my older sister, Lahmu Kipa, with her husband and two daughters, and, being younger, they decided to come with me.

At Thyangboche the expedition was coming back in sections from the mountain, and everything was excitement and confusion. One of the worst problems was to get enough porters for the return trip, for the monsoon rains would soon be beginning, and few people wanted to go.

Also there was almost as much complaining as rejoicing that Everest had been climbed, for now they were afraid there would be no more expeditions and no more jobs. And the lamas (who had never encouraged its climbing) were afraid that our success would bring bad luck from the gods. After a little while, though, we got at least some sort of organization, and made ready to leave. Colonel Hunt said that he was going ahead of the main party, to make various arrangements, and that one of them would be to take me to England. This idea had not occurred to me before. If I had thought anything about the future it was only that I would go back to Darjeeling and rest, and, later, if I had enough money, build a small new house. I still hadn't any notion at all of what was going to happen to me.

It was not long, though, before I began to see that things were going to be very different from before. Already at Thyangboche there was a cable for me from Sir Winston Churchill, and from then on the messages were like a flood. Also there was one message I wanted to send myself—to Ang Lahmu, asking her and the girls to meet me in Kathmandu—and I spoke to Major Wylie about this, saying I would pay for a special runner. As always, he was kind and helpful: the message was sent at expedition expense. And in the days that followed, as we took the long trail to Kathmandu, he was good to me in many ways—giving me sound advice, helping me with strangers, and even acting as a sort of secretary for me with all the messages that were coming in. "Now you see what sort of life you have to face," he told me. But this was just the beginning, and I was still to learn my lessons the hard way.

Up and down we went across the hills and valleys of Nepal. And each day there were bigger crowds and more excitement. After about ten days, when we were some fifty miles from Kathmandu, I received word that Ang Lahmu and the girls had arrived there—and that was fine news. But most of the people who came out were not bringing news, but looking for it, and soon I was walking along in the middle of a whole parade of journalists. Some were Nepali, some Indian, some British, and some American, and, in addition to the story of the climb, many of them wanted me to make all sorts of statements about nationality and politics. Major Wylie had warned me this might happen, and told me to be careful, and I tried to be.

It was not easy, with so many people crowding round and asking questions all at once, and half the time, it seemed to me, they were not only asking the questions, but giving the answers too. At a place called Hukse I had a good interview with James Burke, of *Life* magazine, which had bought the American rights to the expedition story from *The Times*. And a little farther on I met John Hlavacek, of the United Press Associations, with which I later signed a contract for a series of articles. The English climbers could not do anything like this. Before starting out they had signed an agreement that all stories and photographs would belong to the expedition as a whole, which in turn had its contract with *The Times*. But, though I was on the expedition, I had not been asked to do this, so that now I was free to deal with whom I chose. When we reached Kathmandu, and later New Delhi, there was some discussion and argument about this. *The Times* had the rights to all dispatches sent by members of the expedition, and Colonel Hunt tried to get me to sign the agreement. But I declined to do this. For the first time in my life I was in a position to make a considerable sum of money, and I could not see why it was not right and proper for me to do so.

This, however, was only a small trouble. The big one started at a place called Dhaulagat, a little before Kathmandu, when a crowd of Nepali came out to meet me and almost tore me away from the rest of the expedition. I have often been asked since if they were Communists, and this I do not honestly know. But I do know that they were nationalists, with very strong ideas, and what they were interested in was not Everest at all, or how Everest was really climbed—but only politics. They wanted me to say that I was a Nepali, not an Indian. And also that I got to the top ahead of Hillary. I told them I was not concerned with politics or arguments with the British. I begged them to leave me alone. "Up till now," I told them, "nobody cared about my nationality. Why do you care now? Indian—Nepali. What difference does it make?" I tried to say again what I had said in the interview with James Burke: "We should all be the same—Hillary, myself, Indian, Nepali, everybody."

But they would not stop. They drove me almost mad. They put answers in my mouth and made me sign papers that I could not read. And all the time the crowd grew bigger and bigger. I was separated from my companions, pushed and pulled about like some sort of child's toy. What are they going to do with me? I wondered. If I had known it was going to be like this I would have stayed up in Solo Khumbu. When, on June the 20th, we walked down the last hills into the Valley of Nepal they were still pushing and pulling. At Bonepa, where the road begins, they put me into a jeep and made me change into Nepali clothes, and by this time I was so exhausted and confused that I let them do as they liked. In every town and village through which we passed there was a big celebration. People crowded round, waving flags and banners. "*Tenzing zindabad!*" they shouted. "Long live Tenzing!" And in a way it was wonderful to be so warmly greeted. But I confess I would rather have returned simply and quietly, as from every other expedition on which I had ever been.

Three miles outside Kathmandu my wife and daughters were waiting for me, and we had warm embraces of happiness and victory. Ang Lahmu put a *khada,* or sacred scarf, round my neck. Pem Pem and Nima covered my shoulders with garlands, and I told Nima with a smile that I had put her pencil where she had asked me to. Later I learned that, during those past few weeks, things had been almost as confused for them as for me. They had first heard the great news on the morning of June the 2nd, a rainy, gloomy day in Darjeeling, from friends who had been listening to the radio; and from that minute on their lives had changed completely. Important officials had come to call on them. There had been all sorts of messages, many plans and counter-plans. Pictures of me, they said, were all over the town, and my friend Mitra had had a poet compose a song with music about me that was soon being sung up and down the streets. It had all been wonderful and exciting for them, but what they had wanted most of all was to hear from me, and the message I had sent telling them to come to Kathmandu had never arrived. Ang Lahmu, on her own, had wanted very much to come, but had been afraid I might be angry if she did so unexpectedly. "Why is there no wire from my husband?" she had kept asking. "I will pay ten rupees to the boy who brings it from the telegraph office." But still my wire did not come (what went wrong I have never found out), and after waiting eleven days she decided to come, anyhow. She had neither money nor proper clothes, but Mitra gave her a hundred rupees he had made from the sale of my photographs, and later, with the help of Mrs Henderson, of the Himalayan Club, and other friends, he raised another four hundred rupees towards the expenses. She and the girls had left Darjeeling and flown to Kathmandu by way of Patna, arriving four days before me. With them had come Pasang Phutar (still a third one), a veteran mountain man who is both a close friend and relative of ours, and Lhakpa Tshering, an educated Sherpa who came as representative of our Sherpa Association.

But there was little time to talk of any of this on that mad day when I myself reached Kathmandu. After a few minutes I was pulled away from my family. I was taken out of the keep and put in a sort of big chariot pulled by horses; and now many of the other climbers, whom I had not seen for some time, were there too, and Hunt and Hillary were also put in the chariot. Then we were moving into the city, and the crowds were thicker than ever. They threw rice and coloured powder and coins, and the coins kept bouncing off my skull until I thought I was going to get a headache. But there was nothing I could do about it, because I could not look in all directions at once. Most of the time I just stood in the chariot smiling, with the palms of my hands together and the fingers upward, in the ancient Hindu greeting of *namaste*.

So many things were happening that it is hard to remember what came first and what afterwards. Still in our dirty old expedition clothes, we were taken to the royal palace and welcomed by King Tribhuvana, who awarded me the Nepal Tara (Star of Nepal), the highest decoration in the country, and gave two other medals to Hunt and

Hillary. As with so many things at this time, the question of honours, and who received what, caused difficulty and misunderstanding. For at about the same time that I was given one Nepalese award, and Hunt and Hillary another, lesser one, word came from England that the Queen had conferred knighthoods on them, while I would simply receive the George Medal. The fuss that this caused was not only unfortunate, but foolish. Since winning its independence the Government of India, like that of the United States, has not permitted its citizens to accept foreign titles, and, if anything, it would probably only have embarrassed both myself and my country if the Queen had offered such an honour. For me it was *kai chai na*—no matter. Would a title give me wings? And after I·understood the reasons I in no way felt slighted or offended.

Politics—politics: suddenly they were making trouble everywhere. The Nepalese were wonderful to me. They gave me a welcome I could not forget in a hundred lifetimes. But in their effort to make me a hero they went too far: they almost ignored the British, instead of treating them as honoured guests; and too many of them said foolish things and tried to twist the facts for political reasons. There were all sorts of wild stories about: that I had dragged Hillary to the top of Everest, that he had not got there at all, that I had practically climbed the whole mountain all by myself. And unfortunately there were the foolish statements I had been made to sign, without knowing what I was doing, when I was picked up by that mad crowd outside Kathmandu. Finally the whole thing had got too much for Colonel Hunt. He lost his temper and announced that, far from being a hero, I wasn't technically even a very good climber. And this, of course, was like pouring petrol on a fire.

Nepalese and Indian journalists kept after me all the time. People with political motives tried to get me to say things against the British, and because I was hurt at what Colonel Hunt had said I too made a few statements that I later regretted. Luckily, though, there was much more good will than bad will in our hearts. Neither the British nor I wanted to see our great adventure made into something small and mean. So on the 22nd of June we met together in the office of the Prime Minister of Nepal and prepared a statement that we hoped would put an end to all the trouble. One copy was signed by me for Hillary, one by Hillary for me, and this second one, which I still have, reads:

> On May the 29th Tenzing Sherpa and I left our high camp on Mount Everest for our attempt on the summit.
> As we climbed upwards to the south summit first one and then the other would take a turn at leading.
> We crossed over the south summit and moved along the summit ridge. We reached the summit almost together.
> We embraced each other, overjoyed at our success; then I took photographs of Tenzing holding aloft the flags of Great Britain, Nepal, the United Nations, and India.
>
> (*signed*) E. P. HILLARY

Everything in the statement is true. Certainly nothing could be truer than that we reached the top *almost together*. And that is how the matter has been left until this time—when, for reasons I have already given, it seems right to me to tell all the details.

Besides the question of who reached the top first, there was much talk and argument about my nationality. "What difference does it make?" I kept asking. "What do nationality and politics have to do with climbing a mountain?" But still the talk went on, and so I spoke about this too to the Prime Minister, Mr Koirala. I said to him, "I love Nepal. I was born here, and it is my country. But for a long time now I have been living in India. My children have grown up there, and I must think of their education and livelihood." Mr Koirala and the other Ministers were kind and considerate. They did not, as some others had, try to put pressure on me, but only said that if I decided to stay in Nepal they would give me a house, along with other rewards and benefits; and they wished me luck and happiness, whatever my decision might be. I am still deeply grateful for their helpfulness when I was in a difficult situation. As I said then to the Press, "I was born in the womb of Nepal and raised in the lap of India." I love both. And I feel I am the son of both.

We stayed in Kathmandu for about a week. And every day there were new events, new celebrations—and new problems. This time we Sherpas slept, not in a garage, but in the Nepalese Government guest-house; so there was no difficulty there. Or if there was it was only in trying to keep out the crowds of people who wanted to swarm all over us. One evening there was a reception at the British Embassy. I was invited, but declined to go; and since this, like so many other things at the time, caused much loose talk, I shall explain the reason. It was that, the year before, when I was in Kathmandu with the Swiss, I had had an unpleasant experience there. On a certain night there had been some sort of mix-up in the expedition arrangements; I found myself with no place to sleep, and, having stayed at the Embassy with Tilman in 1949, I went there and asked for shelter. It was a mistake, though. Colonel Proud, the First Secretary, turned me away. My feelings were badly hurt. And since Colonel Proud was now still at the Embassy, I saw no reason to accept its hospitality. This was the only reason I did not go that evening, and it was in no way intended as an unfriendly gesture to my comrades of Everest.

When I left Kathmandu it was for Calcutta, in the private plane of King Tribhuvana. There was just myself and my family, with Lhakpa Tshering, who was now acting as a sort of adviser to me. The others were going down to India in different ways. At Calcutta we were put up at Government House, and there was more excitement, more receptions, more *zindabad*. Among those who met us there were my good friend Mitra, whom I had wired to come down from Darjeeling, and one of the first things I did was to give him Raymond Lambert's red scarf and ask him to send it to Switzerland. Also while in Calcutta I told my story to the United Press, with whom I had now signed a contract. For a few days, at this time, it looked as if I would not be going to England after all, because I had decided it would not be right to go without Ang Lahmu and the girls, and the expedition had no money to take them. Meanwhile the *Daily Express* offered me a big tour, with all expenses paid; but after thinking it over I refused, because I was afraid it would have some sort of political significance, and after my experience in Nepal this was the one thing, more than anything else, that I wanted to keep away from. Instead I went from Calcutta to New Delhi, where the rest of the expedition was gathered, still hoping that something could be worked out.

In Delhi it was the same as in Kathmandu and Calcutta. Only more so than ever. At the airport, when we arrived, there was a great welcome, with the biggest crowds I had seen in my life. Then we were driven to the Nepalese Embassy, where we were to stay, and that same evening there was a reception given by Pandit Nehru. This was a great moment for me—the moment Professor Tucci had spoken of long ago in Tibet, and that I had thought of that night in my tent, high on Everest. And in every way it came up to what I had hoped and dreamed it might be. For, from the very first, Panditji[1] was like a father to me. He was warm and kind, and, unlike so many others, was not thinking of what use he could make of me, but only of how he could help me and make me happy. The day after the reception he invited me to his office, and there he strongly advised me to go to London. There had already, he thought, been too much trouble and argument about the climb; Everest was better without politics; and he hoped everything possible would be done to heal any wounds that had been caused. With this I agreed with all my heart. And then, to make everything wonderful, he said it would be arranged that my wife and daughters could go to London with me.

Nor was this all Panditji did. Later he took me to his home, and, since I had hardly any clothes of my own, he opened his closets and began giving me his. He gave me coats, trousers, shirts, everything—because we are the same size they all fitted perfectly—and also some things that had belonged to his father, and on which he placed great value. To Ang Lahmu he presented a fine pocketbook and a raincoat, saying with a smile that it rained a lot in London. And as still another gift for me there was a briefcase, so that I felt, "Now I am no longer a poor Sherpa at all, but a business-man or a diplomat." About the only thing to wear or carry he did not give me was one of his white Congress Party caps; for that would have had

[1] A term of affection and respect often applied to Nehru by Indians. —J.R.U.

political meaning, and he completely agreed with me that I should stay out of politics.

While I was in Delhi there was also the question of a passport, which, in spite of all my travelling, would be the first I had ever had. As it turned out, I was given not one, but two—one Indian and one Nepalese—and this was just the way I wanted it. Then, a few days later, we flew off towards the West. There were no other Sherpas with us, except Lhakpa Tshering, who was still acting as my secretary and adviser. The climbing Sherpas had not even come to Calcutta or Delhi, but had gone straight home from Kathmandu to Darjeeling. But most of the English expedition members were also aboard the plane, and, besides Ang Lahmu and the girls, there was also Mrs—or now Lady—Hunt, who had flown out to meet her husband while we were still in Nepal. We flew in a B.O.A.C. plane, and our first stop was Karachi, where we stayed for an hour while another great crowd came out to see us. Then we went on to Baghdad, Cairo, and Rome, and I was at last seeing the world beyond India and Pakistan that I had dreamed of so often in the past.

In Rome we were welcomed by the Indian and British Ambassadors, and then, because of engine trouble with the plane, we spent the night there. The next morning, when we boarded the plane again, Colonel Hunt looked upset about something, and soon I found out what it was. The newspapers had just published the first part of my story, which I had given to the United Press, and in it I had told something of the difficulties that had arisen during the expedition between the British and the Sherpas. As we flew north he came over and spoke to me, and we talked frankly about the things that had happened. I told him how hurt I had been at his statement to the Press that I was not an experienced climber, and he in turn explained the problems he had had to face. Major Wylie had already spoken to me of these matters. He had pointed out how important it was that there be no ill-will because of them, and I had agreed with him. And this I now said to Colonel Hunt. There *had* been certain difficulties during the expedition and afterwards. There was no use denying it, and I had simply told the story from my own point of view, as honestly as I could. But this did not mean that I bore any grudge, or that I was trying to make an issue of these difficulties, as certain others had done for political purposes. Our talk was candid and friendly, and I think we both felt better for having had it.

After Rome our next stop was Zurich. Though we stayed there only a short while, it was a wonderful time for me, for many of my old Swiss friends were at the airport to meet me. Best of all, Lambert was there, with a big embrace and a welcoming "*Ça va bien*," and I told him about the final climb with Hillary, and how I had been thinking of him when I stood on the summit. Then we flew on to London. Just before we landed Colonel Hunt asked if it was all right with me if he came out of the plane first, carrying a Union Jack attached to an ice-axe, and I said, "Of course it is all right." So that was the way it was, and soon all of us were out on the landing-strip and in the middle of another great reception.

In London my family and I stayed at the Indian Services Club, and we were wonderfully looked after by the Indian Ambassador, Mr B. G. Kher. Immediately after we arrived the other expedition members scattered all over England to visit their homes and families, so that I was almost the only one left in the city; but I was certainly not at a loss for things to do. Just meeting people and shaking hands seemed to take up most of the time, and in between there were newspaper interviews and posing for pictures and touring London and all kinds of public appearances. The English people were tremendously kind and considerate. Their welcome to me, a stranger from a far country, was every bit as warm as that to their own climbers, and I could not help comparing this with the rather indifferent reception the British had had from the crowds in Nepal. I went to so many places I could hardly keep track of them. I spoke on the radio. I appeared on television, before I had ever even seen a set. And the interviews went on and on. Finally there were so many of them, and I had been asked so often, over and over again, how I had felt on the summit of Everest, that I began to get dizzy from it. "Look, I have a suggestion," I finally said to the newspapermen. "The next time *you* climb Everest and let me be the reporter. When you come down I'll ask you one thousand and one times how you felt on top, and then you'll know how I felt—and how I'm feeling now."

We spent sixteen days in London, and they went by as if we were in a dream. The only bad thing that happened was that Pem Pem took ill soon after we arrived and had to spend most of the time in a hospital. But Ang Lahmu, Nima, and I went everywhere—to theatres and shops and places of interest. Once we went to a fair and rode on the scenic railway, and I had a fine time with the ups and downs. In fact, it reminded me of skiing. But Ang Lahmu got so excited she kept pounding my hand with her fists, and when the ride was over she said, "What are you trying to do—kill me?" Being a woman, she had her own best times in the shops, and soon we had a great collection of things to bring back to India. Also, people were all the time offering us presents, but, though I appreciated their kindness, I did not think we should accept too many. "Why not?" Ang Lahmu and Nima would say. "Because it's not right," I would tell them. And then there would be a family argument. I especially remember one day when we were at a camera shop, and the dealer offered us our choice of cameras as a gift. Nima immediately picked out an expensive Rolleiflex, but I told her, "No, no, that isn't nice. You take a simpler one." Later, back in Darjeeling, she said to my friend Mitra, "Papa was mean. He wouldn't let me have a good camera." To which I answered, "It wasn't I who was mean. It was you who were greedy. That's the trouble with you females—you're always greedy."

Colonel Hunt invited us to come to his home in the country. Though we would have liked to go, we did not feel it right to leave London while Pem Pem was still ill; but we made two visits to Major Wylie and his wife, who lived close by. Also I saw many old friends, such as Eric Shipton and Hugh Ruttledge, with whom I had fine talks about the old days. And I was deeply touched when Dr N. D. Jacob, who had been so kind to me out in Chitral during the War years, made a journey of 500 miles just to see me. With all these things, the time passed very quickly. Sometimes, when I was not meeting people or being taken to places, I would manage to go out on my own to look round the streets of London, and this I enjoyed greatly. For these walks I would wear Western clothes, in the hope that I would not be recognized; and sometimes it worked. But for official events I wore mostly the Indian things that Pandit Nehru had given me in New Delhi.

After several days the other expedition members began to come back from their homes, and then came the biggest

event of our London visit, which was our presentation to
the Queen. As we drove to Buckingham Palace the streets
were full of crowds, and I was very impressed by the
Guards, with their red coats and big fur hats. Before
meeting the Queen we went to a tea-party on the Palace
lawn, and there was a great crowd there too—so much so
that we were all pressed together, and I felt that my insides
might be squeezed out. But then I thought, No, I shouldn't
complain. At least I'm thin. But what's happening to poor
Ang Lahmu, who isn't? When the outdoor party was
over we were taken into a big reception room in the Palace,
where we met the Queen and the Duke of Edinburgh. All
the expedition members and their families were there, and
the Queen and Duke presented us with medals and
awards. Afterwards there were refreshments, and for a
minute I almost thought I was back on Everest again,
because what I was drinking was—lemon-juice! The
Queen was very friendly and interested, and asked me
several questions about the climb, and also about my other
expeditions. Colonel Hunt, who knows Hindustani,
started to translate for me, but I found that I could understand and answer all right in English, and this pleased me
very much.

After the reception there was a stag dinner, given for us
by the Duke, and we were all wearing our decorations
from here to there. Later there was another reception.
And the next day, and the day after, there were still more
receptions, most of them given by various Ambassadors.
For a while that was all life seemed to be—one big reception—and I thought, What would happen to me if this
was *chang* I was drinking all the time, instead of just tea and
lemon-juice?

At last the time came to leave London. The Hunts, the

Wylies, and many others came to see us off, and anyone who saw our good-bye would not have to be told that there was no ill-feeling between us. The English people had been wonderful to me. The English climbers were fine men, and my friends. In spite of the minor difficulties, and the trouble-makers who had tried to make them big, we had had a great and successful expedition. And if Colonel Hunt ever leads another expedition back to the Himalayas he will find me ready to help him in every way, even though it might not be possible for me to go with him myself.

"Good-bye! Good luck! Happy landings!"

Then we were in the plane flying back towards Switzerland, and the expedition was over at last, for now there were only myself and family and my assistant, Lhakpa Tshering. It had been arranged that we should spend two weeks in Switzerland on the return trip, as guests of the Swiss Foundation for Alpine Research, which had organized the two expeditions in 1952, and when we arrived there was a big welcome and reunion all over again. But this time it was not to be just crowds and receptions and interviews. After only one night in Zürich I went off to the mountains with some of my old friends, and I had a chance not only to see, but climb, the famous Alps. Mr Ernst Feuz, of the Swiss Foundation, and his wife made all the arrangements, travelled with us, and gave us a wonderful time.

First we went to the little mountain resort of Rosenlaui, where the well-known guide Arnold Glatthard runs a school of climbing, and there we went up a nice rock-peak called the Semilistock. Then we went over to the Jungfrau, rode up to the hotel on the Jungfraujoch on the mountain train, and the next morning climbed the peak itself. One of my companions was Raymond Lambert, and as we stood on top, looking out over the earth, I think perhaps the same thought was in both our minds—that with a little better weather, a little better luck, we could have done this together a year before, on the top of the world. These were the only real climbs there was time for, but I enjoyed them very much, and liked the sound, firm rock of the Alpine peaks. One thing that especially impressed me was how similar the high Swiss valleys were to those of my old home in Solo Khumbu, though, of course, in the Alps the heights and distances are much smaller than in the Himalayas. And I was also interested to see how many people there were who went climbing— men and women, old and young, and even very small children.

Later we spent a day in Chamonix, across the French border. Here I met several members of the Lyons expedition to Nanda Devi, with whom I had climbed in 1951, and also Maurice Herzog, who had led the great ascent of Annapurna in 1950. He was a fine man, who had come through his hard experiences very well, and I much admired the way he drove his own car, even though he had lost all his fingers and toes. Unfortunately there was time only to look at Mont Blanc, not climb it. But I doubt if we could have fitted on to it if we had tried. On the day we were in Chamonix it was so crowded with climbers that it looked less like a mountain than a railway station.

So the two weeks passed, almost before they had seemed to begin. And then I had bid my friends good-bye and we were in a plane again, bound for home. ... Home, I thought. What will it be like after all this time? ... I had left Darjeeling on March the 1st; now it was early August, and in those five months I had hardly for a minute stopped moving. I had reached the top of Everest. I had come down from Everest into a different world. I had travelled half-way across that world, and been cheered by crowds, and met Prime Ministers and Queens. Everything has changed for me, I thought. And yet nothing has really changed, because inside I am still the same old Tenzing. . . . All right; I was going home now. But home to what? What would I do? What would happen to me? . . . First there would be more receptions, more interviews, more crowds, more *zindabad*. But then what?

I had climbed my mountain, but I must still live my life.

20

FROM TIGER HILL

INDIA AGAIN. . . .

In New Delhi I once more saw Pandit Nehru and Dr Rajendra Prasad, the President of the Republic of India, who listened to the story of my travels and gave me good advice for the future. More than ever now I felt that Panditji was like a father to me, and I resolved that if ever I had bad problems or was in trouble it would be to him that I would go.

Then at last, after so many months and miles, I returned to Darjeeling. Our old house in Toong Soong Busti was so full of gifts that had been sent to me that we could no longer fit in it. First we lived in a hotel, then moved to a small apartment and began making plans to buy a new home of our own. Meanwhile there were reunions with the other Everest Sherpas and with the rest of my old friends in Darjeeling. There were, of course, the crowds and receptions and interviews. There was always activity and excitement, and it was a wonderful way to be welcomed back home. But there was not much of the rest that I so badly needed. The days, and then the weeks, went by as if in some sort of mad dream.

Some time before, while I was still in Nepal, my friend Robi Mitra had written to Dr B. C. Roy the Chief

Minister of West Bengal (where Darjeeling is), and suggested to him the idea of an Indian mountaineering school, of which I would be head. Both Dr Roy and I thought it a good idea, and soon after my return home we got together and discussed plans. It was decided that the school would be called the Himalayan Institute of Mountaineering, and its purpose would be to develop a love and knowledge of mountains among Indians themselves, and to give our own young men a chance to learn how to become real mountaineers. I would be in charge of instruction and training, and the administration would be handled by N. D. Jayal, my old climbing companion on Bandar Punch and Nanda Devi, who had now risen to the rank of major in the Indian Army. The headquarters of the school were to be in Darjeeling, but since there are no big mountains close to the town, it would also be necessary to find a base for the actual climbing, and it was decided that the obvious place for this was in the great range to the north, near Kangchenjunga.

Needing the best expert advice on such matters, we got in touch with the Swiss Foundation for Alpine Research, and Arnold Glatthard, head of the climbing school at Rosenlaui, came out to work with us. In October, about two months after my return home, he, Major Jayal, and I took a trip up into the Sikkim Himalayas to look for a good place for our base of operations. After much reconnoitring we selected a spot in the region of Koktan and Kang Peak, which I had visited with George Frey two years before. For here were not only the usual snow mountains, but also many good rock areas, and the terrain was just right for all sorts of climbing and training. After we returned and made our recommendations the work of financing and organizing the school was begun, with the plan of actually opening it in the autumn of the following year.

Meanwhile my family and I began living our life again in Darjeeling, and we could see at once that it was to be a new life, for hardly anything was the same as before. There were still crowds, crowds, crowds. There were still the receptions and interviews. And though I was deeply grateful for the attention and honour I was given, it was sometimes almost enough to make me desperate. I had always loved to walk in the streets of Darjeeling, but now I found that I had to go out before dawn in the morning if I was not to be followed by a whole procession. Visitors came to my home not only by invitation or at the regular hours, but at all times of the day and night, sometimes even forcing themselves in through the doors and windows. People came from all sorts of firms and organizations, wanting me to sign this and endorse that. And the newspapermen never let me alone for a minute. As often as not they would twist the stories I told them for their own purposes, so that what was later printed in the papers was nothing like what I had said; and I could well understand why Colonel Hunt had lost his temper in Nepal, when every one had been pushing and pulling him and putting words into his mouth. One of the questions I was asked most, of course, was which expedition I would go on next. And finally I used to answer, "I am on an expedition right now. An expedition of interviews and photographs." Half the time I felt like an animal in the zoo. Perhaps the lamas of Thyangboche were right after all, I thought, and now I am being punished by the Lord of Everest.

There were other troubles, too. I had been paid a good sum of money for my stories to the United Press, and there had also been generous purses from many Indian cities and organizations; so that it was no longer necessary for us to live in our former poverty. Some people were kind and understanding about this, but others were jealous, and there were even comments that Ang Lahmu was "stuck-up" because she now carried an umbrella on rainy days. Still another thing that went wrong was with Lhakpa Tshering, who had been acting as my adviser. There is no point in going into details. But I soon found that he did not have my best interests at heart, and our association ended. Out of this, at least, came one good thing, for his place was taken by Robi Mitra, who gave up all his other interests to help me. And since then his hard work, good advice, and unselfish devotion have done more than I can tell to make life easier and happier.

The new home I bought was on a steep hillside on the outskirts of Darjeeling, with a wonderful view across Sikkim towards the snows of Kangchenjunga. But it needed much rebuilding, and it was some time before we could move into it. Ang Lahmu, who had been *ayah* to many English families, knew all about Western-type furnishings, and these were what she wanted, including all sorts of modern gadgets for the kitchen. We had the usual husband-and-wife discussions, and I kept saying, "We've done all right so far. Don't try for too much. Let's keep our lives simple." But I'm afraid it is not as easy to do as it is to say. Even for myself, who wants little, I have heard criticism of the collection of things I have made from my many expeditions and travels. "He should get rid of the stuff," people have said. "His house is like a museum." But it is not a museum. It is the place to keep the things that are near and dear to me.

Our home is full and busy. Besides my wife, my

daughters, and myself, there are my two young nieces,[1] who help with the housekeeping. Their mother and father, Lahmu Kipa and Lama Nwang La, with whom they had come from Solo Khumbu, live in our old house in Toong Soong Busti, but often come to us; and Nwang La is in charge of the prayer-room which I have built and furnished. Almost every day there are interviews and correspondence. Pasang Phutar and many other relatives and friends helped in the rebuilding of the house, and, now that it is finished, come and go frequently. There are always visitors—some friends, some strangers—by the dozens and hundreds. And, as boss of everything, there is Ghangar, my Lhasa terrier, with *his* big family. The only one who does not sometimes walk into the living-room is my horse, who lives in a stable, and is quickly eating himself out of any chance of winning races.

One thing that had always concerned me greatly was the education of Pem Pem and Nima. For several years they went to a Nepalese school, but now I have been able to enter them in the Loreto Convent in Darjeeling, where they are learning English, getting a good modern education, and meeting people of all different kinds. To improve my own English I have bought a Linguaphone, and, with the help both of this and of many conversations, I am glad to say I am becoming always more fluent. Dearly would I like to do something, also, about reading and writing. But life is so short and so busy. I now know all the letters in their different forms of printing and script, but still have trouble in putting them together into words. ... Except for my own name, of course. By now I have signed my autograph so often I think I could do it with my left hand in my sleep.

[1] And now my mother.

Starting as soon as I returned home, there were many invitations to visit other parts of India and the East. Some of them, such as to Burma and Ceylon, I was regretfully unable to accept, but I made trips to Calcutta, Delhi, Bombay, Madras, the Punjab, and many other places. As I had found it in Darjeeling, it warmed my heart to receive the welcome and devotion of so many people, but, as there too, the constant crowds and receptions and interviews were a great strain. And there were many incidents and experiences that could not have happened in the Western world. People were always wanting me to tell stories of supernatural things on the summit of Everest, and I had to disappoint them. Many wanted to touch me, thinking that by doing so they would be cured of their illnesses. There were those who insisted on calling me a second Buddha or a reincarnation of Lord Siva, and once, in Madras, several old women lit camphor-lamps and prostrated themselves before me. All I could do was to speak kindly to them and try to help them to their feet again.

There were many opportunities to make money. Not a maharajah's fortune, to be sure, but a great deal compared with what we had been used to. Besides the fee from the United Press and the gifts from cities and organizations, I had offers from many commercial firms for endorsements and other services, but I accepted only two of these, and then decided it was better not to get further involved. I have mentioned the stones I picked up just below the summit of Everest—the highest to be found in the world. Also I had other specimens from only a little lower down; and once this was made known in the Press I was offered large sums by people who wanted them as souvenirs. But I would not sell them. I gave some to Pandit Nehru and kept the rest myself. And, except for Lambert's scarf, which I had sent to him, I would not part with any of the clothing or equipment I had with me on the final climb. Everest was too dear to me, and too great, to be made cheap use of in such a way.

Early in 1954 I received an invitation to visit the United States as guest of the Explorers' Club of New York. It was sent through my friend Prince Peter of Greece and Denmark, who lives in near-by Kalimpong, and was introduced to me by Heinrich Harrer; and, though in many ways I would have liked to accept, I finally felt it advisable to decline. There were several reasons for this—all simple and wholly personal. For one thing, I was then in the midst of building my new house, which (like most houses) was costing twice as much as expected, and I felt I should be there to supervise. Also there was work to be done for the Mountaineering Institute, for which the West Bengal Government was already paying me a salary. It would have been impossible to take my wife and daughters with me, and the Explorers' Club said they could not afford the travelling expenses of Robi Mitra, whom I felt would be necessary to me as interpreter and adviser. And, finally, it seemed wiser to me to postpone my American visit until the publication of my book, which was then being planned, and for which I held high hopes. "If I go now," I wrote to Prince Peter, "I will be only a dumb-show, and people will have the wrong impression of me."

To me all these reasons seemed simple and innocent. But once again there was a storm of politics, and it was said that I had been forbidden to go because of the strained relations between India and the United States over American military aid to Pakistan. This upset me greatly, for I do not like to be dragged into things of this sort or to be made use of for propaganda. All I can say here is what

I have said before. There were no political, but only personal, reasons for my not going. Neither Pandit Nehru nor anyone else in the Indian Government forbade or even influenced me. I told this at the time to the American Ambassador, Mr George Allen, when he came to Darjeeling to see me, and I say it again now, as strongly as possible. Mr Allen was a very kind and understanding man, and when I explained my situation he put no further pressure on me. Later, when he came to Darjeeling to award me we Hubbard Medal of the National Geographic Society, the were warm friends, and talked much about how and when I would visit his country. For I can think of few things I want more to do than visit the United States. It is so big, so vital, so full of people and things and ideas. Among the other things that will be on my mind when I go are a jeep and a ciné-camera and driving on the great open roads. Most Americans I have known like speed, and so do I. If I learn to drive myself before I go there I will probably end up with what they call a "ticket."

I have just spoken of my book—and this is a very important thing to me. Through all my climbing days I have been with men who have written books. I have appeared in many. My home is full of them. And since the climbing of Everest I have wanted more than anything else to have a book of my own. But unfortunately there were many delays and difficulties. Since I could not write it myself, a collaborator was needed, and at first it seemed to me best that he be an Indian. The United Press, however, whose contract with me included the rights to a book, wanted a Westerner, because they thought he would write it more suitably for a world-wide audience. An Englishman seemed most logical to them, and several were suggested, but after much thought I decided against it. Like almost everything else that has happened since the climbing of Everest, this has been twisted and misinterpreted. The reason was not at all that I do not like the British or am prejudiced against them, but only that I felt that, if an Indian was not the ideal nationality for a collaborator, then neither was an Englishman. After all, there had been certain difficulties and problems on the last climb. And though—as I have said over and over again—they themselves were not important, it *was* important that I be able to tell my own story, simply and honestly, without either causing or feeling embarrassment. Because of all this there were unfortunately long delays in getting the book under way. Sometimes I almost despaired that there would be a book at all.[1] In the end, however, arrangements were made with the American novelist and mountaineering writer, James Ramsey Ullman, and in the spring of 1954 he came to Darjeeling to work with me. As it happened, the day on which we began was also the day known in my faith as Buddha Purnima (or Full Moon Day)—the thrice-blessed anniversary of the date on which the Lord Buddha was born, attained godhead, and died. And I said to Jim Ullman, smiling, "Well, I hope it will mean luck for us."

During the early part of the year I received many invitations to go out with new expeditions that were then being organized. After the great work and strain of three Everest attempts in a little more than a year I could not have considered still another major climb, but I would very

---

[1] Meanwhile, to make matters worse, an unauthorized book about me was published in France, and later translated into other languages. Written by a journalist who had interviewed me for about half an hour while I was in Switzerland in 1953, it was full of errors, strongly prejudiced against the British, and has caused me much embarrassment because of the false impressions it gave, both of the Everest climb itself and of my own feelings about it.

much have liked to go with some of the smaller parties—
especially the British-and-Indian one that was going up
into the Everest region to look for the Abominable
Snowman, or *yeti*. With all my obligations, however, it
was impossible for me to get away. Besides everything
else that spring, there was the first showing in India of the
film *The Conquest of Everest*, and I had been so cordially
invited and urged to attend the openings in Delhi and
Bombay that it would have been impossible for me to
decline. As it turned out, unfortunately, it was a mistake
for me to go. After the strain of Everest there had been
the ever greater strain of the endless crowds, receptions,
and interviews. This had been going on now for some
ten months, I had lost nearly two stone in weight, and my
health was undermined. In Bombay, during a heat-wave,
I fell ill, with great weakness and fever. Unable to continue the tour, I returned home, and Dr B. C. Roy (who,
besides being Chief Minister of West Bengal, is one of
India's leading physicians) ordered me to take a thorough
rest. For the next few weeks my only activity was to work
quietly on my book. I kept away from crowds and excitement, and slowly regained my weight and my health.

When *The Conquest of Everest* opened in Darjeeling I
was well enough to attend. This was on the 29th of May,
the first anniversary of the climb, and a big celebration had
been planned. But at almost the same time word came
through from Nepal that Sir Edmund Hillary, who this
year was leading a New Zealand expedition to Makalu II,
had been taken ill up on the mountain. Fortunately he was
soon all right again. But at that time it sounded as if his
illness might be critical, and I asked that, out of respect to
him, most of the celebration be cancelled. In the theatre,
before the showing of the film, I spoke a few words in

Nepali to the audience. "I am deeply sorry that my friend Hillary is ill," I told them. "This is not the time to rejoice, but to pray for his quick recovery. The climbing of Everest was an achievement of teamwork, and I send my warm wishes and greetings to my companion in victory." Once again, may I make the point that is so important to me? Would I have spoken in such a way of one towards whom I felt ill-will and resentment?

The new Himalayan Mountaineering Institute was to open in the autumn, and it had been arranged that Major Jayal and I would spend the summer in Switzerland, as guests of the Foundation for Alpine Research, to study advanced climbing techniques and methods of teaching. Luckily, by early June I was well enough to go, and soon I was back in the Alps with my old friends of earlier climbing days. There was still a certain amount of *zindabad* —of crowds, receptions, and interviews—but much less than the year before, and I was able, on the whole, to live quietly, enjoy the mountains, and do the work for which I had come. First we went to the village of Champex, in the Valais, where young Swiss climbers were taking their examinations for guiding licences. There, unfortunately, there were certain difficulties, because I felt that I was being treated like a novice; but they did not amount to much, and soon everything was going well. As before, I loved Switzerland, and once I was up in the mountains I felt almost as if I were back home again in my own Himalayas. It is just like Solo Khumbu, I found myself thinking many times. But that was not when I was looking at the roads and railways, bridges and power-plants.

Later in the summer six other Sherpas came on from India. They too had been invited by the Swiss Foundation to receive a course of training for their future work at the new mountaineering school, and I had selected the men before leaving Darjeeling. They were the veteran Ang-tharkay and Gyalzen Mikchen, who was also a top sirdar; Da Namgyal and Ang Tempa, of the Everest expeditions; and my two nephews, Gombu and Topgay. After their arrival we all went to Rosenlaui, where Arnold Glatthard has his climbing school, and for several weeks had much valuable experience in every sort of mountain-craft. Then, towards the end of the summer, we returned home again, to continue the preparations for our own school, which was officially opened on November 4, 1954, by Pandit Nehru.

In this first season, of course, only a beginning could be made with the mountaineering instruction. Towards the end of the year, when the weather grew too cold, I was for a time free again, and now I made a trip that for a long while had been close to my heart. This was back to Solo Khumbu again; but this journey was different from any before it, because I took with me my daughters, Pem Pem and Nima. Leaving Darjeeling on Christmas Day, we went by car and train to Jaynagar and Dharan, near the Nepali border, and from there on we went on foot, with the girls carrying packs on their backs like any other Sherpa travellers. It was an absolutely new experience for them, and we had lots of fun. But also, more seriously, it was a sort of pilgrimage, for they had never before been to the home country of our people or seen their grandmother— my mother—who was now eighty-four years old. When we reached the Sherpa land there was great rejoicing, with feasting and dancing. After we had stayed awhile in Namche Bazar and Thamey we went on up farther to visit the famous Thyangboche and other monasteries. And then I took my daughters up almost to the site of the 1953 base camp, where they paid homage to Everest, which had made the Sherpas great—and us happy.

While in Solo Khumbu we twice had a very interesting experience, for it was now, for the first time in my life, that I saw the actual remains of *yetis*, or Abominable Snowmen. Both occasions were at monasteries—one at Khumjung, the other at Pangboche—and in each case the remains consisted of a skull, rather pointed in shape, with scalp and hair still attached. The hair of the Khumjung skull was dark and coarse, like that of a hog; that of the Pangboche skull somewhat lighter, giving the impression that it might come from a younger creature. Both were looked upon by the lamas as important and powerful talismans. But they had been there so long that no one knew where they had come from, and the mystery of the living *yeti*, and what he is like, still remains to be solved.

Also on this trip there happened another thing I had wanted for many years. I brought my mother back with me to Darjeeling. Since she was a Sherpa, she made the long trip on foot very well, even at her great age; but she had never before been to the outside world, and when we came to India she had fantastic and surprising experiences. One of these was when, for the first time in her life, she rode in the train from Jaynagar. A little while after the train had started she suddenly asked me with great surprise, "Tenzing, where is that tree I saw in front of the waiting-room at the station?" My daughters and I burst into laughter, and I explained to her what a train is. Then, with a sigh of relief, she said, "I have never in my life seen a whole house moving like this from place to place."

So now, for the first time, almost our whole family is

together in Darjeeling. And that is where things are at as I finish this story of mine. Just what the future will bring I, of course, cannot tell. There will be my work at the Mountaineering Institute, in which I hope I may help to give a knowledge and love of the high places to many young Indians. There will be other work with the Sherpa Association, of which I am now president, and which is expanding its functions to include the supplying of Sherpas to expeditions and the regulation of their wages and conditions of employment. Also I want to be of use, as much as I can, to my people in general. I have come to where I am now from a very low position. I know the problems of poverty and ignorance, and want to help them improve and educate themselves towards a better life.

Especially I would like to help and teach young people with their lives before them. What I can teach is not from books, to be sure, but from what I have learned in living my own life: from many men, many lands, many mountains—and, most of all, from Everest. Some of it has to do with physical and material things. But not all of it; for I think I have learned other, and more important, things as well. One is that you cannot be a good mountaineer, however great your ability, unless you are cheerful and have the spirit of comradeship. Friends are as important as achievement. Another is that teamwork is the one key to success, and that selfishness only makes a man small. Still another is that no man, on a mountain or elsewhere, gets more out of anything than he puts into it. . . . *Be great. Make others great.* That is what I have learned, and all men may learn, from the great goddess Chomolungma.

A question I am often asked is if I think Everest will be climbed again. The answer is yes, of course it will. How soon the next ascent, or even attempt, will be made no one knows; but in time it will be reclimbed, I think, not only from Nepal, but from Tibet, and perhaps even by a traverse from one side to the other. The question that always follows—can it be climbed without oxygen?—is a harder one. But my guess here is also yes, provided preparations and conditions are exactly right. For one thing, I am convinced that a still higher camp would have to be set up between our 1953 Camp Nine and the summit, for at that height and without oxygen men can climb only a very short distance in a day. And also there would have to be five consecutive days of good weather for the climbers to get from the South Col to the top and back again alive. So that, if it is ever done, it will be a matter not only of great skill, endurance, and planning, but also of tremendous luck. For no man—sometimes one almost thinks no god—has control of the weather on Everest.

Do I myself want to climb again? The answer here is: on other, smaller mountains—yes. On Everest—no. On such a peak, as on any of the true Himalayan giants, to be both a high climber and a sirdar, with the two different responsibilities, is too much for one man, and there will be no more such ordeals in my life. In the past it was different. In 1953 I felt that I must either get to the top of Everest or die, and the victory was well worth the struggle. But now that victory has been granted I cannot feel the same way again, either about Everest or about any mountain equally formidable. I am now forty, which is not so old—but neither is it so young—and I do not long for any more "tops of the world" to conquer. Most certainly, though, I want to return to the mountains again, for the mountains are my home and my life. I want to go back many times—on small expeditions, for good climbs with good companions. Most of all, I want to do some more good climbing with my dear friend Raymond Lambert.

Besides climbing, I should like to travel. When this book is published there I hope to visit the United States. I hope to go back to England and Switzerland, where I have had such wonderful welcomes, and also to see many places where I have never been before. From my travels so far I feel that I have learned a great deal, and not only about cities and airlines and geography. I have learned that the world is big, and that you cannot see all of it from one little corner; that there is good and bad in all of it; that because people are different from yourself it does not necessarily mean that you are right and they are wrong. It has often been said that Westerners are more materialistic than Easterners, but could it not be that they are also more honest? In my own experience, at least, with officials and tradesmen, this was very much the case. Also, we of the East often pride ourselves on our hospitality; but the reception I received in London almost made me blush when I compared it with what the British climbers were given when they returned to Kathmandu. By these two small examples I do not mean that I am against my own people. On the contrary, I am proud to be both an Indian and a Nepali. But I think that much harm has been done by narrow prejudice and nationalism, that Everest itself has been harmed, and that my own people are at least partly to blame. The world is too small, Everest too great, for anything but tolerance and understanding: that is the most important of all things I have learned from my climbing and my travelling. Whatever the differences between East and West, they are as nothing compared to our common humanity. Whatever the difficulties that arose about Everest, they are as nothing beside the common cause and the common victory, and to my English companions—to Hunt and Hillary and the others and all their countrymen—I reach out my hand across half the world.

Since the climbing of Everest my own people have been good to me. Every one has been good to me. But, as for all men, I suppose, there have been good and bad, rewards and problems, all mixed up together. Sometimes the crowds around me have been so thick, the pressures so great, that I have thought gloomily that a normal life is no longer possible; that my only chance for happiness is to go off with my family to some solitary place where we can live in peace. But this would be a defeat and a retreat, and I pray it will not be necessary. If only people will leave me alone politically things will be all right. If only they will not push and pull at me for their own purposes: asking why I speak this or that language, why I wear Indian or Nepali or Western clothing, why the flags were in one order instead of another when I held them up on the top of Everest. It is not so much for my own sake that I feel this as for the sake of Everest itself. For it is too great, too precious, for such smallness. What I hope for most for the future is that I be allowed to live my life honourably, and not disgrace Everest. Future generations will ask, "What sort of men were they who first climbed to the top of the world?" And I want the answer to be one of which I would not be ashamed.

For it is just this, I think, that is the real importance of Everest: that it is the top not merely of one country or another, but of the whole earth. It was climbed by men both of the East and the West. It belongs to us all. And that is what I want also for myself: that I should belong to all, be a brother to all men everywhere, and not merely a member of some group or race or creed. As I have said at the beginning of my story, I am a lucky man. I have had a dream, and it has come true. All I can now ask of God is that I may be worthy of what has been granted me.

So Everest is climbed. My life goes on. In this book I have looked back at the past, but in living one must look ahead.

Once—only once—in my new life have I done what I did so often in the old—climbed up in the dawn to Tiger Hill, behind Darjeeling, and looked out across the miles towards the north-west. There are no tourists with me now; only a few friends. And no need to talk or explain, but only to stand quietly and watch the great white peaks rise up into the morning light. But as I watch it is no longer the same morning or the same year. I am back on this hill long ago, with my seven American ladies, and I am remembering what I said to them. "No, it is not that one. That is Lhotse. Nor that. That is Makalu. It is the other one. The small one."

"The small one." . . . Perhaps that is a strange name for the biggest mountain on earth. But also not so strange, and not so wrong, for what is Everest without the eye that sees it? It is the hearts of men that make it big or small.

You cannot see it for long from Tiger Hill. Soon the sun is up; the clouds come. It is neither big nor small, but gone. And now I go too—down to Darjeeling, my home and my family, my new life, which is so different from the old. One of my friends asks, "Well, what is it like? How do you feel about it now?" But I cannot answer them. I can answer only in my heart, and to Everest itself, as I did on that morning when I bent and laid a red-and-blue pencil in the summit snow:

Thuji chey, Chomolungma.

I am grateful.

INDEX